## YOUTH AND THE FUTURE

# YOUTH AND THE FUTURE

*The General Report of the*

## AMERICAN YOUTH COMMISSION

AMERICAN COUNCIL ON EDUCATION

WASHINGTON, D. C.

1942

# FOREWORD

---

IN THIS book the American Youth Commission rounds out the formulation of its recommendations in regard to youth. Hitherto the recommendations of the Commission, based on staff research, other available information, and the active and long-continued discussions of the members of the Commission, have been adopted in the form of brief statements and have been published in pamphlet form. In this general report, many new recommendations of major importance are presented for the first time, while the topics previously considered in the briefer statements are here placed in the setting of a comprehensive treatment of the whole field and are restated from a longer-term point of view.

In the preparation of this report, the major objective has been a philosophy which would be applicable both in war and in peace. The Commission foresaw the likelihood that the United States would be drawn completely into the war, and was acutely aware of the changes which have been taking place with increasing momentum ever since the outbreak of war abroad in September 1939. Now that we are actually in the war, it seems likely that it will become increasingly difficult to think calmly and clearly about the conditions which must be established after the war and which must be prepared for during the war. It is fortunate, therefore, that the Commission was able to utilize the last remaining months before this country became an active

v

belligerent to prepare a program which is directed to the post-war future as well as to the urgent situation of the present.

The American Youth Commission came into existence in 1935, when the American Council on Education appointed the members and they agreed to serve. As originally constituted, the Commission included seventeen members, of whom twelve have served continuously throughout the life of the Commission. The Honorable Newton D. Baker was chairman from the beginning until his death in 1937. Mr. Owen D. Young, who had served previously as vice chairman and acting chairman, became chairman of the Commission in 1940, at which time Mr. Henry I. Harriman became vice chairman. Dr. Miriam Van Waters has served continuously as secretary. Of the other original members, Dr. Lotus D. Coffman died in 1938; Mrs. Edgar B. Stern resigned in 1938, Dr. Robert M. Hutchins in 1938, and Mr. Ralph Budd in 1939. Dr. Henry C. Taylor became a member in 1937, and Dr. Clarence A. Dykstra and Dr. Mordecai W. Johnson became members in 1939. The members and officers as of the date of adoption of this report appear on a preceding page.

Dr. Homer P. Rainey, previously president of Bucknell University, served as director of the Commission during its first four years, resigning in the spring of 1939 to become president of the University of Texas. The undersigned was appointed director at that time.

The present report was discussed by the Commission in the form of an outline and partial draft at a meeting in May 1941, and a preliminary draft was considered in September. At a meeting held on October 8 and 9, 1941, the recommendations were completed and the report was adopted, subject to the necessary editorial revisions in preparing it for the press. After the declaration of war, editorial changes were made in recognition of the changed situation.

Various members of the Commission and of the staff participated actively in the writing of sections of the draft. In particular, the Commission has a special debt to one of its members, Mrs. Dorothy Canfield Fisher, who prepared Chapter XVIII, which comprises Part IV, the concluding part of the report. The content of this chapter represents a refinement of her thinking over a period of years as well as the result of group discussion in many Commission meetings.

The organization of the report as a whole, the drafting of Chapters I through V in their various stages, and much of the drafting of other chapters throughout the report were the work of Dr. Paul T. David, who has served the Commission since 1939 as associate director and chief economist.

In closing this foreword, it seems appropriate to emphasize the great amount of labor and unselfish interest which the members of the Commission have put into the present report, as well as the active contribution to all aspects of the work which they have made throughout the life of the Commission. If this report proves to be a document which lives and has influence, it will be because it expresses the final outcome of the group thinking carried on over a period of six years by one of the most outstanding groups of men and women in America.

FLOYD W. REEVES
*Director*

# INTRODUCTION

By

## OWEN D. YOUNG

*Chairman of the Commission*

I<small>T IS</small> the purpose of the American Youth Commission in this report to set forth a program in regard to youth—a program based on the experience of the past, adjusted to the harsh realities of the present, and adequate to foreseeable needs of the future.

This has not been an easy time to prepare such a report. When the members of this Commission began their term of service, the future seemed obscure. It is less predictable now. Yet the task of planning for youth and the future must be faced.

The Commission was appointed in 1935, and found its origin in the circumstances of the period. Thousands of youth were roaming the country as destitute young tramps. High schools in almost every community were swamped with sudden increases in enrollment at a time when school taxes often remained unpaid and school budgets were being drastically cut. No one knew exactly what was happening to the millions of oncoming youth who were unable to remain in school, yet it was obvious that they were not moving smoothly into employment.

As the major social institution dealing directly with masses of youth, the schools could not avoid becoming aware of the impact on young people of the forces let loose by the depression. It was thus natural that the emerging "youth problem" first received extensive attention from the major educational organizations. In particular, the American Council on Education came to the conclusion that the problem had reached the level of a crisis requiring an extraordinary effort to find solutions. As a part of that effort, the present Commission was formed by the Council. Funds to finance activities for a term of years were provided by one of the major educational foundations, the General Education Board, and the members of the Commission were given the utmost freedom to determine the scope of their inquiry and to formulate far-reaching recommendations.

In its proposal for the creation of an American Youth Commission, the American Council on Education made the following statement:

Recent social and economic changes in the United States have given rise to difficulties in the care and education of young people with which existing institutions are quite unprepared to deal adequately. The changes not only have greatly intensified the problems which confront the schools, but also have created an urgent need of protection and further education for millions of youth whom the schools are not now reaching. Without some provision for basic planning to meet this situation, there is serious danger that present conditions may constitute a fundamental threat to the national welfare. It is believed that both the public and the great majority of workers interested in this field are deeply conscious of this danger, and would welcome a comprehensive and thoughtfully conceived program for meeting it.

When first appointed as members of the Commission, we were aware of the truth of these generalizations. But to acquire an impression of the actual situation both vivid and comprehensive, factual information was necessary. Much of the needed information did not exist in any specific form at that time and, in some cases, research had not even progressed to the point where it was possible to identify the decisive factors for orderly investigation.

The first task, therefore, was to seek information. This was done in a variety of ways, partly by assembling the research of others, partly by organizing conferences at which members of the Commission were able to receive expert testimony at first hand, and partly by carrying on extensive field investigations through the Commission's own staff. Among the most important of these investigations was the Maryland Youth Survey, the report of which was published in 1938 under the title, *Youth Tell Their Story*. This report is still the most important single handbook of factual information in its field. It continues to be used both as a source of information concerning the status and attitudes of American youth and as a model for new inquiries.

As a source of quantitative information concerning youth unemployment, *Youth Tell Their Story* has been superseded in part by later official censuses. It was, however, the first publication based on large-scale field investigation to suggest the conclusion that during the depression years the number of unemployed youth might be as large as 4,000,000, a conclusion later confirmed when the official estimates based upon the 1937 federal census of unemployment were published.

Although we began our task with much more than an academic interest in the economic situation of young people, we were both startled and shocked by the findings of the Maryland Youth Survey. Our first reaction was to hope, as most Americans have hoped when confronted with similar facts, that general processes of economic recovery would soon reduce many elements of the problem to a more manageable size. Meanwhile, it seemed imperative to make as thorough as possible an exploration of the extent to which youth unemployment could be ameliorated by improving the social facilities which are intended to smooth the path of young people from schools to jobs.

A cooperative project was therefore organized at the beginning of 1938 to test out community programs of occupational adjustment in four cities and in a like number of rural counties. This project was carried on for eighteen months, ending in the summer of 1939.

Much was learned from the cooperative occupational adjustment project, as well as from the other investigations and demonstrations which had been carried on from the beginning under the auspices of the Commission. As the facts accumulated, we were compelled by the coercive quality of the data to come to many unwelcome conclusions. It became apparent, for example, that even if the social services of occupational adjustment could be brought to a state of perfection, the employment problem of young people would not be measurably solved under conditions such as those prevailing from 1930 to 1940. Moreover, as we shifted our attention from one aspect of youth to another, taking up questions in the fields of secondary education, use of leisure time, marriage and the home, health and fitness, juvenile delinquency, citizenship, and the special problems of rural youth and of minority groups, we found ourselves meeting the economic situation at every turn.

Through this process it became apparent that major attention must be given to the problem of employment opportunity for youth in all of its manifold ramifications. Studies were being made of the possibilities for a revival of private employment opportunity for young people when, in September 1939, the war began abroad. Against the background of the war situation and the President's declaration of a limited national emergency, we adopted the brief statement on youth and war, employment, health, and education which was published in pamphlet form as *A Program of Action for American Youth*. Some of the paragraphs of this statement dealing specifically with youth unemployment were as follows:

> The Commission feels obliged to emphasize the fact that, whether in war or at peace, any nation interested in self-preservation must see to it that the young have a proper chance to grow into useful citizens. . . .
> In view of the crisis in world affairs and the necessarily slow adjustment of business to current conditions, the Commission concludes that in many states and communities the present gap between the number of jobs for youth and the number of youth who need and want jobs cannot be closed without the aid of the federal government. Every young person who does not desire to continue in school after 16, and who cannot get a job in private enterprise, should be provided under public auspices with employment in some form of service.
> The Commission believes that all young people should be required

and enabled to attend full-time schools up to the age of 16, but that it would be undesirable to compel the attendance above that age of young people who would prefer to go to work. Above the age of 16, many young people who would benefit from the training of a job would be wasting their time in school.

The Commission is impressed with the success of experiments that have been made with combinations of part-time schooling and part-time employment. This device for bridging the years between full-time school and full-time job should be extended as rapidly as practicable. The Commission recognizes, however, that the opportunities even for part-time work are limited, and that this admirable method of introducing youth into industry cannot solve the general unemployment problem of youth in a short time.

Public work for young people should be planned with special regard to its educational quality. It should be superintended by persons who are competent to train young people in good work habits as well as in specific skills. It should be carried on in a spirit that will give to the young worker a sense of being valued by and valuable to his country. Finally, it should provide an opportunity to try various kinds of work, so that the young person may find his own aptitudes and abilities and may be given some guidance in preparing for private employment in a field where he can be most useful and successful.

In its emphasis on public work to fill the gap for the youth who were unable to find opportunity for other types of employment, this statement focused attention upon a recommendation which was essential at the time, as it is still; but we also continued our discussions of the ways and means of expanding opportunities in the normal channels of employment. As additional statements were adopted and issued by the Commission, increasing emphasis was given to the importance of fundamental economic remedies. In the present report, they are the subject of one of the longest chapters.

In every statement which the Commission has adopted and published since September 1939, including the one just quoted, the war has been a major factor in our thinking. After the fall of France, a statement was issued in July 1940 under the title *Youth, Defense, and the National Welfare,* in which we advocated selective compulsory military service. By the time when we began the active preparation of this report, most of us were convinced that the United States would soon be completely in the war, and we prepared our report accordingly. Now that the war is actually upon us, many of the recommendations of this report are even more timely and urgent than before, while others which look to the post-war future do not lose importance as we gain a better conception of the magnitude of the eventual post-war readjustments.

The recommendations of the Commission have not been the easy product of a group of like-minded persons. On the contrary, in the earlier meetings of the Commission, the possibility of unanimous agreement on important recommendations at times seemed remote. We continued our effort, however, because of the firm conviction that unless representative Americans can reach agreement on problems such as those we have faced, the future course of this country may be perilous indeed.

In this report, the Commission of necessity looks mainly to the future. The problem of how best to induct youth into the responsibilities and opportunities of adult life will be very largely conditioned in the future by factors which can be foreseen only dimly if at all. Yet, these are times that call for action, and wise action must be influenced by some conception of things to come. After careful consideration, the Commission therefore adopted the following general assumptions as a basis for this report.

The Commission assumes:

1. That the successful prosecution of the war is the most important problem confronting the American people today.

2. That in the post-war period, economic reconstruction to achieve sustained full employment under peacetime conditions will be the most difficult problem and the most urgent objective of the American people.

3. That the changes in the basic structure of the American economic system which have taken place during the last fifty years, and which in some cases are now being accelerated, will not present insuperable barriers to the achievement of peacetime full employment but will undoubtedly make necessary many fundamental readjustments.

4. That for some years after the war, efforts to achieve sustained peacetime full employment through the expansion of private employment will be only partially successful, and that meanwhile it will be necessary to carry on substantial programs of public work for the unemployed.

5. That because of necessity the trend both during and after the war will continue toward an increasing use of government to regulate economic affairs and in particular that government will be given increasing responsibility for the peacetime stimulation of a balanced expansion of productive activity in the basic industries producing for interstate commerce.

6. That under democratic government and without giving up the liberties we prize, the American people will have it within their power to bring about a continuing abundance of available employment opportunity in future times of peace, with a rising standard of living for all who contribute to the productive effort of the nation.

In stating these assumptions, the Commission does not assume either that we are completely at the mercy of fate or that we shall reach our desired goals without sacrifice and effort. It is assumed that the American people will continue to exercise their native qualities of good will, courage, and foresight, and that progress will thus continue toward the realization of the American dream of universal opportunity in a land of peace and freedom.

# CONTENTS

# PART II
## Other Basic Problems

*Part I*

EMPLOYMENT OPPORTUNITY
FOR YOUTH

# CHAPTER
# I

## YOUTH UNEMPLOYMENT
## AS A CONTINUING PROBLEM

SINCE the summer of 1940, the American people have been devoting an increasing share of their energy to the expansion of the Army and the Navy and to the production of munitions of war. Now we are actually at war; and the armaments boom of the months before we entered the war has become a full-scale war effort in every aspect of life.

In our current preoccupation with the war, the problems of the depression years from 1930 to 1940 seem increasingly remote. Many of the problems doubtless still exist in one form or another, but it has become relatively easy to dismiss them from consideration.

Even if tempted to forget the past, however, we cannot disregard the future. When this war is over, it may represent even more of a great dividing point in the course of history than the war of 1914–18. Though we cannot predict the future in any detail, we have an imperative duty to plan for it on the basis of the soundest assumptions we can devise. Among other things, we must plan for the care and education of youth in the post-war world, as well as during the difficult period of uncertain length which stretches ahead.

3

When finally the war does come to an end, there will be a demobilization of military forces and of the war industries now expanding so rapidly. Any such demobilization will release for other employment large numbers of young men and women under 30 years of age. A large percentage of the soldiers and workers who will need new jobs will be under 25. The demobilized group will in itself be a "youth problem" until it can be assimilated into peacetime pursuits.

During the reabsorption of the demobilized group, it will be exceedingly difficult to maintain normal placement of the oncoming annual classes of beginning workers. Those demobilized from the war effort will have many special claims to consideration and in many cases will be given preference in filling such jobs as exist.

Undoubtedly the extent of youth unemployment in the post-war period will depend primarily upon the extent of general unemployment. But it appears certain that whatever the general rate of unemployment, the rate will be higher among the work-seekers under the age of 25, and especially high among those under the age of 21. Unless we can find and adopt more effective policies to promote full employment than those tried experimentally during the 1930's, a piling-up of several million jobless, inexperienced new workers seems very likely to happen in the coming years after the war.

In view of this prospect it is clear that we must plan policies to reduce the extent of unemployment, and we must prepare programs of action which will adequately care for youth unemployment on a large scale if it does come. In this chapter the discussion is begun by presenting first some of the more important general factors that have affected the position of youth in American economic life. The greater part of the chapter is then devoted to the recent trends in youth employment, the effects on young workers of long-continued periods of unemployment, and the extent of social responsibility in regard to the problem of youth unemployment.

## BACKGROUND FACTORS IN YOUTH EMPLOYMENT

The American people have long prided themselves on the independence, vigor, initiative, and self-reliance of the individuals who built this country. All these virtues and characteristics are important. They are not confined, however, to the residents of any one land.

It behooves us, therefore, to search back into our beginnings for the special reasons for the rapid economic development of this country. First of all were the great natural resources—virgin timber, a rich land ideally adapted to agriculture, a profusion of minerals. Second was an expanding and vigorous population, recruited from all the peoples of the Old World and enlarged by a high rate of natural increase. Third was the American form of government, a government close to the people, responsive to their welfare, committed to the fostering of free enterprise, and with no obligation to any self-perpetuating aristocracy.

Fourth was the fortunate and timely development of science and technology. Without the steam engine, the railroad, and the steamship, coming at the time they did, our rate of early progress would have been impossible. Throughout our entire national life, our material progress has been enhanced and carried along by a whole series of fruitful inventions. Moreover, the expansion which has been characteristic of our system has made it particularly easy for us to take fullest advantage of those inventions. They not only have raised the levels of living for our growing population. In their importance and timing, they have had much to do with the characteristic optimism of this country.

Fifth was the comprehensive use of the corporate form of business enterprise, which became a characteristic feature of American economic life at an earlier date than was the case in other industrial countries. This has had various results, not all good. Nevertheless, it facilitated the easy and flexible mobilization of great amounts of capital. It also spread the risks attendant upon so rapid a development of our resources. Without it we would have smaller units of manufacturing, transportation, communication, and trade. Almost certainly we would have a much lower although possibly a more stable level of living. In any event, we would live in an entirely different economic world.

A sixth and closely related factor has been the development of new techniques of industrial organization and management. These have not been as spectacular as the important mechanical inventions, but in the aggregate they have had a tremendous influence on production. Without them, our large industrial and commercial organizations would hardly be workable, and surely would not be very efficient.

The widespread diffusion of knowledge throughout the population is a seventh characteristic factor in American development which is too easily taken for granted but which deserves special consideration. Public education at an early date, a newspaper and periodical press of exceptional coverage, dissemination of knowledge and skills through the migration and mixing of diverse peoples, all have played their part in forming a population which ranks high in the proportion of individuals who are literate, articulate, and adaptable. This has had many consequences, not the least of which is a major contribution to productive efficiency.

The economic forces of modern times plus the special factors just noted have given us the present economic system of the United States. That system has a very pervasive influence on our lives.

The importance of industry and trade as contrasted with agriculture constitutes a major feature of our present situation. We have a great agriculture, but it has been declining in relative importance for many decades. The market for agricultural products has not proved as expansible as that for other goods and services. Scientific progress has increased the productivity of agricultural workers and decreased the number needed. The geographic frontier has disappeared, and little new land remains for exploitation.

The country has become a single economic unit, although still politically diverse, by virtue of a network of transportation and communication facilities of unrivaled extensiveness. These have made possible the large industrial enterprises and the nation-wide marketing of products. They also have greatly affected the distribution of the areas of commercially successful agriculture.

The development of transportation and the predominance of industry and trade are making us increasingly a group of urban people. This in turn reacts upon the character of the economic system, particularly by further segregating industry and agriculture.

The industrial and commercial side of our economic system is characterized by large-scale private economic activity. We have many small enterprises and we must keep a place for more, but they do not give our system its dominant note. The large corporation is the most conspicuous factor in most fields of industry, transportation, commerce, and finance. Many of these corporations market their products throughout the United States, if not the world.

In the large corporations, management has tended to become separated from ownership and managers have become the representatives of an impersonal entity. The personal relationship and the face-to-face bargaining which still exist between, for example, the typical farmer and the typical hired hand have been wholly lost in large corporate enterprise.

The development of large corporate employing interests and of associations of employers has been paralleled by the development of unions through which employees have mobilized their economic strength in order to approach equality in bargaining over the terms of employment. The development of unions has not proceeded as far as the development of corporations and of associations of employers, but the expansion of union membership has been rapid in recent years. The time may not be far distant when most of the workers employed in the large units of production will be organized into unions.

From the standpoint of the individual, perhaps the most fundamental result of all these changes is the drastic decline in opportunities for self-employment, coupled with increasing personal dependence upon the general operations of the economic system. Opportunities for self-employment in the production of goods either for use or for sale remain on a large scale only in agriculture and even there have been greatly curtailed.

Satisfactory opportunities for living on the land on a completely self-sufficing basis have vanished, although desirable forms of live-at-home activity in agriculture are receiving increasing emphasis. Most of the farm population is at least partially dependent upon commercial farming. The income from the sale of products is often small, but it is essential unless some cash income can be obtained in the form of wages for part-time work off the farm. Even though self-employed to a large extent, the farm groups are highly dependent upon pervasive economic forces.

The productive activities of the home, formerly a major field of self-employment, have dwindled away with the development of manufacturing and service enterprises outside the home. With the transfer of work from home to industry, girls and women, married and unmarried, have increasingly entered the market for gainful employment.

The great mass of the population has thus become dependent upon work for wages as its sole means of livelihood. This is now so much an accepted fact that it has no novelty. When viewed in historical perspective, however, it is obvious that such a situation is much less conducive to stability in the social order than was the situation which prevailed a hundred years ago.

This observation becomes especially pertinent when attention is directed to the unstable character of the economy in which we live. Chronic cycles of prosperity and depression have been a major characteristic of the so-called "money economy" as far back as our economic records run. There is no doubt that more and more of the population has been drawn within the direct influence of these fluctuations. This is an obvious result of the decline in opportunities for self-employment. It is a fact of the utmost importance.

Our material progress has been remarkable. For a long time the influence of the setbacks which did occur was not sufficiently great to result in any general loss of confidence. Occasional years of difficulty were accepted as the necessary price of progress without engendering much fundamental criticism.

From 1930 to 1940, however, we struggled through a period of economic adversity which made us all very conscious of the elements of instability in our economic system. Much thought was given to ways and means of providing new influences which would be conducive to greater stability, as well as reduce the amount of shock suffered by individuals in the midst of economic catastrophe. Many new governmental action programs which had these objectives were developed and put in operation.

The efficacy of these programs can be determined only through years of experience. Some of them offer hope for the future. Meanwhile, however, the period of war through which we are passing is involving major changes in the social and economic life of the nation. When we emerge from this period of strain, it seems more than likely that the problems of economic instability will be as acute as they have been during any period of the past.

## TRENDS IN YOUTH EMPLOYMENT

Most people recognize that when large numbers of adults are unemployed, something is wrong with the economic system. Strangely enough, many of these same people apparently feel that when large numbers of youth are unemployed, something must be wrong with the young people.

Because this feeling is so common, the American Youth Commission has made elaborate studies to determine whether deficiencies in the care and education of youth have been responsible in any large degree for the extensive youth unemployment of recent years. Through these investigations, it has become apparent that much could be done to improve the employability of many young people. The Commission has become even more certain, however, that the major causes of youth unemployment are to be found in basic economic trends rather than in social and educational institutions for youth. Very few youth are so unemployable that they cannot be employed when jobs are available. The best evidence of this is the rapid rate at which they have been moving into the war industries.

Although unemployment as a problem of youth first became conspicuous only recently, the roots of the problem run back for many years. A century ago, most young Americans entered employment by beginning to work as a part of the family unit on farms or in small workshops. It was taken for granted that parents had a comprehensive responsibility for the vocational, social, and moral training of their children until they reached a marriageable age and were settled in homes of their own.

In rural areas, parental responsibility in these matters still bears some semblance to the older pattern. Children who grow up on family farms still begin work under parental direction. Often it is assumed that they will leave home in search of more ample opportunities as soon as they reach maturity, but if conditions are unfavorable, they can remain for a longer period. Meanwhile, they can contribute to the economic basis of family life without necessarily obtaining wage employment.

About two-thirds of the population, however, live in cities and other incorporated places. With the development of present forms of urban economic activity, it is no longer generally assumed that children will begin their working life by spending several years in employment under the direction of their parents. For young people other than those living on farms, the arrangements of the present social order are based upon the assumption that when they reach the point in their development where they are ready for work, opportunity will be forthcoming from some quarter in the form of wage employment.

Since about 1910, the proportion of young people in gainful employment has been declining most of the time. Frequently it is assumed that this trend away from employment is merely a reflection of the trend toward increased school attendance; but the relationship is not so simple.

Much of the increase in school attendance has undoubtedly been caused by the desire of parents to give their children a better start in life than they received themselves. The customary age of school-leaving has been rising slowly for several generations, largely because of this desire on the part of parents. It is worthy of note, however, that between 1920 and 1930, when the number of youth 15 to 19 years of age in school increased from 3,668,000 to 5,779,000, there was seldom any suggestion of a shortage of juvenile labor. Nor was there evidence of any decline in the number of youth 15 to 19 years of age who were not in school and not working.

American employers were evidently becoming increasingly reluctant to hire young workers even before the recent years of depression. So-called "boys' jobs" were being eliminated one by one with changes in methods of production and the introduction of additional machinery. The tendency was to hire a young person only when he or she seemed mature enough to do the work of an adult, and to avoid whenever possible the training costs involved in hiring beginning workers.

With the advent of the depression years, these tendencies were intensified. Young people entering the labor market, sometimes prematurely because of family necessity, found themselves in competition not only with other youth of their own age but also with millions of competent, experienced, unemployed adults. In many communities, the employment operations of the largest employers consisted exclusively of laying off and rehiring the workers who had been employed before the advent of the depression. Young workers without experience or accumulated seniority rights were shut out of employment in some plants for years at a time.

Under the circumstances, it is remarkable that so many oncoming youth were able to obtain employment for even a part of the time. By 1935, it is probable that of the 21,000,000 youth 16 to 24 years of age, over 4,000,000 of those who were out of school were unemployed. The special unemployment census of 1937 demonstrated conclusively that the rate of unemployment was higher among young workers between 20 and 24 than in any older age group, and highest of all for the young people under 20 who were out of school and seeking work. The regular decennial census of 1940 reported a smaller amount of unemployment, but a continuation of the disproportion between age groups, with 35 percent of the unemployed under 25 years of age, although only 22 percent of the employable population was reported as under 25.

In general, the lower the age, the higher the rate of unemployment among the youth who are out of school and in the labor market. In the Maryland Youth Survey in 1936,[1] for example, the following percentages of unemployment were found at the various ages:

| Age | Percentage unemployed |
|-----|----------------------|
| 16  | 56 |
| 17  | 49 |
| 18  | 39 |
| 19  | 29 |
| 20  | 29 |
| 21  | 25 |
| 22  | 22 |
| 23  | 20 |
| 24  | 20 |

The figures just given, it must be remembered, represent the percentage unemployed of those out of school and working or seeking work. Since there is much variation in the age of leaving school, it is also desirable to look at the percentages of *all* youth who are unemployed at the various age levels. The pattern of unemployment among youth, including emergency workers, as found by the 1937 federal census of unemployment, was as follows:

| Age | Percentage unemployed of all youth | Percentage unemployed of those in the labor market |
|-----|-----------------------------------|---------------------------------------------------|
| 15  | 3.5  | 41.4 |
| 16  | 10.6 | 50.0 |
| 17  | 17.5 | 46.5 |
| 18  | 24.1 | 41.6 |
| 19  | 23.4 | 34.7 |
| 15–19 | 15.8 | 41.2 |
| 20–24 | 17.3 | 24.3 |

[1]Howard M. Bell, *Youth Tell Their Story* (Washington: American Council on Education, 1938), 273 pp.

The specific distribution of unemployment by single years of age in the youth age group is of importance because the legal requirements in regard to compulsory school attendance and the regulation of child labor are organized mainly in terms of definite minimum and maximum ages. Twenty years ago, 14 was the age in many states up to which school attendance was compulsory and employment during school periods was prohibited. The age of 14 is now sometimes specified as a minimum age for employment outside of school periods in non-manufacturing occupations, but 16 has become the age up to which school attendance is frequently compulsory, and it is also the age now commonly set by child labor laws as the minimum for full-time employment in manufacturing industries. Below age 18, employment in certain hazardous occupations is often prohibited, and employment in other occupations is often subject to special restrictions that cease to be effective at the age of 18. The key ages in child labor regulation have thus become 14, 16, and 18.

In terms of the customary practice of employers, the important ages are 16, 18, and 21. Apparently many urban employers give no consideration whatever to the employment of young people under the age of 18, and in some occupations the attainment of the age of 21 has been made a significant factor by law or custom. This gradation of ages at which employment opportunities become less restricted is undoubtedly a significant factor in the high rates of unemployment among the youth who leave school and seek employment at the earlier ages.

In rural areas, irregular school attendance followed by early withdrawal from school is much more common than in cities. The result in terms of unemployment statistics, however, is not the same. Out-of-school youth in farm families are frequently reported by the census as "unpaid family workers," and are thus classed as employed rather than unemployed. When there is work to be done unpaid farm youth contribute real labor and are a definite part of the family economic unit. Very often, however, their labor could be readily dispensed with.

So-called employment as an unpaid family worker is frequently merely a stopgap pending the availability of some other form of employment.

The number of farm boys who reach maturity each year is more than twice the number of farms that fall vacant annually through the retirement or death of older farmers. Moreover, the limited number of available farms is not the only factor restricting opportunity in agriculture. It is probable that many adult farmers could be spared and many farms could be taken out of production without impairing the supply of agricultural products. It seems likely that for some years to come, from 300,000 to 400,000 oncoming farm youth, boys and girls, will annually become available for nonagricultural employment. At times when these young people remain on the farm because of a lack of opportunity elsewhere, they may not be counted as unemployed, but they will nonetheless constitute a surplus population in farming areas.

In general, the farm youth who find it easiest to migrate away from the farm are the ones who could remain with the largest chances for a successful and satisfactory farm life. The greatest problems are presented by the young people growing up in the farm families dependent upon public relief, the youth in the families of migratory farm laborers, and the youth who live in the cutover, eroded, and generally submarginal rural areas. Geographically, the difficulties are concentrated among the youth of the old cotton belt and in the southern highlands, although equally disadvantaged farm youth can be found in smaller numbers in other parts of the country. Many of the surplus farm youth of the cotton belt are Negroes and are faced with special difficulties in attempting to solve their problem through migration.

In recent months, young people have been moving into the new war industries and the Army in increasing numbers. In some cases they have gone directly from high school and college, and a tendency toward lower school and college enrollments has become apparent. In most cases, however, increases in employment have been accompanied by a decline in the number of unemployed youth.

In the industrial centers of the northeastern states and on the Pacific Coast, it is probably fair to say that youth unemployment is no longer a problem for competent youth 18 years of age or older, except in the case of Negroes and other minority groups for whom opportunities are restricted by discriminatory practices of employers and of organized labor. In many other urban areas which so far have not participated much in war industries, youth unemployment continues. Rural youth in some parts of the country are moving rapidly into industry, but the largest numbers of available rural youth, white and Negro, live at great distances from the centers of industrial activity and are being reached only at a slow rate.

The outlook for the immediate future is for a continued reduction in youth unemployment as long as the industrial and military activity of the war continues to increase. Over the longer future, it seems probable that after the war the trends which have resulted in youth unemployment in the past will again assert themselves.

### EMPLOYMENT AS A FACTOR IN PERSONAL GROWTH

No one is likely to assume that when young people leave school a long period of unemployment will provide a satisfactory introduction to their new life. But our ideas need clarification as to the specific effects of unemployment upon youth who are just reaching the threshold of maturity. Since unemployment is a negative condition, perhaps the discussion may best begin with a consideration of the effects of employment.

Employment has two major aspects—work and wages. Both are important.

Work is important because it provides the focus for a new organization of life habits. The best hours of the day must now be given over to an activity more purposeful, more controlled, and often more tiring than school. Fellow workers become the principal associates, and the supervisor or foreman enters life as a dominating influence; a new code of personal behavior must be assimilated. The work routine must be mastered, and skills must be learned in the use and care of tools and equipment. The concept of an honest day's work acquires meaning, and punctuality becomes something more than an old-fashioned virtue.

The care, energy, skill, and foresight of successful workers are habits. Like all habits, they can best be learned by a considerable amount of relatively unbroken practice. Like other habits, they can be learned more easily before incompatible practices have become too firmly implanted.

Wages are important because they provide an index of status on the job and a basis for the organization of life off the job. For young people, wages provide for the first time an income which is peculiarly their own. A part of that income, at least, is almost always left completely within their own control, even while they remain in the parental home. Training in the management of income is thereby provided in the only effective way, namely through practice; and the major restraining influence becomes not the external control of parents but the internal effect of the effort which went into earning the money. At this stage the dependency of childhood is often reversed by the initiation of contributions to family support, and at a later stage earnings begin to be considered as the possible foundation for marriage and the establishment of a new home.

The desire for independence of parental control is ever-present in youth. When parents cede control while at the same time providing financial resources for a wide range of activities, the results are sometimes detrimental to the best development of character and personality. When, however, young people obtain income under the steadying influence of a job and the income is dependent on the job, self-control, self-reliance, and self-support become linked together in the normal adult pattern.

As a part of the process of growing up, young people must eventually achieve the position in which they take complete responsibility as adults for the direction of their own personal activities. Work and wages together provide the basis for the achievement of this major personal goal.

Not all jobs are equally good as training for beginners. If the work and the supervision are irregular, the habits inculcated are likely to be the same. If the hours are excessive, the pay low, and the working conditions bad, the wages received may not be sufficient to perform their proper function and the work may be so poorly regarded by the young worker and his mates that the contribution to a self-respecting status may be very nearly nothing. The point need not be labored, but it should be remembered that many of the jobs available to young people during the depression years, as indicated in the report of the Maryland Youth Survey, were not much better than no jobs at all.

Nevertheless, with assimilation into even an inferior form of productive activity, young people come to feel a new respect for those who work. They learn anew the lesson of every oncoming generation, that work is the only basis for self-respecting participation in the working world of adults. As this new standard of values is acquired, adult valuations become intelligible, old friendships are likely to be reassessed, and personal relations with other people, young and old, begin to follow new channels.

Through the experience of work and association with those who work, youth who are reasonably well employed develop a new outlook on life possibilities, an outlook which is realistic but also characterized by a modest optimism. Every study of the vocational aspirations of adolescent youth in school has demonstrated the extent to which wishful thinking is a prevailing disease. Unemployment out of school has a sobering effect and may induce deep pessimism, but daydreaming about impossible life outcomes is likely to continue and may even be intensified. Employment, on the other hand, provides a sharp but necessary disillusionment for many young people. After the readjustment of ideas has been completed, the possibilities for small but definite gains in status then come to the fore and provide an effective incentive for effort. Such possibilities are the basis for the limited but real optimism which is characteristic of normal adults in ordinary circumstances.

To summarize, employment is necessary for most youth for the completion of the psychological process known as maturation. It is true that some girls may complete the process successfully by learning to take responsibility as homemakers, first in the parental home and later in homes of their own. Moreover, in the older form of family economic unit which still survives on the farm, both boys and girls may reach an effectively mature level of personality development without necessarily passing through any period of wage employment. But under modern conditions of urban life, it can be stated without qualification that all youth, young men and women alike, need and will usually profit from the experience of a job—a real job for which they receive wages and on which they take orders, do work whether it is pleasant or unpleasant, and adjust their own likes and dislikes to the requirements of the job, the boss, and the fellow workers.

### THE EFFECTS OF UNEMPLOYMENT UPON YOUTH

When young people leave school, they usually begin immediately to search for work, if they have not been able to arrange for employment even before leaving school. From a personal point of view, the urgency of the search is usually intensified by the fact that many other youth are leaving school at the same time—if one does not hasten, the jobs may be gone.

During most of the depression years, perhaps half of the new workseekers were successful in obtaining some employment within three months after leaving school. Usually the employment was part time or temporary, but at least it was a start. The remaining group moved into employment very slowly; half or more of those unemployed at the end of three months were still unemployed at the end of a year, and had never had a job.

The longer the period of unemployment for those never employed, the more unfavorable their situation became. Other youth who had left school at the same time, even if again unemployed, had the advantage of some working experience. Still other youth who had left school more recently were at least not under the stigma of long-continued unemployment. As the years of the depression wore on, there was undoubtedly an increasing carry-over from year to year of unemployed youth who had obtained no substantial work experience and whose chances for getting it in private employment were small indeed as long as employers could draw upon an abundant supply of oncoming youth fresh from school. In the Maryland Youth Survey, it was found that half of the unemployed youth had never had a full-time job. Some of them, interviewed in 1936, had been out of school and continuously unemployed for as long as seven years.

Any attempt to assess the influence of unemployment upon youth must take into account other factors which operate at the same time. The most important of these is probably the family situation and especially the impact of unemployment upon the family as a whole, since the typical young work-seeker is still living in the parental home. He or she usually occupies the position of a would-be supplementary wage earner in a family mainly dependent upon some other primary wage earner. Usually this is the father, although it may be the mother or an older brother or sister. In some cases both parents may be working or seeking work and there may be several supplementary wage earners. Disregarding these possible variations, the four situations most commonly found during a period of severe unemployment are as follows:

1. Father working, youth working
2. Father not working, youth working
3. Father working, youth not working
4. Father not working, youth not working

In the first of these situations, unemployment has not struck the family and there is no problem. In the second situation, the father is unemployed, but the older boy or girl is working. This is obviously not a case of youth unemployment, but under depression conditions it is a common situation in which unemployment is undoubtedly having an important effect upon the young person or persons concerned. Frequently schooling has been cut short, marriage has been postponed, a lower level of living is being endured, and the family as a whole is passing through a period of acute strain. But the young person who is the employed member of the family has come to grips with adult responsibility in full measure, has become a central member in the family councils, and in the end may become a better adult citizen for the experience.[2]

In the two major types of case where the young person is unemployed, the father may or may not be working. The situation in which the father is unemployed, when there are no other employed wage earners in the family, is clearly the most desperate of the four major typical situations from the standpoint of the family as a whole. Under urban conditions of life, few families can withstand this situation for more than six months to a year without resort to the social welfare agencies or to public assistance in some form.

If direct relief is the only alternative, the family finds that it is first required to complete the process of pauperizing itself by cashing any insurance policies, selling any remaining possessions of value, and moving to a lower grade of housing, if that is possible. The family next learns that it is best to make its expenditures in accordance with the views indicated by the social worker. Finally, the longer the family stays on direct relief, the more thoroughly it is taught by experience that every aspect of its welfare is dependent upon its efficiency in proving as often as necessary that it is quite unable to do anything for itself. The bad results of such an environment upon the development of young people in their formative years can readily be imagined.

In spite of many deficiencies as commonly administered, work relief in the form of WPA employment for the head of the family was a major upward step for millions of families previously on direct relief during the depression years. As work for a worker, WPA employment

[2]For case histories illustrating this specific point, as well as for his general analysis of the effects of unemployment, see the recent books by E. Wight Bakke, *The Unemployed Worker* and *Citizens Without Work* (New Haven: Yale University Press, 1940), 465 pp., 311 pp.

was often considerably less than satisfactory, but wages were paid. The head of the family was able to resume his position as the provider of income, the family resumed control over expenditure of the available income, and the normal pattern of family life could be reconstituted. There is substantially no evidence that unemployed young people in WPA families were in a worse position or in any essentially different position from unemployed youth in other low-income families where the primary wage earners had some form of regular employment.

The unemployed young people who lived for a period on direct relief had personal experience with one of the worst phases of the depression history in this country. But in most cases and especially in recent years, the typical unemployed young person is found in a family where the primary wage earner has employment, private or public. It is therefore especially important to explore the results of youth unemployment in this relatively common situation.

The most obvious aspect of the situation is the fact that young men and women who would normally become self-supporting are instead compelled by circumstances beyond their control to remain in the dependency of childhood. In most cases they are in no danger of being thrust out of the parental home, but as long as they are unable to obtain work and to produce income, they are likely to be treated as children. Parents may be sympathetic, but the young person who has reached the age of employability and who is out of school with nothing to do is increasingly made aware of the fact that he or she occupies a parasitic relationship.

Under the spur of this situation, few young people fail to make vigorous efforts to secure employment during the initial period out of school. Under depression conditions, those efforts necessarily will be unsuccessful for a considerable number. As time wears on and all of the possibilities are exhausted, further search seems futile and the sense of failure increases. Eventually the search is likely to be given up completely, although the merest rumor as to possible openings will usually stimulate a new effort to obtain work.

For youth of no more than average ability, the result of long-continued unemployment is usually an attitude of apathy and defeatism. A loss of interest in all forms of active life is one of the commonest tendencies. It shows itself in a reluctance to meet new people, in a lack of energy for vigorous sports, and sometimes in a failure to keep up previous reading habits even when the reading materials are available. The feeling grows that nothing which one does will have any important effect upon himself or anyone else, and that therefore nothing is worth doing.

The more able the young person, however, and the better his prospects before the onset of unemployment, the more likely it is that failure to secure employment will provoke a reaction of anger rather than of apathy. The revolutionary youth movements of Europe during the last twenty years found their spearhead and leadership, not in the unemployed youth of the masses, but in the unemployed graduates of the universities who had looked forward to brilliant careers in the law, in medicine, in governmental service, and in the other professions. These frustrated young people, convinced of their own ability by years of scholastic success and prepared only for highly specialized forms of intellectual activity, found themselves in thousands upon thousands of cases with literally no outlet for their costly training.[3] In this country we had no such problem during the 1920's. We had much more than a beginning of it during the 1930's among our unemployed young engineers, architects, chemists, lawyers, and other unemployed graduates of colleges and universities.

Whether apathetic or rebellious, a common outcome in the attitudes of unemployed youth is a loss of confidence in existing economic and social arrangements. Here it needs to be remembered that every person who is involuntarily unemployed must find some explanation for that fact, if he is to remain rational. Those who are unemployed for a long time have only two alternatives: they can blame themselves or blame

[3]For details see Walter M. Kotschnig, *Unemployment in the Learned Professions* (London: Oxford University Press, 1937), 347 pp. Although its relation to youth may not be immediately apparent from the title, this is in fact a book on youth unemployment.

the system. They can take the blame themselves only at the price of an acceptance of personal failure which may easily reach psychopathic levels. If they blame the system, they may develop lifelong tendencies toward radicalism, which may or may not be a good thing, but at any rate they save themselves and are not likely to become insane.

The least that can happen to a young person who is unemployed for a long period after leaving school is a postponement of growth and a failure to achieve a well-adjusted maturity of personality. In every case, postponement is at the peril of a distortion of individual development which may leave a twisted personality for life. In some cases there is great danger that hope, courage, and ability may disintegrate so completely under the stress of long-continued unemployment that a restoration at a later date will be very difficult, if possible at all.

### RESPONSIBILITY FOR YOUTH EMPLOYMENT

A high measure of social responsibility must be recognized for all forms of unemployment. In some cases the responsibility is greater than in others. In particular, when the unemployment of primary wage earners strikes at the basis of family life and endangers the livelihood of young children, the necessity for some appropriate form of social action is widely accepted.

The primary concern of the American Youth Commission is for youth. It therefore seems appropriate to reassert the principle, as old as history, that adults are responsible for providing suitable conditions for children and youth. In the present era, this means, among other things, that adults are responsible for providing opportunity for employment through which young people may undertake responsibility at a proper stage in their development. Since most adults are no longer in a position individually to provide self-employment, much less to provide employment for their children, the age-old responsibility for assuring youth a start in life has become largely a social responsibility.

As previous parts of this chapter have indicated, there is no longer any assurance that this social responsibility for young people will be discharged without conscious thought and action. The disturbing tendency to exclude juvenile beginners from employment, even when there is work for adults, goes back for many years. In recent times of general unemployment, youth have been conspicuous in the ranks of the unemployed. In the post-war period of readjustment, there is every reason to believe that unemployment will bear with special severity upon younger workers. Over the longer future, it is quite likely that as we work toward a condition of full employment, the youngest workers, especially those under 21, will be among the last to move into regular full-time employment.

The Commission recommends, therefore, that in the formulation of public policy at all levels, explicit recognition be given to the social responsibility of seeing to it that all young people are constructively occupied up to some appropriate age. The Commission believes that 21 is the age which ought to be recognized for this purpose. In so far as any specific age can do so, it corresponds to a real point in the process of maturation for a very large number of individuals, and it has been imbedded in law and custom by centuries of usage.

Emphasis on responsibility for youth under 21 does not imply that young people should be neglected above that age. In recent years a number of youth programs have been provided which included young people up to varying ages above 21. Under the circumstances and in view of the previous lack of attention, this probably was desirable. But in the future, if young people have previously received proper care, education, and training, by the age of 21 they should be as able to take care of themselves as most adults. As in the case of older adults, assistance may be needed in some cases.

The special social obligation to youth under 21 can be met mainly in three ways: by providing schooling, by efforts to expand normal employment opportunities, and by appropriate programs of public work.

The Commission believes that adequate facilities for schooling should be provided and that all youth should be required and enabled to attend school up to the age of 16. Above that age, many youth should continue in school for varying numbers of years in accordance with their own needs and those of society. Many youth now forced to leave school prematurely who would benefit from additional years of education should be assisted to continue. Likewise, many youth who now continue full time in school or college far beyond the point beneficial either to them or to society should be strongly advised to discontinue their full-time formal education when employment opportunities are available.

For many youth, only work and wages can provide the experiences most urgent for their further personal development after they have finished the tenth grade. For all youth, it would be a great improvement over the present condition of affairs if the principle were widely accepted that formal education should not be continued beyond the twelfth or thirteenth grade without several months of experience in some realistic form of gainful employment. Certainly a period of at least six months of full-time or twelve months of half-time experience would not be too much to expect at this point in personal development.

A generation ago, it is probable that the majority of youth entering college had met the test of work through the accumulation of part-time, summer, and other employment. Since then, the proportion of youth who continue their education beyond the period of adolescence has greatly increased, but the proportion who obtain the toughening experience of employment along the way has greatly declined.

Sometimes parents who have the financial resources to continue the education of their children appear to have some fear that if the children are employed for a year at some point between the ages of 16 and 20, they will develop new standards of values and a new independence of spirit which together will result in a refusal to resume formal education. To this it may be said quite simply that if that proves in fact to be the result, it may well be to the best interests of all concerned. On the other hand, every mature teacher of youth welcomes especially the youth who have adjusted to the hammering experiences of a real job and have then decided that they need and will benefit from further education. The greatest misfits among youth today include many of those who have good minds, but who have pursued the absorptive processes of reading, listening, and studying so long and so uninterruptedly that their personalities have taken on the major characteristics of a sponge.

It is recognized that whenever employment opportunities are limited, it will be difficult to secure general acceptance for the view that for each youth full-time formal education should cease at the point where he or she would profit more from a job. Doubtless many young people might well remain in school a year or two longer or drop out a year or two sooner than would otherwise be desirable, in accordance with the degree of probability that suitable gainful employment can be secured.

For those young people, however, who have reached the point where realistic employment is urgently needed as a maturing experience, if not also as a permanent basis for adult life, school is a very poor substitute. This is certainly true of the schools as they now exist, and it will probably remain true under any state of affairs that can readily be imagined. If the school should adopt the purpose of producing goods and services, turn itself into a factory, pay wages, hire foremen, and in other respects conduct itself as an employing institution for masses of young people, perhaps the school might be able to perform the function of an employer in the development of youth. But would such an institution be a school?

The solution which would be universally acceptable and which is greatly needed would be the maintenance of regular employment opportunities at a level such that when young people need jobs, they could obtain them without undue difficulty. But to provide this solution, we must solve the problem of full employment for all, young and old, under modern economic conditions. Moreover, it must be solved not merely through the military and economic activity of war but on a basis which will give some assurance of continuing full employment under peacetime conditions.[4]

[4]See Chapter V of this report.

The Commission believes that in future years it will be a major objective of the American people to manage our economic system so effectively that a sustained level of full employment can be achieved through the regular channels, including employment in necessary governmental services as well as in private economic activity. We can and should begin to work toward that objective without waiting for the return of peace. At the end of this war it should be possible to avoid any large amount of chronic peacetime unemployment, although some years of additional effort may be needed to achieve full employment on a permanent basis.

Meanwhile, it will be essential to provide a program of public work for young people which can be contracted and expanded in accordance with the extent of the need. In conjunction with attendance at school and with employment in private industry and in the regular branches of government, the program of public work for unemployed youth should be sufficiently extensive at all times to make it possible for all young people to be constructively occupied up to the age of 21.

No fully adequate peacetime program of public work for unemployed young people has yet been provided in this or any other country.[5] Major attempts to meet the needs of youth have been made, however, through the distinctive special youth work programs of the Civilian Conservation Corps and the National Youth Administration. We turn, therefore, to a consideration of those programs.

[5]For a description of European youth work programs prior to the present war, see Kenneth Holland, *Youth in European Labor Camps* (Washington: American Council on Education, 1939), 303 pp.

# CHAPTER

# II

## EXPERIENCE WITH YOUTH WORK PROGRAMS

O F THE two major agencies to provide employment for unemployed youth, the Civilian Conservation Corps is the older and better understood. It was established in 1933 and has employed more than 2,500,000 young men, as well as a considerable number of unemployed war veterans who have been assigned to special camps. The National Youth Administration was established in 1935 and has provided part-time employment for more than 1,750,000 out-of-school young people as well as administering a student work program through which more than 1,800,000 needy youth in school and college have been assisted.

### THE CIVILIAN CONSERVATION CORPS

The Civilian Conservation Corps[1] was established initially to provide work relief and to conserve and develop natural resources. The new agency was headed by a director appointed by the President, but most of the work of organizing and administering the Corps was

[1] For an earlier but more detailed presentation of the Commission's findings and recommendations, see *The Civilian Conservation Corps*, adopted December 6, 1940, and published in pamphlet form. The descriptive statements of the present chapter have been revised as of October 1941.

carried on under the general supervision of the ccc director through older federal departments. The Departments of Agriculture and Interior laid out the work projects and organized the project supervisory force. The War Department built the camps to house the enrollees, organized the services of transportation and supply, and took all responsibility for camp administration, including the supervision of the health, welfare, and discipline of the enrollees.

The physical organization and character of the ccc has been determined from the first by the nature of the work to be done. Conservation work cannot be done in a workshop; it has to be carried on at the points where the natural resources in need of conservation are located. Work projects for the ccc have been established accordingly throughout the national forests, the national parks, and the other public lands of the United States; on state forest and park lands; and in soil conservation districts where privately owned lands are being improved under agreements between the owners and the United States Department of Agriculture.

Projects have been authorized for prosecution in accordance with their general importance and urgency. Project priorities have been influenced by a desire to spread the work somewhat evenly throughout the country, and to avoid concentrating large numbers of camps in any one area, but the geographic distribution of the public lands and of other major areas of conservation activity is such that the distribution of ccc work projects necessarily departs widely from the general geographic distribution of the population of the United States.

Each standard ccc camp is built to provide housing for a group of 200 enrollees in barracks of 40 each. Since enrollees must be transported daily between camp and the points where work is currently in progress, each camp must be located so far as possible at the center of the area throughout which project activity is to be carried on. Ordinarily a camp is not established in any area where there is not enough work needed to justify operation of the camp for a period of five years.

The enrollees who make up the working force are recruited by state selecting agencies, usually the public assistance divisions of the various states. For a number of years only unemployed youth in relief families were eligible for admission as junior enrollees. The requirements have since been relaxed to admit any unemployed young man between the ages of 17 and 23 who is in need of work and training, but selection continues to be carried on by the public assistance authorities.

The age of the enrollees is lower than is commonly realized. Most of them enter camp at the age of 17 or 18; of those currently in camp, 44 percent are 17 and another 39 percent are 18 or 19. Enrollees sign up for periods of six months and may re-enroll for periods up to a total of two years.

The enrollees come predominantly from a low-income family background, whether urban or rural, and their records at the time of entering camp indicate many deficiencies in the care, education, and training they have previously received. The typical enrollee has completed a little more than eight grades of school in the course of ten to eleven years of school attendance. A considerable number of the enrollees have not progressed in literacy beyond the fourth-grade level, although others have been graduated from high school, and a few have attended college. Important segments of the ccc youth population include the 20 percent of enrollees with foreign-born parents, the 10 percent who are Negroes, and the 37 percent from broken homes. About 70 percent have had no significant work experience before entering camp, and most of the others have had only a few months of previous employment.

As the characteristics of the enrollee group have become more widely known, public policy has moved toward the point of view that conservation work should continue to be the major activity, but in the conduct of such work and in the administration of the Corps generally, the welfare and training of the enrollees should be a primary objective. This view was reflected fully in the most recent legislation extending the life of the Corps, and in the executive action transferring the Corps to the Federal Security Agency when that agency was established.

In the day-by-day operation of the projects and camps, however, enrollee welfare has seldom been made the central objective, although it has received more attention in recent years than was given to it at the beginning. The project supervisory forces have continued to operate under the direction of the Departments of Agriculture and Interior, and have been primarily concerned with advancing the objectives of those departments. The tendency at first on the projects was to treat the enrollee groups in the same manner as any other common labor force. It soon became evident, however, that the enrollees needed a large amount of job training by the supervisors, and that if the number of salaried foremen was to be held within reasonable limits, the more talented enrollees must be rapidly developed for service as semiskilled workmen, gang leaders, and subforemen. In recent years there has been much highly commendable effort to improve the quality of supervision and to provide more thorough training for enrollees on the work projects.

Camp administration has been the responsibility of the War Department. That department has taken pride in its administration of the CCC camps and has provided a high standard of institutional care for the enrollees. At no time has there been any serious complaint concerning the food, shelter, clothing, or medical care; safety standards and sanitation have been maintained at high levels. This has been no small achievement, particularly in view of the number of camps and the isolated areas in which many are established.

The construction of barracks and other camp buildings, an activity in which enrollees might well have participated, was performed exclusively through the employment of workmen from the usual building trades. Most of the work of camp maintenance and operation, however, has been carried on by the use of enrollee labor. In each camp a number of enrollees are detailed to work full time in connection with camp operation, and all enrollees participate in some phases of camp housekeeping, in addition to their work on the projects.

A leisure-time educational program has been carried on in the camps under the joint auspices of the War Department and the United States Office of Education, with a full-time educational adviser assigned to each camp. Most enrollees spend several hours a week outside working hours in attending classes in vocational or academic subjects. The educational program has been frequently criticized in educational circles on grounds that it was not being well administered, and there has undoubtedly been some basis for such criticism. In the camps where a good program has been provided, it has usually been the result of special competence on the part of the educational adviser or unusual interest on the part of the company commander or project superintendent.

Since the beginning of the program, about one enrollee in five has ended his camp experience through desertion or for disciplinary reasons. This proportion seems unnecessarily high, although in many colleges the percentage of entering freshmen who fail to go beyond the first year is as high or higher. There is some reason to believe that many CCC enrollees who are especially immature or who are unable to adjust rapidly to new conditions are discouraged and repelled by the impersonal manner in which they are treated at the induction centers, on arrival at camp, and in many of the processes of camp administration. More individual attention and a more friendly spirit on the part of some officials would be helpful.

The majority of the enrollees who remain for an entire six months' enrollment or for longer periods are benefited greatly. The benefits include the experience and training on the work projects, conspicuous gains in health and physical fitness, improvement in morale and self-confidence, and in many cases a generally beneficial reorganization of personal habits and attitudes.

With the expansion of private employment in recent months, employers have been turning increasingly to the CCC as a source of labor supply. It has become apparent that former CCC enrollees are as eagerly sought by employers as any other group of available young men with comparable qualifications. The reason for the outspoken approval of many employers seems to be that in the CCC the conditions of employment approximate those of private industry somewhat more generally than is the case on other public work programs or on most school-administered programs of work or vocational education. Most CCC enrollees unquestionably do learn to work a full day, to carry out directions, and to take pride in their work. In some cases they also have opportunity to learn specific skills which are of value.

In addition to benefiting the enrollees, the CCC has contributed greatly to the maintenance and development of the natural resources of the United States. The value of the work accomplished during the first eight years of the CCC has been officially estimated to be in excess of $1,500,000,000. Any such estimate necessarily includes speculative elements, but the accomplishment has undoubtedly been very large. For the first time in their history, the major conservation agencies of the federal government were provided with a labor force approximating the size of their task. An immense amount remains to be done, and it is evident that large labor forces will continue to be needed if our national estate is to be maintained adequately on a permanent basis.

In a previous statement, the American Youth Commission called attention to the fact that Negroes have been largely excluded from supervisory and administrative positions in the CCC, except as educational advisers in camps for Negro enrollees.[2] In the year which has elapsed since this statement was made, the general occupational problems of Negroes have received more public attention than in any previous period, and there have been specific attempts on the part of administrative officials to improve the situation in the CCC. The effort which has gone into these attempts has been praiseworthy, but the amount of actual improvement appears to be small. In particular, there is still a general reluctance to promote Negroes above the posi-

[2] *The Civilian Conservation Corps*, pp. 18–19.

tion of leader enrollee, although many white enrollees have been promoted to positions in the supervisory and administrative group in recent months. The Commission again affirms its previous recommendation of vigorous action to increase the use of Negro supervisory and administrative personnel in camps for Negro enrollees.

The beginning years of the CCC were years of great and rapid achievement. It became one of the most popular of all governmental agencies. A tendency then developed to rest on the laurels of early accomplishment, and the rate of progress became markedly slower. More recently the program has suffered from an excessively high rate of turnover on the part of the company commanders and subalterns who operate the camps, and the preoccupation of the War Department with problems of military defense has perhaps led to some deterioration in the parts of the program for which it has been responsible. On the other hand, however, there have been specific efforts by the CCC administrative officials to improve the general administration of the program and to adapt it to the requirements of the present period, and there has probably been some continuing improvement in the day-to-day operation of the work projects.

If the CCC is to be continued on even a skeleton basis for the duration of the present war effort, it may be necessary to modify the program in many particulars. With vigorous and alert administration, however, it is probable that the CCC can continue to combine important forms of national service, such as safeguarding the national forests, with types of experience which are essential for many 17- and 18-year-old youth.

## THE NATIONAL YOUTH ADMINISTRATION

The principal function of the National Youth Administration is to provide employment for unemployed young persons on public projects of various types. It also administers a program of student work, through which funds are provided for the part-time employment of needy young persons in schools, colleges, and universities to enable them to continue their education. In this part of the report, the Commission is concerned with the NYA only as an agency to provide employment for unemployed youth.[3]

In its original form, the NYA was a relief agency constituting a part of the Works Progress Administration, the predecessor of the present Work Projects Administration. Since 1939, the NYA has been a part of the Federal Security Agency.

The NYA program of work projects for unemployed out-of-school youth began in 1935 as a sort of junior WPA. It was established by the same administrative officials who were in charge of the WPA. They had become conscious that many unemployed youth in relief families could not be given access to WPA employment because such employment was confined mainly to heads of families. On a special youth work program, it seemed likely that it would be possible to provide more appropriate supervision for younger workers and a greater variety of desirable types of work experience, while at the same time accomplishing light construction work and other projects for community betterment.

In view of the later criticism of the duplication resulting from the existence of two federal youth work agencies, it may be noted that the NYA was created by deliberate executive action after the CCC had already been in operation for two years. Certain limitations in the CCC program had become evident. At that time it was operating at an annual cost per enrollee of about $1,200 a year. This restricted the possibilities for CCC expansion. There was also the fact that many young men who otherwise might have enrolled in the CCC were unwilling to leave their home communities, and the further consideration that unemployed young women were not eligible for CCC enrollment.

The NYA was founded on the belief that by allowing unemployed young men and women to remain in the parental home and by using community facilities to the utmost, a desirable youth employment pro-

[3]For a review of the NYA work program, as well as a general discussion of the major issues involved in the operation of such a program, see Lewis L. Lorwin, *Youth Work Programs: Problems and Policies* (Washington: American Council on Education, 1941), 195 pp.

gram could be provided on a part-time basis at costs per youth very much lower than those of either the CCC or WPA. For several years, the NYA succeeded in keeping its total expenditures for each part-time youth worker under $225 a year. The program was less than adequate in many respects, but the total accomplishment for the amount expended was substantial.

The work projects carried on by the NYA have been so diversified that it is not easy to describe the program. In former years, construction projects provided the largest amount of employment for young men. Thousands of small public buildings have been constructed—rural schools, vocational education workshops, community center buildings, and recreation structures and buildings of many types. Roads, sidewalks, parks, airports, and river banks have been improved. Young women, on the other hand, have been employed mainly in clerical and service types of activity. Clerical workers and other assistants have been provided in schools, hospitals, libraries, and social work agencies of all sorts. Both young men and women have been put to work in production workshops. Quantities of clothing, household articles, hospital supplies, school furniture, playground equipment, and other articles have been produced or repaired in the NYA production units.

Most of the projects have been sponsored by school boards, city governments, and other local public and private nonprofit agencies. Sponsoring agencies have supervised much of the work and have frequently contributed materials and equipment. Youth have been put to work in their own communities, usually in small groups ranging from one to thirty persons on a project. The whole program has been extremely flexible and highly decentralized.

In 1937 the NYA began to experiment with so-called resident centers, to which rural young people could be brought for work and training in agriculture and home economics. These centers were usually established in conjunction with educational institutions. Later the NYA began to establish centers which specialized in shop training for industrial and mechanical occupations. The resident center program has been a significant developmental activity for several years, although at no time have the resident centers included as many as 15 percent of the youth on NYA work projects.

Since July 1939, when it became a part of the Federal Security Agency, the NYA has developed rapidly and has changed in character to a considerable degree. Previously, many administrative functions of the NYA had been performed for it by WPA administrative personnel both at the national headquarters and throughout the states. With the complete segregation of personnel, functions, and activities, the NYA established a clear-cut identity of its own for the first time. It has set up its own machinery for recruitment, selection, and assignment of youth personnel. Relief status has been dropped entirely as a condition of eligibility for NYA employment, although the youth workers are still required to be unemployed members of low-income families.

Beginning in October 1940, the NYA was given special funds with which "to provide employment for needy young persons between the ages of 17 and 24, inclusive, in resident and workshop projects which furnish work experience preparatory to employment in defense occupations." This defense work program is at present limited to not more than 100,000 youth at any one time, and $60,000,000 was appropriated for the fiscal year ending June 30, 1942. The unit cost of the defense program will be much higher than that of the regular program and will exceed $600 per youth worker a year, although this is to some extent a misleading figure. Youth move through the program into industry so rapidly that most of them do not remain on the program longer than three months. Among other productive activities, youth workers on this program produce articles and equipment for the military services. They are trained for specific war industry occupations through careful supervision on the job, with related instruction provided by public vocational schools. The program is proving effective as a means of providing workers for the war industries.

During most of its existence the major limitations of the NYA, as well as much of its pioneering, have grown out of the fact that it is an attempt to cover as much as possible of the out-of-school youth problem of both young men and young women with a relatively small amount of money. The program has been spread so thin that the quality of performance has necessarily suffered.

The major means of spreading the program has consisted of employing youth on a part-time basis, averaging around 60 hours a month in former years with average compensation of about $16 a month. In most cases these payments were not sufficient to represent a self-supporting contribution to the family budget for youth who were living at home as members of low-income or relief families. Moreover, the hours worked on the regular program were so few that the employment was discontinuous, difficult to organize and supervise, often inefficient and unproductive, and not always fully conducive to the establishment of the best work habits.

On the special defense work program, the youth workers must devote 160 hours a month to a combination of work on the projects and related instruction provided by educational authorities, with a minimum of 80 hours of work a month. Recently the regulations of the NYA were revised to provide for a minimum of 80 hours of work a month by the youth workers on the regular program, with small upward adjustments of the monthly rate of pay.

These were commendable steps, but a half-time work program should not be regarded as adequate for most unemployed youth. It is particularly inadequate unless a supplementary educational program is also provided by some appropriate agency to complete a program in which unemployed young people may be constructively occupied on a full-time basis. An educational program has not yet been provided for a majority of the youth on the regular NYA work projects.

### RELATIONS BETWEEN CCC AND NYA

As the years have gone by and the CCC and NYA have developed their respective programs, the expediency of maintaining two separately organized youth work agencies has been more and more called in question. The transfer of both establishments in 1939 to the new Federal Security Agency was a step in the direction of coordinated planning for their activities. So far, however, each youth program has continued to maintain a high degree of autonomy.

At one time or another, the NYA has carried on many of the types of productive activity in which the CCC engages. Although it has not operated large residential conservation projects in isolated areas, it has carried on a variety of conservation work, usually in small units and with youth workers remaining at home. On the other hand, the CCC has not confined its operations to work in areas where housing for the workers was a requisite of successful operation. Housing and maintenance account for much of the cost of the CCC, yet in some instances it has established camps in areas where unemployed youth and adults living at home could have been mobilized at less cost for the same work.

The NYA resident work centers have more elaborate training and instructional programs than the typical CCC camp. But in connection with its central motor repair shops, the CCC has established resident training centers for enrollees which have much in common with the NYA industrial workshop resident centers.

As such instances of similarity and duplication multiply, it becomes increasingly clear that the total amount of funds provided the two programs could be used more effectively under unified responsibility for program planning and administration. This is not only true in connection with the over-all planning of work projects, the establishment of priorities, and the decision as to which projects will include housing and which will utilize local unemployed youth living at home. It is even more evident in connection with the recruitment, selection, assignment, job training, and eventual placement of the youth in private employment.

In general, any youth who is eligible for enrollment in the CCC is also eligible for NYA employment. Many CCC enrollees have been on NYA rolls either before or after their CCC experience, and most young men who participate in one program or the other have to choose between them. The choice for many young men has been influenced by such factors as the aggressiveness of the respective selecting agents, the extent to which youth are well informed concerning both programs, differences in cash allowances, and other factors either irrelevant or only partially relevant to youth welfare and national welfare.

In the present period of expanding opportunities for employment in the war industries, the CCC is having increasing difficulty in recruiting enrollees in most states. This is due only in part to the decline in unemployment. Unemployed youth who might otherwise enroll hesitate to do so because of the isolation of the camps from normal employment opportunities, and because it is not possible to provide experience and job training on most CCC work projects for the kind of employment which is becoming available in the war industries. The NYA has been having much less difficulty so far in recruiting youth workers in most parts of the country because it is able to give employment, experience, and job training to unemployed youth who would otherwise move into industrial employment at a slower rate. Youth on local NYA work projects can and do continue to seek other employment while employed on the projects.

The present difficulties of the CCC could be overcome to a considerable extent if the activities of the CCC and NYA were integrated. It would not be necessary to alter the major functions of the CCC. The camp activities would become a part of a larger program with strong roots in the communities where youth live. In the larger program, the camp projects would be joined with the employment and job-training activities of the NYA. Unemployed youth could then be transferred back and forth between the camps and other parts of the total program on the basis best adapted to their individual development for employment in the war industries, for military service, and for normal civilian occupations. In such a total program, the physical isolation of the CCC camps and the nature of the conservation work projects would be less of a deterrent to enrollment.

If present enrollment trends continue, the CCC may soon be left with no immediate reason for continued operation as a youth employment program. Yet it will continue to have a high potential usefulness as long as there are substantial numbers of unemployed young men between the ages of 17 and 21. The most recent statistical analyses indicate that unemployment in this age group is still far from ended in most parts of the country.

Moreover, although some conservation projects can be deferred without great loss until some later period of more severe unemployment, the complete cessation of the ccc conservation work for the duration of the present emergency would be a disaster for which generations would pay in depleted soil and forest resources. In particular, fire losses would probably become severe, since emergency fire-fighting crews are especially difficult to recruit during periods of high industrial activity. The problem of adequate fire protection in the national parks and forests had not been solved before the ccc. An adequate solution probably cannot be found without an equivalent of the ccc.

The American Youth Commission recommends the consolidation of the ccc and the nya into a single youth work projects administration. The existing work programs of both agencies should be continued by the new agency, and it should conduct any other major work programs for unemployed youth that may be found appropriate. Within the consolidated youth work projects administration, it would be desirable to maintain the Civilian Conservation Corps as a somewhat distinctive work program for young men on conservation projects where housing of the workers is required, but with unified administration of all matters pertaining to youth personnel. A variety of approaches to the problem of youth unemployment through several different types of work program would be highly desirable provided there is adequate central planning and control to prevent unwise duplication of effort and conflicts in administration.[4]

[4] On October 27, 1941, Federal Security Administrator Paul V. McNutt announced to the press that he had been requested by the President to prepare plans in cooperation with the Bureau of the Budget for the consolidation of the ccc and nya, including plans for such legislation as might be necessary, as well as plans for transferring from the War Department to the Federal Security Agency all administrative duties in connection with the operation of the ccc.

Consolidation of the ccc and nya was first recommended by the American Youth Commission in the statement entitled *The Civilian Conservation Corps*, adopted December 6, 1940, and published at that time. The Commission again affirmed this recommendation at its meeting in May 1941 and in the final adoption of the present report on October 9, 1941.

# CHAPTER
## III

# WORK PROGRAMS FOR YOUTH
# IN THE FUTURE

---

IN SOME quarters it is being suggested that all programs to provide public work for the unemployed should be abandoned for the duration of the war because of the overwhelming increase in federal expenditures required to carry on the war effort, and the decline in unemployment which is largely the result of those expenditures. It is argued both that we cannot afford to provide public work for the unemployed and that the work is no longer needed. Some of the suggestions for economizing have been particularly directed at the youth work programs of the CCC and NYA.

No one contends, least of all the American Youth Commission, that anyone should be kept on any public job that can be dispensed with at a time when his services are needed more elsewhere. This principle is far more widely applicable than merely in connection with the work programs. On those programs, in so far as they exist to relieve unemployment, obviously activities should be reduced whenever unemployment declines to a point where the activities are not fully needed. But the measure of need is the remaining amount of unemployment.

In some industrial centers with large war industries, unemployment has vanished. In such areas, the work programs should be brought to a close, unless it is found that they are carrying on essential activities or providing training that cannot be provided as effectively in any other way. Such a finding would not be strange in some cases, in view of the amount of civilian training and necessary productive activity that is being carried on under the work programs.

In most parts of the country, unemployment still remains and is even being increased from time to time as priorities on materials and equipment bring about the curtailment of employment in peacetime industries. Because of this factor, progress toward full employment is neither as rapid nor as regular as had been expected. Until full employment has been reached generally throughout the country, and not merely in limited areas, work programs for the unemployed will be needed and should be continued on a scale proportionate to the needs.

We shall not come to financial disaster by maintaining an adequate amount of public work as long as it is needed. The work programs are a form of productive activity. At a time when nothing should be wasted, they utilize human labor that would otherwise run to waste. They are carrying on activities that are useful, that are steadily increasing in usefulness, and that will be sorely missed whenever the labor ceases to be available for them because it is needed more elsewhere.

With the current intensification of war effort, it is probable that we shall reach full employment in most areas before another year has passed. Some shifting of population will be required, and undoubtedly a considerable amount of economic dislocation will continue and will retard the expansion of employment.

In the event of full employment, we shall be faced with two principal alternative courses of action in regard to the work programs. They may be liquidated and dispensed with. Or for the time being they may cease to have any function of unemployment relief, but may be continued nevertheless as agencies through which to prosecute various types of civilian defense activity; perhaps in some cases they may continue peacetime activities which are essential to long-range national welfare and which would not seem likely to be cared for in any other manner.

If we could be assured that we would never need them again, much could be said for winding up the work programs at the earliest date at which we reach full employment. All activity for the war would then have to proceed on its own merits and through such organizations as might seem most appropriate for the purpose.

But the prospective situation is not likely to be so simple. If we reach full employment during the present period, it will be under circumstances which can only be regarded as highly abnormal. We shall continue to hope for other times and other circumstances, in which employment will not be sustained by military expenditures on a tremendous scale, and in which we shall revert to problems no more difficult than those of recent years. In such times, we shall again need the work programs to relieve unemployment while we continue to seek better solutions of the problem of full employment under peacetime conditions.

This may seem to offer the possibility of a dilemma, if we admit on the one hand that the work programs may cease to be needed to relieve unemployment but on the other hand we wish to see them maintained in some form against a later day of need. Actually, this dilemma is not likely to develop, in view of the tendencies that are already apparent.

The Public Works Administration, previously on the point of decease, was revived to administer certain kinds of national defense construction work. The Work Projects Administration, although greatly curtailed, has increased its concentration upon military construction and civilian defense until about one-third of the WPA workers are on such projects. The NYA has become mainly an agency to provide preliminary experience and job training for war industry occupations. The CCC is carrying on some military construction work and has a backlog of essential conservation work that should be continued on at least a limited scale under almost any conditions.

These agencies will always have enough important work during the present period to justify their continuation on at least a small scale. As unemployment declines, the less important projects are being and should be curtailed. If unemployment vanishes entirely, it may be necessary for the agencies to change their employment policies and even to recruit labor forces in the competitive labor market, in order to continue activities which will be regarded as essential and which they will be as well qualified to carry on as the new agencies that would otherwise be necessary.

In any event, the Commission feels impelled to warn against forms of retrenchment which would in effect abandon the remaining young men and women who need assistance, merely because the number is smaller than in former years. In a time of crisis such as the present, it is imperative to maintain the morale of the whole population, and especially of youth, by seeing to it that everyone is useful and that no one is left out. The total need for assistance to youth is smaller than it has been for ten years, but the need for action in regard to the part of the problem which still remains has never been more acute.

## POST-WAR PUBLIC WORK FOR YOUTH AND ADULTS

Whenever we are able to reach a period of general demobilization of military activity and the war industries, several million workers will be released for a return to the occupations of peace. Other millions who provide goods and services for the war industry workers and who are dependent upon their expenditures for consumption will likewise be affected. The present geographic redistribution of population will be reversed to some extent. The whole process of readjustment will be difficult.

At the very least a period of one or two years of inadequate employment in private enterprise would seem likely. The period will be much longer unless governmental economic policies are handled with great skill and unless there is a general disposition on the part of private economic leadership to proceed rapidly with the work of reconstruction.

Undoubtedly there will be a backlog of demand for new housing, for durable consumer goods, and for the general rebuilding of the capital equipment of this country, as well as for assistance in reconstituting the economic life of other countries. A post-war sequence similar to that of 1919–29 is far from impossible.

But the post-war outlook after this war will not be the outlook which followed the first World War, partly because the recollection of the chronic unemployment prior to the present war will still be vivid. Moreover, if for any extended period of time unemployment is again allowed to mount to the level of 10 or 12 million or more, the strain will be so great that it may become disastrous.

Accordingly, steps must be taken. But what steps? First and most important is the formulation of measures to bring about a rapid expansion of employment in the peacetime industries. The adoption of specific governmental measures for planned industrial expansion under peacetime conditions would be desirable. In any event, the general economic policies of government must be directed to that end.[1]

There is not much doubt, however, that employment in the war industries can be curtailed more rapidly than employment in private peacetime industries can be expanded. It is always easier to produce unemployment than to produce employment. To tide over the gap and to hold unemployment within the lowest practicable limits, we shall need provision for peacetime public work, to be carried on as long as needed.

If our advance planning is expert and our economic management in the interim is skillful, the need for public work might be temporary and on no larger a scale, for example, than the programs conducted in 1938 and 1939. It is more likely that we shall not be so fortunate, and that the necessary programs will have to be larger and to be continued for a considerable number of years.

The unemployed workers who will need the work programs will include millions of the younger workers between 21 and 30 who are

[1]See Chapter V of this report.

now going into the war industries and the military services. As the Commission has already pointed out, these younger workers when demobilized will constitute a "youth problem" in a very real sense. They will have strong claims on the attention of their country. If those claims are not met, these young people will not rest in silence. Every post-war movement of social unrest will cater to this group. Any movement which received their united allegiance could rapidly assume revolutionary proportions.

For this group, however, the answer will not be a special youth work program. They will belong on a program for adults, and an adequate program for adults in which they can participate should be provided.

An adequate program will not consist entirely or even largely of innumerable small projects, carried on mainly by hand labor with little material or equipment. This is an immense country with unrivaled potentialities. We have never had enough labor to accomplish the things we want done. Whenever unusual amounts of labor become available for public work because they are not employed elsewhere, we should seize the opportunity to proceed as rapidly and as efficiently as possible with the conservation work, the great construction projects, the rebuilding that is required on every hand, and the innumerable other tasks that will advance the common interest.

Early in the period of unemployment from 1930 to 1940, we started feebly and with many misgivings to carry on a small emergency program of public works, mainly under private contract. In 1933, we provided substantial funds for the purpose but also provided so carefully for their expenditure that the effect was delayed for years. Then, because the effect obviously was delayed, we again provided large funds and proceeded to spend them by hiring the unemployed and putting them to work at whatever task offered, without waiting to plan large construction projects or to deal with private contractors. For convenience, the first effort may be called the PWA type of activity; the second effort was the WPA type.

Through the irony of circumstance and the inadequacy of our knowledge, we began our attack on unemployment by using the type of heavy construction program which takes longest to come to fruition, and then at a later date transferred our major emphasis to the type of program which can be started most quickly. Then we kept on using the short-time type of program year after year because we continued to think that the emergency was almost over.

In any similar future period, we shall find a place for both types of program. If we could develop enough foresight, however, it would seem desirable to reverse the order in which the two types of program are given importance. In other words, for any period of severe unemployment lasting as long as two or three years, it would seem wise to start with a WPA type of program and then to shift the major emphasis as rapidly as feasible to the PWA type, which accomplishes projects often of more evident value, puts more people to work in private employment both directly and indirectly, and tends more effectively to restore the processes of private enterprise.

The foresight problem may not be as difficult as it seems. During any period of rapidly declining private employment, such as may come when the war ends and there is a return to conditions of peace, it should not require much foresight to expand a WPA program rapidly, especially if there is some advance planning of projects. On the other hand, if unemployment is once allowed to become large, it ought to be assumed as a basis for planning that it will continue for a proportionate length of time. Whenever unemployment is in excess of 6,000,000 persons, for example, it would be reasonable to assume that private employment will not expand more rapidly than an additional 3,000,000 jobs a year. Accordingly, there should be no hesitancy whatever about organizing and prosecuting a PWA type of program whenever unemployment has become large.

### SPECIAL YOUTH WORK PROGRAMS

In any program which brings about an expansion of normal private employment, young people will participate to some degree. Likewise, in public works carried on by the regular government construction agencies, such as the state highway departments, and in emergency PWA type programs carried on through contractors, the participation of young people will be similar to their participation in private industry. In WPA type programs, however, relief standards of eligibility for employment are likely to persist for a long time. Even if the principle should become widely accepted that a job should be provided for every unemployed worker, the application of this principle in the case of adults is likely to remain highly restricted for many years. As long as this is the case, it is probable that unemployed young people will be able to participate in WPA type programs only when they are heads of families or primary wage earners, and usually only if they have a previous record of employment or military service.

The question arises, therefore, as to what more is needed; and it is evident that there will continue to be need for special youth work programs. If such programs were to be abolished, it would probably become necessary to reconstitute them for the same reasons that obtained when the present special youth work programs were originated: discrimination against youth in private employment in the interests of those already at work as long as private employment is below a full employment level; no assurance that the major public work programs can or will make an adequate place for youth; and a general belief in the advantages of separately organized work programs for unemployed beginning workers. These advantages include the opportunity for special supervision and job training on the one hand, and a lower cost per worker on the other hand because of the fact that beginning workers do not earn an adult wage and, if living in the parental home, do not need an adult income.

If, however, special youth work programs are to continue to exist side by side with much larger programs for the general group of unemployed workers, how shall they be differentiated?

Age limits for eligibility are the first and most obvious means of setting apart the youth work programs. The Commission believes that in the future, these programs should be limited to youth 16 to 21 years of age, or 16 to 20 inclusive. Exceptions should be made for youth workers who become assistant supervisors or key workers necessary for efficiency. These should receive a higher wage and be allowed to continue beyond the age of 21. However, even they might well be required to leave by the age of 25, except when promoted to positions normally filled by adults.

Within the age limits specified, there should be no requirement as to relief status or financial need. One of the major reasons for providing youth work programs is to make certain that young people will be able to obtain the maturing experience of employment at the right stage in their personal development. The need for this experience is not confined to youth in low-income families. On the contrary, many sons of wealthy parents have a special need for the type of experience they would obtain in the ccc, and it would be equally desirable to provide opportunity for the daughters to participate in a program from which they would derive similar benefit. There is some reason to believe that many young people from upper-income groups would participate gladly in distinctly grueling work programs if given opportunity.[2]

The selection of work projects to be carried on through the youth work programs is a second major factor for consideration. Several different types of projects appear to be particularly appropriate.

Much, although not all, of the work now carried on by the Civilian Conservation Corps would seem to be especially suitable for a labor force of unmarried young men. When projects are to be carried on in isolated areas, when the locally available labor supply is inadequate, when special housing in camps must be provided for the labor force, and when the work to be done requires few highly skilled workmen, the conditions all point to the ccc. The same work could be done by older unemployed workers with families and settled community ties

[2]Kenneth Holland, *Work Camps for College Students* (Washington: American Council on Education, 1941), 32 pp.

only at greater cost or with much disruption of normal family life. On the other hand, when the locally available unemployed labor force is adequate and special housing is not required, the CCC is obviously not appropriate. Undoubtedly it has been used in some such cases, largely because government agencies having access to CCC labor were unable to obtain access to funds for expenditure in the more appropriate manner.

Conservation projects which do not require housing for the labor force would seem equally appropriate for youth and adults. Most soil conservation projects, as well as many others, fall in this class. As a general rule, the smaller projects would seem likely to provide more diversified experience and to be more adaptable to the purposes of a youth work program.

Construction work typically requires skilled workmen, large amounts of material, and special equipment. Large construction projects are therefore likely to be outside the normal scope of a work program for beginning workers, although the CCC and the NYA have both carried through a number of construction projects of surprising size and quality. Both agencies have demonstrated that small construction projects can well be prosecuted by youth labor forces, and that a very large number of small public buildings may usefully be provided.

The production or repair of goods and equipment for public use is another type of appropriate activity. At present, the NYA is producing many articles for the military services. In former times it has built or rebuilt thousands of desks and other equipment items for rural schools.

Assistance in the operation of public and nonprofit services, especially services for children and youth, has been a major field of NYA activity. There is almost no limit to the amount of human energy which can be usefully applied to the social services under proper supervision. Young people may well be made conscious of the amount of labor involved in providing the services from which they profit. By assigning youth workers to these services, many desirable objectives are served.

Finally, mention may be made of one more major field of useful public work, namely the production of goods for the use of such portions of the people as are unable to purchase necessities in adequate quantities. This field of activity must be so administered as not to bear harshly upon any particular branch of private competitive activity. But the total market for private enterprise need not be reduced by such a social program, because the low-income families in need of additional commodities will undoubtedly continue to spend such money income as they have available. Accordingly, under proper administration this is an appropriate field of public work for youth and adults, and one which ought to be expanded during any period of unemployment and distress.

### THE PROBLEMS OF PLANNING AND COORDINATION

There is no lack of useful work to be done by unemployed youth, and there will be no lack at any time within the foreseeable future. But if the available energy of the unemployed, both youth and adults, is to be utilized most effectively, there is need for a very large amount of advance planning of work programs and of coordination in their operation.

In the discussion of the relations between the CCC and the NYA in Chapter II, the difficulties in planning and coordination which result from the existence of two separate youth programs were pointed out. But the problems of relationship between CCC and NYA differ only in degree and not in kind from the problems of relationship which also inevitably arise between special work programs for youth and work programs for adults.

The difficulties arise mainly at two focal points: the assignment of the available labor force to the various programs, and the assignment of work projects for prosecution to the various agencies.

For the reasons indicated on a previous page, the Commission believes that special youth work programs are desirable even though they introduce complexities in over-all planning and coordination. But so far as the assignment of labor forces between other programs and the special youth programs is concerned, this is not a difficult problem to solve. It is assumed that anyone eligible for an adult program will prefer that program and will secure placement through it if possible. Those not eligible for the adult program or who cannot secure a place on it, and who are under the age of 21, will find their place in the youth programs.

In practice, there has been no serious difficulty in distinguishing the clienteles of the WPA on the one hand and of the CCC and NYA on the other. The difficulties have arisen between the CCC and NYA. They have come about because for young men there is no basis for a significant difference in eligibility requirements between the two agencies. That is why recruitment for the two youth work programs should be brought under a unified administration.

The problem of assignment of work projects to the various agencies for prosecution presents somewhat greater difficulty. So far as the youth work programs are concerned, the problem can be solved to some extent by specifying the types of project in which they may engage, but a substantial area of overlapping jurisdiction will inevitably remain. A public building in a state park, for example, might at one time have been built with assistance provided by the PWA, WPA, CCC, or NYA. Many projects fall within the spheres of at least two of these agencies, and the problem of allocation and coordination is therefore important.

One possible solution of this specific problem would take the form of transferring the youth work programs for administration to the Federal Works Agency, which already includes such other major public work agencies as the Work Projects Administration, Public Works Administration, United States Housing Authority, and Public Roads Administration, instead of leaving the youth work programs in the Federal Security Agency, where they are associated with the Office of Education, Public Health Service, Bureau of Employment Security, Bureau of Public Assistance, Bureau of Old-Age and Survivors Insurance, and other administrations and divisions.

By definition, the primary function of a youth work program is to provide work. From the standpoint of functional organization and administration, much could be said for the point of view that all public work intended to relieve unemployment should be carried on by or under the auspices of the Federal Works Agency. But the same reasons which justify the continuation of youth work programs separate from those for adults indicate that the question of assignment among federal departments should not be settled exclusively in terms of the leading function.

For any service of employment specifically for youth, there will be a special problem of coordination with other services for youth, notably services of education, occupational counseling and placement, and health. In the federal establishment, these services are represented primarily in the Federal Security Agency. In recent months the amount of discussion devoted to problems of coordination within the Federal Security Agency has been somewhat indicative of internal friction, but it also indicates effort to solve a problem. Any comparison of the situation today with that which existed before the various organizations were brought together in the Federal Security Agency will demonstrate conclusively that progress toward improved coordination of youth services is taking place.

After an extensive discussion of the factors involved in a continuation of special youth work programs and of their location in the federal establishment, the American Youth Commission reached the conclusion that in the future it will be highly important to maintain special work programs for youth under a unified youth work projects administration, that the question of whether the youth work projects administration is assigned to the Federal Works Agency or the Federal Security Agency is of much less importance, but that on the whole it appears desirable to continue the youth work programs in the Federal Security Agency, where they are at present.

It is important to point out that such measures of administrative consolidation as the transfer of the youth work programs to the Federal

Works Agency would be wholly inadequate to solve the most important long-range problems of the planning and coordination of public work. These problems involve most agencies of government at federal, state, and local levels. They go far beyond decisions concerning particular projects to the general consideration of what types of public work are most urgent and to the determination of the type of public agency through which various kinds of needed public work may best be prosecuted at any given time.

When we consider the range of public work in the present usage of the term, at one extreme we find work which would be done even in a time of labor shortage, and at the other we find work which should be done only at a time when labor will go to waste if the work is not done. In our concentration on the consideration of public work as a way of providing work for the unemployed, we are in danger of forgetting the original meaning of the term "public works." Mainly it meant large construction and conservation works which were prosecuted solely because of the need for the facilities they would provide. We still have need, as we always shall, for such works. We shall continue to build them when unemployment is no longer a problem; but until then, at least, the planning of their building can never be disassociated entirely from a consideration of employment, however important in their own right they may be.

The basic problem of public work planning is the problem of what work shall be done first—the problem of priorities. In general, three levels of priority may profitably be distinguished. First are those public works which for one reason or another must be carried on at once, regardless of the economic or employment situation. Second are those which will be needed within a few years, but for which the timing is flexible. Third are all of those forms of public work, construction and otherwise, which would be unnecessary or unjustified under conditions of full employment, but which are useful and justified at a low priority rating in any time of general unemployment.

To a superficial observer, it may seem that all public works of the first class are carried on by the regular agencies of government, and only by them, while all work of the third class is conducted exclusively by the emergency work agencies which exist to provide work for the unemployed. But this is far from the actual situation. Whenever an emergency work agency is in existence with a suitable available labor force, it can and probably will be used to prosecute public works of the first and second classes, if this can be done without displacing regular government employees. Likewise, when one of the regular construction agencies of government is found with little work of first or second degrees of importance on its schedule at a time of general unemployment, it is likely to be given work to do which would otherwise not be undertaken.

From this it follows that the long-range planning of work to be carried on by the unemployed cannot be prosecuted effectively in isolation from the long-range planning of public works to be carried on by the regular construction agencies of government—federal, state, and local. Moreover, long-range public work planning of both kinds must be coordinated with the general economic and fiscal policies of government.

The planning agencies in the Executive Office of the President, notably the National Resources Planning Board and the Bureau of the Budget, would seem to be the only possible place in which to centralize the necessary general planning of public work policies and programs. A good beginning in the direction of such planning was made in January 1941 when the National Resources Planning Board published the first of an anticipated series of annual revisions of a program for the development of resources and the stabilization of employment in the United States.

If the youth work programs continue to be located administratively in the Federal Security Agency, where they are the only major public work activity, it would seem especially important for them to be included in planning processes through which they may be assigned a coordinated place in the general programming of all forms of public work.

# CHAPTER
# IV

## RELATIONS BETWEEN SCHOOLS AND YOUTH WORK PROGRAMS

In the years since the establishment of the CCC and NYA, school people have watched the development of these agencies with much interest and some misgivings. Almost from the beginning, the youth work programs have had some educational aspects. "Training" has been one of their announced objectives, and as time has passed, training in one form or another has seemed to become constantly more conspicuous.

The concern of the school people has arisen out of fear that we were developing a federal system of education which would undercut and eventually displace the established public high schools of state and local school systems. With the more vigorous administration of the NYA which has come since 1939, this fear has been accentuated.

The American Youth Commission has given very extensive consideration to the problems of relationship between the youth work programs and the schools. In order to clarify its analysis, it has attempted to formulate certain general principles which appear to be applicable.

## GENERAL PRINCIPLES

1. Appropriate amounts of useful work are desirable elements in the experience of children and youth of all ages. During the years of compulsory school attendance, such work should be subordinated to the requirements of schooling. In many instances, productive manual labor and other forms of useful work should be introduced into the school program as an element on a par with other major elements of a well-rounded curriculum.

2. In the personal development of every young person there comes a time when, in his or her own interest and in the interests of society, employment should replace school attendance as his or her major occupation. For many young persons this time comes at the age of 16, the age up to which school attendance should be compulsory. Other persons should continue to devote their time primarily to formal education up to 18, 20, 22, or still higher ages, in accordance with their respective interests and capacities, the needs of society for specially educated persons, and the development of suitable programs in schools and colleges.

3. After they have passed the point up to which schooling should be their major occupation, young people should normally be able without undue difficulty to enter private gainful employment. When the opportunities to do so are not adequate in numbers, it is a function of government to provide the necessary additional opportunities.

4. Persons employed on public work programs because they are unable to obtain other employment, from which they would normally expect to derive income, should be paid a suitable wage. On public work programs which have a distinct training value for those employed, a relatively low wage for beginning workers may be appropriate.

5. It is desirable that beginning employment, whether private or public, be so administered by the employing concern or public agency that the developmental effects for young workers will be as great as possible. Public work programs for unemployed youth should provide gainful employment, production of needed goods or services, experi-

ence, and some degree of training through supervision on the job. In the assignment and rotation of the available labor force on every public youth work project, requirements of production should be balanced against those of experience and job training. Factors of experience and training should be given a high value; but productive accomplishment is the indispensable objective and distinguishing characteristic of a true work program.

6. Young people on public work have the same needs for a part-time educational program which they would have in similar private employment. Unless they left school prematurely, their need for education is distinctly subordinate to their need for employment. Public education authorities have the same obligation to provide appropriate supplementary educational services for youth on public work that they have for similar youth in private employment.

7. Any form of work or gainful employment may have educational effects. In this respect employment is not different from such other major aspects of life as those involved in marriage, citizenship, community participation, and, at present, military service. The fact that an experience does or may have educational effects does not necessarily make the supervision of such an experience an educational function in general or a school function in particular.

8. The public function of providing gainful employment for the unemployed, whether young or old, is not an educational function. Like other noneducational, governmental functions, in some cases it may appropriately be carried on through school authorities.

9. In view of the fact that the administration of programs of gainful public employment for the unemployed is not an educational function and the further fact that many specialized problems and contentious issues will always be involved in their administration, it would seem advisable for school authorities to avoid the administration of such programs, either for youth or adults. Programs of unpaid school or community service are another matter, as are special programs of wage employment which have primarily educational objectives.

School authorities may very properly carry on such incidental programs in connection with their main task of educational administration.

10. Because of the fiscal strength of the federal government, its responsibility for the regulation of interstate commerce, and its other broad powers, the primary responsibility for governmental measures relating to unemployment has devolved upon it. In order to maintain the necessary flexibility for adjustment to changing conditions in private employment throughout the country, major programs of public work for the unemployed, both youth and adults, should continue to be planned and administered by the federal government.

11. The control and administration of public schools to be attended by children and youth during the period of compulsory school attendance is the function of the states and local communities, and not of the federal government. Other public educational facilities are by custom maintained chiefly by the states and local communities, in some cases with the assistance of the federal government. But the federal government is not prohibited by law or usage from providing additional educational services which youth and adults may utilize on a voluntary basis under appropriate circumstances, and the federal government has compulsory powers of education and training for national defense.

12. It is clearly desirable to avoid so far as possible the establishment of competitive and duplicative public educational services. Accordingly, where supplementary educational programs are to be provided for youth and other persons employed on public work programs, such programs should be provided so far as possible by the established educational authorities. Federal grants to the states for such supplementary educational programs are desirable and should be supplied.

### THE CIVILIAN CONSERVATION CORPS

Direct relationships between public schools and the Civilian Conservation Corps have been significant but mainly confined to camps located in areas accessible to large high schools and vocational schools.

Relations between the ccc and the schools have on the whole been friendly and cooperative.

There has, however, been some tendency to regard the ccc with disfavor on grounds that it is a federal educational agency, and therefore suspect. It is regarded as an educational agency for three principal reasons: There is an officially designated educational program in the camps, consisting of classroom instruction and other activities, organized mainly by a full-time official in each camp known as the educational adviser, and carried on in the leisure time of the enrollees. In the operation of the ccc work projects, considerable emphasis has been placed on training on the job by supervisors. Camp life under supervision is an experience which undoubtedly has distinct educational effects.

It is clear that the purposes of the ccc are in part educational, but it is equally obvious that it is a multiple-purpose program. The major purposes in the order in which it is usually desirable to give them importance appear to be as follows: (1) employment for unemployed young men, (2) conservation of natural resources, (3) improvement of health and physical fitness, (4) job training, (5) training through supervised camp life, (6) remedial education for illiterate enrollees, and (7) constructive leisure-time educational and recreational activity. At present, the officials responsible for the administration of the ccc are making specific efforts to provide training which will be useful to enrollees who later enter war industries or the military services.

As previously noted, the ccc program has been distinctly expensive as a means of relieving unemployment, ranging in cost from $1,000 to $1,200 per enrollee a year. Against this cost, however, the program should be credited with productive accomplishments which may aggregate as much as $700 per enrollee a year, in addition to the benefits to enrollees and the contribution to the support of their families. In the future, some minor economies might be made, but no substantially different level of costs will be achieved as long as the program includes the present standards in regard to food, shelter, clothing, health service, enrollee compensation, and project materials and equipment. Moreover, the more important the conservation work which is accomplished and the more isolated the areas in which it is prosecuted, the more expensive the program will be.

The cost of the program can be justified only by obtaining all of the possible benefits. In terms of other alternative means of providing education and occupational training, only a fraction of the CCC cost could be justified. It is evident, however, that a large part of the cost may properly be charged off to conservation activity, and in any time of unemployment most of the remainder may be charged to the relief of unemployment.

The major purposes of employment and conservation will vary in relative importance in accordance with the amount of unemployment. When there is a large amount of unemployment, the size of the Corps may appropriately be increased by undertaking more conservation work. When there is little or no unemployment, the purpose of providing employment becomes unimportant or nonexistent. Under such conditions, the Corps should shrink to the point where all of the work is sufficiently important to need no other justification.

It is the belief of the American Youth Commission that a *civilian conservation corps* of unmarried young men is so peculiarly fitted for certain types of essential conservation work that a CCC should be maintained under any conditions that can now be foreseen. It should fluctuate in size, in accordance with employment conditions and conservation needs. An authorized strength of 300,000 enrollees is perhaps a suitable upper limit. The Commission does not have available the technical knowledge of conservation requirements to recommend a lower limit above which the CCC should be maintained if possible, but would not expect such a limit to be under 50,000 enrollees, and it might be distinctly higher.

For a number of reasons which seem conclusive, the CCC should continue to be administered by the federal government. Much of the work is carried on in the national parks and forests, and much of the remainder although conducted on privately owned farm land is a part of the important federally administered program of soil conservation. The work on state park and forest lands might appropriately be left to the states, but much can be said for the present arrangement. Because of the location of the work, the enrollee labor forces must frequently be transported across state lines and to points at considerable distances from their homes. Finally, there is the consideration that any program as large as the CCC, both financially and in numbers of persons affected, is necessarily an important element in any general program for combating unemployment and promoting national development. Accordingly, it would seem appropriate that it continue to be administered by the federal government, even aside from the special characteristics of the CCC work projects and labor force.

In the future, if the CCC is limited to the conservation projects which seem particularly appropriate for it, namely those on which it is necessary to provide housing for the labor force, relations between the CCC and public school authorities are likely to become even more limited than they are at present. Large school systems which can effectively provide evening and week-end classroom instruction for CCC youth are found only in the thickly settled parts of the country, where there is seldom a valid reason for the establishment of a CCC camp. In any event, most of the camps will remain beyond the reach of such school systems, as they are now.

Accordingly, in most of the CCC camps, the camp educational and recreational program must continue to be carried on by the federal government if it is to be maintained at all. The Commission does not believe that the specifically educational functions of the camps will ever be more than a minor aspect of the CCC, unless it is distorted to the point where it ceases to be a program primarily for the carrying on of *conservation* work projects. But young men at work full time on conservation projects in isolated areas have the same needs for related instruction and for a constructive educational and recreational leisure-time program which they would have on private construction projects in similar areas. The Commission believes that those needs should be adequately met, and that it is the duty of the federal government in administering the CCC to see that they are met.

## WORK FOR UNEMPLOYED YOUTH AT HOME

The NYA has had one or more work projects for unemployed out-of-school youth in almost every community of substantial size in the United States. There has been much more opportunity for direct local relationships between NYA work projects and the schools than between CCC camps and the schools. The opportunities for irritation and friction have been correspondingly greater, and in some parts of the country the relationships between NYA and schools have been distinctly unsatisfactory.

As a cause for general suspicion on the part of school people, there is the fact that the NYA appears to be an institution which is in competition with the schools for the time and attention of youth. In a general way, this may be inevitable, in the same sense that private employment is in competition with the schools for the time of employable young people above the age of compulsory school attendance.

Aside from instances in which there have been specific complaints concerning the recruitment policies of the NYA, school people have been concerned about two major aspects of the program. One is the content of the activities actually provided during the time that young people are paid to work; the other is the manner in which related educational activities are provided.

In some states, there were undoubtedly periods when some NYA supervisors gave cause for reasonable doubt as to whether they were conducting a work program or a school program. There was little evidence of tangible productive accomplishment, the hours of so-called work were short, and a considerable amount of instruction not essential for production was provided on paid time.

During the last year or two, the NYA has tightened up its program considerably and is putting more emphasis upon production than ever

before. Instructional activities not directly related to production have
been eliminated from paid time on the work projects, and it is the
evident intention of the national leadership of the program to make it
a *work* program in every sense of the word. Great emphasis is still being
placed upon training, but upon training on the job through intensive
productive activity under careful supervision. This is in keeping with
the primary function of providing employment for unemployed beginning workers.

As previously noted, most NYA work projects have been conducted
on a part-time basis in order to include as many unemployed youth
as possible. It was therefore urged in many quarters that an additional
part-time educational program be provided for the youth on the
projects.

In some instances a part-time educational program was provided
by the schools. But not all school authorities were prepared to face the
problems of out-of-school youth in a cooperative way, and financial
difficulties were almost universal. In some cases where the schools did
not provide part-time education, provision was made for it by the NYA.

The entrance of the NYA into the provision of a local educational
service, even one limited to project workers and on a part-time basis,
immediately gave rise to controversy. The result of the controversy
was a compromise in the form of an agreement signed July 27, 1940,
between the administrator of the NYA and the United States Commissioner of Education, in which it was agreed that state departments
of education would assume responsibility for developing suitable educational programs for the youth on NYA work projects, and the NYA
would abstain from providing such programs.

In October 1940, Congress provided funds to be administered by
the United States Office of Education and to be granted to the states
for "related or other necessary instruction" under public educational
auspices for youth on NYA work projects. A second appropriation in
the amount of $10,000,000 for this purpose has been made for the

fiscal year ending June 30, 1942. Public school systems throughout the country are now making special provision for NYA youth in many cases, using state and local funds as well as the federal appropriations.

The problem of school-NYA relations in connection with the major program of part-time work projects for unemployed youth thus seems to be moving in the direction of a satisfactory and suitable state of adjustment. The NYA should continue to emphasize training through supervision on the job, and it should continue to develop cooperation with the schools for such other training and education as the project workers may need. The Commission believes that a desirable relation between schools and NYA for many youth on part-time work projects would be very similar to that between schools and private employers under the cooperative plan of education, in which young people work half time in regular private employment and attend school the other half of their time.

As an employing agency, however, the NYA will always be subject to criticism until it makes more adequate use of the available working time of unemployed young people. For many of the unemployed youth 19 and 20 years of age, it would seem that the program properly should be a full-time work program. Most unemployed youth do not want a half-time school program, and some of them do not need it. Much of the value of the CCC has come from the fact that it teaches young men to work industriously on a full-time basis. For at least a part of its regular program, the NYA should operate on a similar basis for young men and women.

Regardless of some temporary and local lapses, the major program of the NYA for unemployed young people living at home has been primarily one of productive work and gainful employment. If it continues to develop along present lines, it will continue to be such a program. Accordingly, it is the opinion of the Commission that the major program of the NYA should continue to be administered by the federal government as long as it is needed.

## SPECIAL PROBLEMS OF RESIDENT WORK AND TRAINING CENTERS

The discussion concluded immediately above has to do only with the NYA program of local work projects for unemployed youth who continue to live at home. In addition to this major program, the NYA operates several hundred resident centers. As of September 1941, about 40,000 youth were being provided with various programs of work and training at these centers.

The first group of these centers was established in 1937 in cooperation with educational institutions offering instruction in agriculture and home economics. Unemployed rural youth were brought to the centers for periods usually ranging from one to six months, were given an opportunity to work part time on various projects, and were provided with part-time instruction, mainly in agricultural and homemaking subjects. Tuition, subsistence, and other costs were worked out on the projects, and in addition a small cash wage was usually paid. Costs were low because the projects were conducted very largely on a self-help basis. In many cases dormitories were constructed by the youth workers themselves, unlike the practice in connection with CCC camps.

Later the NYA began to experiment with resident centers organized around production workshops as a means of providing youth with experience in various mechanical occupations and crafts. Under the current program, the resident centers of this type are being increased in number, and have the special function of facilitating the entrance of rural youth into the war industries. Rural youth who could not readily be given any form of specialized industrial training at their homes are brought to resident centers and are there given about three months of intensive job training and beginning work experience in specific occupations which they immediately enter. Frequently the centers are located alongside shipyards, airplane factories, and other industrial plants.

The agricultural and home economics resident centers are still being maintained, as well as some industrial workshop resident centers engaged in nondefense projects. The centers have not been standardized, and many have distinctive experimental features. But all of the NYA resident centers, including those for war industry training, have certain distinguishing characteristics.

In the first place, the work projects do not determine the location of the centers in the way that the location of a CCC camp, for example, is determined. Most of the resident center projects are of such a character that they could be conducted almost anywhere so far as the work is concerned. Training factors have had much more influence than work requirements upon location.

In the second place, although the youth workers are engaged in productive work of some value and are paid a wage, the work is selected predominantly for its value as practice and the purpose of the wage is largely to provide credits which can be used for subsistence at the center, as well as to provide cash for incidental personal needs. In most of the resident centers which give no special training for war industries, the work program in motivation is more analogous to the in-school student work program than to typical local work projects for unemployed youth living at home.

In addition to the work and job training for which the NYA takes direct responsibility, most of the resident centers include extensive part-time educational programs for the youth workers. Instruction is provided by the staffs of cooperating educational institutions or by vocational education teachers who are assigned to the centers by state boards for vocational education and are paid from state and federal funds. No instructional staff is provided by the NYA.

Most of the centers utilize the opportunities of a residential establishment to emphasize training in community living. In a number of them, self-government by the youth workers in matters pertaining to living arrangements and recreation has been developed to a very high point. As the agency maintaining the residential facilities, the NYA usually has responsibility for such matters. In some instances the center directors are appointed jointly by the NYA and the state board for vocational education, and each agency pays half the salary.

Officially, the resident centers in their employment aspects constitute a part of the NYA work program for unemployed youth, while in their instructional features they are usually parts of state systems of vocational education. Actually, each center is an institution which must be considered as a unit. When the centers are considered as units, bearing in mind the interlocking combination of part-time employment, job training, related instruction, other education, and experience in community living, it is evident that they are primarily educational institutions, although institutions of a relatively new type. By comparison with a typical CCC camp, it may be said that while the CCC work projects provide full-time jobs with housing and training attached, the NYA resident centers provide training and housing with part-time jobs attached. The distinction is important.

If they are to be regarded primarily as educational institutions, the question arises as to whether the resident centers should continue under their present plan of mixed federal and state administration. It may be admitted at once that any clear-cut justification for permanent federal administration is distinctly lacking for many of the centers. On the other hand, the conclusion that the resident centers should forthwith be transferred to the states for administration is not justified.

The centers should be considered in two groups: those which draw their respective clienteles mainly or exclusively from within the state in which they are located, and those which serve a clientele from several states, or at any rate mainly from outside the state in which the center is located.

The problem presented by the first group of centers is relatively simple. It would seem that these centers should be transferred to the states whenever the states can and will make appropriate arrangements for continuing them without impairing their value. These centers would become state vocational schools, operated on a residential basis and emphasizing training through productive work. Most states need such facilities as parts of their state systems of education in order to provide adequate opportunities for rural youth.

In most cases it would be necessary for the state departments of education to take direct administrative responsibility for the operation of the centers. The states should also assume a substantial part of the cost of maintaining them, although the federal government might continue to provide the funds for payment of wages to the youth workers, as it now does in connection with the in-school student work program.

The second group of centers, those with an interstate function, present a more difficult problem. Unless the functions of these centers are changed, they could be brought under state administration only with the greatest difficulty, if at all. Yet it is becoming apparent that they provide an essential means for facilitating the interstate migration of young workers and for guiding such migration along desirable lines.

The Commission believes that all practical measures that can be adopted to improve the processes of migration are of the greatest importance. Moreover, it seems clear that such measures fall mainly within the province of the federal government. Accordingly, the Commission is convinced that resident work and training centers which participate in the planned interstate migration of youth should remain under the administration of the federal government. This conclusion may be based upon a new principle of federal-state relations in the fields of education and occupational adjustment, but the Commission is unable to discover any impropriety in such a principle.

In any event, it is universally admitted by those familiar with them that the NYA resident centers are exceptionally valuable institutions, and that they are still in the experimental phase of their development. They offer the possibility of development into a uniquely American type of folk school, one in which a cooperative self-help program can be provided for oncoming rural youth who have no adequate opportunities for employment or education in their home localities, and who will be especially in need of assistance in the post-war period. Whatever the course of action eventually adopted for the division of responsibilities between state and federal governments for the financial support and administration of the resident centers, it is highly important to avoid any action which would destroy or even delay the development of a type of social institution greatly needed in this country.

# CHAPTER

# V

# THE PROBLEM OF FULL EMPLOYMENT

---

ALTHOUGH neither the fiscal strength of the government nor the tax-paying ability of the people of the United States is unlimited, whatever is necessary to provide public work for unemployed young people can probably be managed. Taxation, after all, is simply the redistribution of income from those who have it to those who receive income from government.

But the problem of youth unemployment will not be solved in any ultimate sense until it is solved permanently by enlarging the normal channels of employment. Under some conditions, employment on a public work program is preferable to continued attendance at school, and certainly it is very much better than idleness while talents decay. From every point of view, however, work in some suitable form of regular employment is much to be preferred to work on a public work program—the experience for the young worker is more salutary, the strain on the fiscal and administrative machinery of government is less, and the confidence of both youth and adults in the prevailing economic system will be maintained to a much greater degree.

Unfortunately, there is every reason to believe that youth unemployment cannot be eliminated through the expansion of normal types of

71

employment except when employment opportunity for adults exists at a level equivalent to a chronic shortage of labor in the industrial sections of the country. In other words, there is likely to be a considerable amount of youth unemployment in the post-war future, even under conditions of relatively full employment for adults, such as those which prevailed in most parts of the United States from 1923 to 1929. More than any other age group, youth are dependent for employment opportunity on a constant flow of new economic activity.

It therefore seems desirable as a part of this report to continue the discussion begun in Chapter I by taking up at some length the problem of full employment in its general economic aspects. In doing so, the American Youth Commission is aware that it may be proceeding somewhat far afield from the immediate interests of those professionally concerned with the care and education of youth. There is no doubt, however, that the most fundamental problem of youth is precisely the problem of full employment under peacetime conditions for all employable workers. Until we solve this problem, we shall continue under the necessity of providing appropriate types of public work programs, and the recommendations of the previous chapters will remain pertinent. The sooner we solve the general problem of full employment, the sooner we shall be able to dispense with the work programs or to reduce them to the point where they are carried on exclusively to provide needed governmental services.

In this chapter, the Commission does not undertake to set forth a formula by which all of our economic troubles may be settled henceforth. The objective is the more modest one of exploring some of the fundamental features of the economic system under which we live and of discussing some of the problems involved in managing that system to secure full employment for every employable person who wishes to work. The analysis is necessarily incomplete, but does lead to a number of definite conclusions. The chapter ends with suggestions as to further steps that might be taken at once to develop the details of a suitable post-war program.

During the recent years of depression, it became a commonplace to remark that unemployment was not due to any lack of ability to produce, since we had the manufacturing plants and other productive equipment for full employment. In the present war effort, we are on our way toward a demonstration in actual fact that a place to work exists or can be made for every employable member of the population. This is true, moreover, even though new labor-saving devices and methods of major importance are constantly being developed. We are demonstrating again that some types of technological advance take place more rapidly in a time of labor shortage than in a time of labor surplus. The progress in technology which was blamed for much unemployment during the depression years was simply a continuation, probably at no more than the normal rate, of the advances which we have been making since the first days of factory organization in America.

To many people, our advancing productivity has seemed to promise an embarrassment of riches. We have been embarrassed, it is true, but not by too much production. Anyone familiar with the consumption capacity of the American people knows well that even under peacetime conditions we could use all of the goods and services which could be produced if everyone were at work at the right kind of activity. The problem is partly one of balancing the various types of productive effort. Even more, however, it is a problem of distributing income in such a way that goods and services will be available to the people who could and would consume them, thus making it possible for production to continue and expand.

## OBSTACLES TO FULL EMPLOYMENT

Beginning in the winter of 1929–30, mass unemployment was a fact in this country. Much could be said as to why severe unemployment began at that particular time and concerning the trends in employment during the following years. Regardless of other more specific factors, however, two aspects of the situation deserve the most concentrated attention.

In the first place, the depression revealed the possible extent of variation over a period of years in the flow of production and income in this country. In 1929 income produced amounted to about 83 billion dollars; in 1930, to about 69; in 1931, to about 54; and in 1932, to about 40.

The decline in money income in each successive year was in part a reflection of declining prices, but it was more largely a reflection of an actual decline in physical production. In terms of 1929 prices, the income produced in 1932 would have been valued at about 50 billion dollars, instead of 40. But the decline in total dollars of income as currently produced and measured is not an inappropriate measure of the severity of the depression. The deflation of values was about as devastating to popular morale and to the actual functioning of the system as the extraordinary reduction in total physical production.

In advance of the evident fact, hardly any person of sanity and judgment would have admitted even the possibility of so catastrophic a decline in monetary valuations and in productive activity as actually took place. Now we know that it is possible for the income produced by private enterprise in this country to shrink more than ten billion dollars a year and to do so for a succession of years.

In a system which has produced income ranging between 40 and 83 billion dollars annually in the years before the armaments boom began in 1940, what can we expect in the future? We are by no means sure that 40 billion dollars was the bottom possibility, and we hope that 83 billion is not the top under normal conditions. But in a system so unstable, no businessman can look to the future for markets with assurance, and no worker for hire can be assured that future employment will be available.

For a long time, we have been accustomed to fluctuations in industrial activity. The amount of human misery caused by these fluctuations in former years was large, but eventually the system always recovered, and it was believed that the system contained within itself forces which would inevitably bring renewed prosperity. Between 1929 and 1933, however, recovery began to seem very doubtful. There was little evidence of the working of automatic forces conducive to a revival of activity.

The relative absence of these forces is the second aspect of the depression beginning in 1929 which deserves special attention. If the belief had not become general in 1932 that matters would become worse if left to themselves, the program of governmental intervention which began in the following year would not have come into existence. In this connection, it becomes important to review the studies which have been made of previous periods of business difficulty in order to determine the factors which led to revival on those occasions.

Unfortunately, there is no area of economic analysis in which there is more disagreement than on the specific problem of the factors which bring about recovery from depression. Much is known concerning the cumulative forces which work together during a period of business expansion. Much is likewise known concerning the difficulties which join together to drag down business activity during a period of decline. Not as much, but a great deal, is known about the danger signals which indicate the approaching termination and possible reversal of a period of expansion. But our understanding of business fluctuations is most inadequate at the very point where a lack of knowledge is most dangerous—in the identification of the factors which will check a decline and institute a recovery.

Among the students who have made searching analyses of turning points in former depression periods, there have been many distinct schools of thought. Two of these appear to deserve special attention at this time. Of the two, one group finds the explanation of the upturn primarily in the events of the time. According to this group, when business is depressed and industrial activity is at a low level, depression will probably continue until there is some special reason for revival, unless, indeed, conditions become worse. For example, the six years of stagnation and acute misery beginning in 1873 were ended in 1879 by a wheat crop of record size at a time of crop failure abroad. The flood of purchasing power released in this country by the event brought a revival of railroad construction and industrial activity, and the cumulative forces of expansion were then at work.

The other group of students is the one which places great emphasis upon the operations of the price system and which constructs systematic explanations of business recovery in terms of automatic forces which involve the price system.

In our economy, the price system has two major functions. As everyone observes, it provides the mechanism through which private income in the various forms of wages, interest, rent, and profits is determined. Most people fail to notice another equally important function of the price system: to serve as the regulatory mechanism through which the flow of production is directed. Under the joint influence of production costs and consumer demand, prices have the function under normal conditions of determining what shall be produced, and how much of it. We rely upon the price system to direct the flow of goods into consumption and the flow of savings into capital formation.

Because the price system has this function, it is easy to assume that a maladjustment of price relationships is responsible when recovery from depression fails to occur. It is equally easy to attribute the apparently self-generated recoveries of former years to the better functioning of the price system in those times. But if the price system is to be required not only to direct the flow of activity under normal conditions but also to bring about expansion under depression conditions, it would probably be necessary for it to have a number of highly special characteristics. For example, it would be necessary for prices to be flexible enough to move finished goods into actual consumption, regardless of the conditions which prevailed currently. It would also be necessary for all of the prices which measure elements of production cost, including taxes, interest rates, and wages, to be flexible enough to keep production on a profit-making basis no matter how much decline occurs in the prices for finished products.

The price system certainly did not have these characteristics in 1930, 1931, and 1932. The extent to which it had such characteristics during the nineteenth-century periods of severe economic depression is a matter of controversy. Those who expound theories of automatic recovery involving price flexibility hold that in former times the price system had such characteristics to a very considerable degree. Those who explain past recoveries in terms of specific events hold that even in former periods, price relationships were most out of line at the very time that recovery began.

In any case, it is evident that for the last fifty years we have been developing an economic system of large-scale private enterprise in which the selling prices of most finished products are "administered." Under the stress of the present war effort, government agencies are participating to an increasing degree in price administration, but most commercial goods and services have been priced for many years through the action of private corporation executives. Basing-point systems, trade association control of cost accounting, and the price leadership of large firms have all had their influence.

Administered prices are decidedly lacking in flexibility, especially downward flexibility. The result is that the prices of manufactured products are largely maintained and production is curtailed if necessary when depression threatens. Prices are maintained partly because costs and costing practices have become inflexible. Charges for fixed plant are often treated as a cost, although no plant has value if its products cannot be sold. Interest and tax payments are heavy and inflexible. Wages and raw material prices were the most flexible elements of cost in 1931 and 1932, but wages have since become much more inflexible because of the progress of minimum wage legislation and of union organization, while the prices of many raw materials have become the special concern of government.

These developments have been defended on grounds that price deflation is not helpful to business recovery, and that it is essential to maintain the flow of purchasing power to wage earners and others who are dependent upon money income. Undoubtedly these contentions contain large elements of truth.

On the other hand, many of the prices which were most inflexible in the face of the depression beginning in 1929 were exactly the ones which were too high before the depression began. In the period from 1923 to 1929, stable prices were regarded as desirable. In many manufacturing industries there was much opposition to any reduction of prices, even though productivity per man-hour in typical manufacturing industries was advancing around 4 percent a year. In numerous cases, price maintenance policies had the effect of increasing profits, but retarded the expansion of markets and of total employment which would have been possible if prices had been reduced in accordance with costs.

After the depression had set in, overhead costs became more burdensome because of reduced output, and the same industries which had already been practicing price maintenance had a further incentive to continue the same policies. But with other prices falling rapidly, the effect was to push the maintained prices out of line with the price system as a whole, and to bring about increasingly unbalanced relationships between all prices, costs, and the flow of income.

The whole subject of wages and their determination is of particular importance in this connection. Wage costs make up a very large part of the price of the finished products of industry. If wages are pegged at a high level in some occupations and industries, the prices into which those wages enter must likewise be maintained at a correspondingly high level. But with other wages and prices falling under the stress of depression, the resulting distortion of normal relationships makes difficult the continued exchange of goods. Those whose incomes have been reduced most severely can no longer buy the products of those who have made no concessions to the prevailing situation. There is not much doubt that the difficulties of the depression would have been lightened if the wages and prices which were most rigidly maintained had been brought into line with other wages and prices, and it is probable that there would have been less decline in production and less unemployment if this had been done.

The distortion of wage-rate relationships was doubtless enhanced by the partial character of unionization in American industry at the beginning of the depression. Organized labor comprised too small a fraction of the total labor force and was too much on the defensive to take any adequate responsibility, even in cooperation with other economic interests, for the over-all planning of an effective program to combat the forces of depression. Instead, each local union defended the walls of its own castle, and in many cases refused to make any concessions on wage rates until its own individual situation had become so desperate that no alternative could longer be considered. During the downward phase of the depression, a greater degree of willingness in the ranks of union labor to think in terms of the maintenance of real wages rather than in terms of the maintenance of specific money rates would have been helpful, especially in view of the far more drastic pay cuts which were currently being enforced upon the ranks of nonunion labor in many occupations, and the great decline in the income of farmers and farm workers.

Organized labor can be of tremendous assistance in the life of the nation when it becomes effectively able to represent substantially all of the wage workers in industry and commerce, provided it will rise to the level of statesmanship required by so great a part in the direction of American economic life. In the long run, union organization will benefit individual workers to the extent that the policies of organized labor are determined in the interest of all working people and of society as a whole, and are not merely an aggregate of the narrowly conceived objectives of a multitude of separatist local unions.

Only a part of the restrictive practices of the depression years originated in labor unions. In some cases unwise policies of price maintenance were carried out by employers who at the same time could and did cut wages. Many forms of collusive activity in connection with prices became more general than they had been previously, and there was a spreading paralysis of restrictive practices by which each economic group, industry, and locality attempted to organize some form of security for itself at the expense of others. The results tended further to retard recovery.

In government circles there was not at first any general tendency to attack these restrictive practices. On the contrary, during the period of the National Recovery Administration, many of the most doubtful practices took on a new dignity and were given the force of law for a time, while the governmental efforts to encourage the organization of labor were not accompanied by as much emphasis as might have been desirable upon the responsibilities of labor when organized.

In more recent years, however, some evidences of a change of heart in government circles have become apparent. In particular, many of the restrictive practices of employers and of unions have been vigorously attacked by the antitrust division of the Department of Justice, both in the courts and before the bar of public opinion. Other economic agencies of the government have given renewed attention to the problem, especially in connection with the investigations for the Temporary National Economic Committee, which recently closed its work.

Enough progress has been achieved to demonstrate how much can be done to restore competitive vitality to areas of the economic system from which effective competition has long been absent. Some of these efforts will doubtless be at a standstill for the duration of the war, although they should be continued in all cases where it is possible, and, in the cases where they must be postponed, they should eventually be resumed.

Even when such commendable efforts can be carried to their maximum development, however, we shall not succeed in turning back the clock to 1890. We are too far advanced in an era of large-scale economic activity. By making prices more competitive and more flexible under normal conditions, we could greatly improve the efficiency with which the price system distributes the results of progress and influences the allocation of consumer demand and of productive resources. But whether or not it ever did in the past, it does not seem likely that in the future the price system will operate automatically to stop a business decline and to start recovery without governmental intervention under depression conditions such as those which prevailed in 1930, 1931, and 1932.

These conclusions will become of the most urgent importance whenever we are next threatened with a major decline in business activity. Such a time may come when there is a curtailment of armament production after the war, particularly if we have had extensive price inflation in the meantime and there is a consequent disposition to expect a severe fall in the general level of prices. Or the time may come eight to twelve years later, as in the case of the major economic difficulties which followed the Napoleonic Wars, our own Civil War, and the first World War.

In any case, unless we succeed meantime in greatly improving the management of our economic affairs, sooner or later we shall again face economic difficulties comparable to those of the early 1930's. When that time comes the present economic system will be in great danger of being destroyed unless some means is found of rebuilding it on a more stable basis.

Throughout the world for the last generation, there has been a general loss of confidence among the masses of the people in the economic system which we have inherited and adapted from nineteenth-century capitalism. It seems obvious that the loss of confidence is directly related to the failure of the present system to provide continuously a sufficient number of opportunities for employment. Young people especially are critical. Their own experience in many cases has included periods of unemployment, and has often been marked by a process of occupational frustration even when they were employed.

Almost no one under the age of 30 has any clear recollection of the economic conditions prevailing prior to 1929. But most young people have a very vivid knowledge of the employment conditions of recent years. Necessarily they judge the system almost entirely in terms of their own experience.

With the gradual deterioration of price competition as a directive mechanism, our economic system has become a ship without a rudder. The problem of economic reconstruction in the United States is basically the problem of how in the future we shall supply direction for our system.

The primary objective is not necessarily a matter of a higher standard of living or of a more equitable distribution of income, although these are objectives of very great importance. People will accept a low standard of living if it is the best that can be had from available resources, and they will put up with great inefficiency and many inequalities if everyone is busy with productive activity. Even an inefficient economy with low-grade resources should be able to find some use for all of the available human energy. In the United States unemployment on any large scale can have no reasonable justification. So long as such unemployment is possible, the operation of the system stands indicted.

### PUBLIC WORK AS A CURE FOR UNEMPLOYMENT

Among the various governmental activities of recent years to promote recovery and expand employment, a major place has been occupied by programs of public work. These programs were originally begun on an emergency basis and have not been made permanent. They have had two major objectives: to provide needed employment directly, and to enlarge the flow of purchasing power, thereby increasing employment in the private consumption goods industries and, it was hoped, also stimulating the flow of private savings into capital formation.

The employment objective has seldom been questioned and is undoubtedly firmly grounded in public opinion. This does not mean that Americans believe more than formerly that the world owes every man a living. What they do believe is that under civilized conditions of life society does owe every man an opportunity to make a living. Consequently, public opinion has been driven to the inevitable corollary that when opportunities for private employment are not available in sufficient numbers, government, as the representative of organized society, must find means of expanding the opportunities in private employment, or itself provide the necessary additional opportunities.

The moral basis of this proposition is secure beyond challenge. It is still, however, a relatively novel doctrine. The attempt to put it rapidly into practice under the conditions prevailing from 1930 to 1940 led to many unanticipated difficulties and adverse repercussions.

The purchasing-power objective of the program especially was a source of much public confusion. Many theories were in vogue as to the alleged causes and cures of inadequacy in the flow of purchasing power. Many of these theories were obviously fallacious, yet they inevitably became involved in the controversies over the work programs. A sound and defensible analysis of spending in relation to purchasing power and private employment has required time for its evolution, and is still far from general acceptance.

Perhaps because of the confusion and misunderstanding of purposes both inside and outside of government, the effects of the work programs indirectly by way of the general flow of income and purchasing power were disappointing. It had been hoped that the income distributed in this way by government would lift employment decisively in the private consumption goods industries, that additional capital equipment would be required, and that the flow of private savings into capital formation would thereby be revived, with further favorable repercussions. Instead, it appears that only a limited amount of additional employment was created in the consumption industries, and that the program was regarded so unfavorably by businessmen and investors that the net effect on capital formation may have been adverse rather than favorable.

The reasons for this unfavorable reception deserve examination. Part of the difficulty was due to the fact that a large-scale program of public work is not easy to operate without competing, or at least seeming to compete, with private enterprise at many points. Even to the businessmen who are not directly threatened, the mere existence of such a program implies the possibility of its expansion to the point where all private enterprise will be superseded.

Another part of the difficulty arose from the fact that the program was financed mainly by borrowing. This prevented a direct drain upon private consumption through taxation, but awakened fears for the future which steadily increased as the deficits accumulated. If a more vigorous attempt had been made to find and levy taxes which would have supported the program at least in part without an equivalent curtailment of private income flowing into consumption, the program might have rested upon a sounder basis.

Still further difficulty resulted from the general atmosphere of antagonism which surrounded the relationships between government and business. The efficacy of spending for public work as a stimulant to private business was certainly not enhanced by its association with a general program of reform legislation, however desirable that legislation may have been in its own right.

Bearing in mind all of these difficulties, one may well wonder what would have happened if the work programs had been expanded to the point where they included from six to eight million of the unemployed. Would private employment have been so stimulated that all of the remaining unemployed would have been put to work? Or would the competitive public work, the enlarged deficits, the prospective increases in taxes, and the heightened controversy have dried up private investment and spending still further, with the result that private employment would have declined and unemployment would have increased?

There is no way by which the answers to these questions can be ascertained; opposite answers have been given by persons equally sincere and well informed. The fact that either result might have eventuated, however, casts doubt on the advisability of relying on the indefinite expansion of public work programs financed with borrowed funds as the major means of escape from severe economic depression.

Instead, it appears that we must search further for solutions. The failures of private enterprise in the field of employment must be solved primarily by improving the operation of the private enterprise system. Unless this is done, it may at times be impossible to provide enough public employment to fill the gap completely, however much we may wish to do so.

Meanwhile, we must continue to reckon with the realities of existing situations. Whenever we have any considerable amount of involuntary unemployment, the moral duty of the state to provide opportunities for employment on public projects is undeniable. For some years it seems likely that a flexible program of public work which can be expanded and contracted in accordance with the need for supplementary public employment will fill an essential place in our economy.

The Commission believes that the need for such a program has become so generally appreciated that many of the difficulties which have been associated with it in the past can readily be avoided in the future. The character of the program and of its various parts should be established by continuing legislation, so that all concerned may have some reasonable basis for accommodating their expectations to its essential requirements. It should be conducted in such a way that the productive accomplishments will be useful and proportionate to the labor expended upon them; no other standard is consistent with the self-respect of the workers on the program or of the country which supports it. The program should be adequate in size; in conjunction with measures to expand and stabilize private employment, it should be large enough to assure employment for all who are able and willing to work.

But we should never reconcile ourselves to the idea that our economic system must continue indefinitely to be propped up with special programs for the unemployed because there is no alternative. Instead, our objective should be to make that system work so well that no emergency program of public employment will be necessary merely to relieve unemployment. Some unemployment will of course always remain because of seasonal factors, shifts between jobs, and the necessities of vocational adjustment, but with good management the amount of such unemployment might ultimately be brought down permanently to the point where it could be cared for by a system of dismissal compensation, coupled with some enlargement of the present system of unemployment compensation.

It will probably be a considerable number of years before this ideal can be fully achieved. The belief that it can be realized in practice requires no small amount of faith in the intelligence and stability of the American people. The Commission is convinced, however, that this is the objective which we should keep before us and toward which we should work. At the earliest possible date, we should adopt measures which will prevent any post-war repetition of the extreme unemployment of 1932–33.

### FOREIGN TRADE AS A BASIS FOR FULL EMPLOYMENT

Much of the recent public discussion of post-war economic prospects has been devoted to the future role of foreign trade in the American economy. In the months before we actively entered the war, such discussion was mainly concerned with the economic eventualities inherent in a Nazi victory. On the other hand, it was also suggested that if we entered the war, a victorious America might come to occupy the position of world trade leadership formerly held by Great Britain. In that position, it was said, we would have full employment and prosperity in this country for the next several generations.

A comprehensive discussion of foreign trade in this document is impossible, but a few comments may be desirable. In a world not preoccupied by active belligerency, international trade would offer two major possibilities: either peaceful exchange of goods and services with the objective of a higher standard of living for all participants, or economic warfare for markets as one country after another seeks to balance its internal economy by dumping surpluses abroad.

It needs little argument to demonstrate the irrationality of a situation in which most countries seek to increase the quantity of useful goods and services leaving their borders and to decrease the quantity coming in. Certainly no direct contribution to domestic consumption can be made by the goods that go out, while the goods which come in may enter into domestic living standards.

Unless a country has solved its employment problem, however, the matter is not so simple. If one looks at employment, it seems clear that increasing the amount of goods leaving a country may increase employment in it, while new imports may bring about the displacement of some workers previously employed. Only in a country which knows how to maintain employment while expanding imports which compete with domestic production is a rational approach to foreign trade possible. Mutually profitable exchange of goods would then be the only concern.

It is conceivable that this country might achieve a world position so dominant that it could reach and maintain a high level of employment for a time through an aggressive foreign trade policy. By supplying the investment funds which many countries undoubtedly will need, we could enlarge our foreign markets, expand employment in the export industries, and provide a situation favorable to increased employment throughout the system. By continually increasing our investments abroad, an expansion of imports could be postponed for a considerable period, thereby avoiding depressing effects upon competitive domestic industries.

Such a policy of export expansion through foreign investment has various difficulties and dangers, and there is a limit to the number of countries that can pursue it at the same time. Obviously not all countries can expand their exports simultaneously, while refusing to expand imports. The effort to do so is a form of economic warfare which inevitably provokes retaliation, and may lead to actual military conflict. For success on a large scale, it must be backed with effective military force. Nevertheless, in one form or another, proposals of this kind are finding support at present among many influential groups in this country.

The American Youth Commission advocates the peaceful *exchange* of goods and services between countries to improve the living standards of all. It advocates the teaching in the schools and the extension through all channels of public information of a greater knowledge of the economics of international commerce. But it vigorously opposes attempts to solve the employment problems of this country by engaging in economic imperialism.

If it proves possible to establish conditions of peace and freedom throughout most of the world, there will be a revival of mutually advantageous trade between nations. In that event the achievement of full employment will be facilitated in this and in other countries. In all countries, however, it will be necessary to emphasize the important relationship of domestic policies to the maintenance of full employment. International economic and political stability will depend in large measure on the extent to which the major industrial countries are successful in setting up internal economic arrangements such that international economic warfare will become unnecessary from their respective points of view.

This country is considerably less dependent on foreign trade than most other great nations. If we are to solve the problem of full employment on any permanent basis and to make our necessary contribution to world economic stability, we must not fail to look to the management of our internal economic affairs for essential solutions.

### CAN A PRIVATE ENTERPRISE SYSTEM BE CONTROLLED?

Faith in private enterprise has been stronger in the United States than in most other countries. Yet there has been a long history of governmental effort to control the operation of economic affairs in pursuit of one or another objective.

Some of the earliest tariff legislation was an attempt to hasten the development of manufacturing industries in this country. Many governmental activities have been carried on to prevent the establishment of monopolies or to control them in cases where their necessity is accepted. The immense volume of social legislation now on the statute books of the various states and of the federal government is largely intended to remove defects in the operation of private enterprise, or to provide compensating influences for deficiencies that cannot be removed.

After many years of recurring financial panics, the Federal Reserve System was organized to strengthen and stabilize the banking system of the United States. As the Federal Reserve System developed and was given increasing powers, it came to be regarded as the major central agency through which the general level of economic activity in the United States might be influenced. Between 1925 and 1933, however, it was demonstrated that the powers of the Federal Reserve System are largely negative—they can be used with greater effect to curtail a speculative boom than to initiate a recovery from depression.

Since 1933, the government of the United States has been given more responsibility than ever before in regard to the management of economic affairs. Dollar devaluation, codes of fair competition, agricultural adjustment, social security, wage and hour regulation, public work programs, and large-scale deficit financing have all been utilized, along with many other less important measures, as means of influencing the operation of the economic system.

For the future, it seems clear that the American people are committed to a belief in the advantages of private enterprise and they wish to see it maintained, but they look to government for such central economic controls as may be necessary to prevent general unemployment, as well as other forms of economic calamity which are capable of causing the most distress to the largest numbers of people.

If government is to discharge these great responsibilities successfully without destroying freedom, the decisions of government must be based upon a correct understanding of the principles of a private enterprise system under modern conditions of technology, large-scale corporate activity, immense productive capacity, and many large individual incomes. But it is exactly in this area that our understanding is still very imperfect.

There is, for example, the present widespread confusion concerning the economic effects of saving money. When individuals refrain from spending all of their income for consumption and save a part of it for investment in the formation of capital, they perform an indispensable economic function. This has always been true and is seldom denied. But in recent years, controversy has arisen over the possibility of too much saving under peacetime conditions.

For an intelligent discussion of whether it is possible to save too much, it is necessary constantly to remember three things: (1) A person who saves money has the option of holding it in cash or in a check-book balance, as well as of investing it. (2) His decision about whether to invest or not is affected by a multitude of influences, especially the prospective rate of return. (3) The rate of return which will be available is also affected by a multitude of influences, and in particular by the amount of capital equipment already available from past accumulations of savings.

Economists have long recognized the possibility that with continued accumulation of productive capital, a wealthy nation might eventually reach the point where the available current savings could be invested completely only at a low rate of interest, such as 1 or 2 percent. When this question was being discussed merely as a problem in theory, however, it was usually assumed that a low interest rate would influence investors to curtail greatly the amount of their savings, but that to the extent they accumulated funds, they would accept the prevailing rates of interest, regardless of how low they might fall.

These are no longer regarded as safe assumptions. Certainly the tendency to save does not seem to be much affected by the interest rate, while many investors will hold funds in cash balances for long periods before they will accept a rate of return which they regard as unduly low. There is, therefore, a possibility of oversaving in the sense that savers may constantly add to balances which they hold in cash because they cannot invest them at rates which they will accept.

One of the most important factors which affect the possibility of such oversaving is the distribution of income. Families in the income group below $1,500 a year save money at times, but in the group as a whole, emergencies take the savings as rapidly as they are made, and there is no net accumulation of wealth by this group. On the other hand, the families with incomes in excess of $5,000 a year are responsible for the greater part of all savings. The large share of the national income which was "saved" during the latter part of the decade of 1920–30 was the result not only of a high level of national income as a whole, but of unprecedentedly high incomes for the families in the saving part of the population.

Those high incomes for some families were in part the result of the industrial price maintenance policies previously referred to. When prices are maintained while costs fall, profits expand, but the benefits are confined to the profit-making groups. In the long run, even they are likely to lose because of the economic maladjustments which result. The very practices of price maintenance which enhance profits for a period at the same time restrict the opportunities for expansion and capital investment, thus increasing the danger that uninvested savings will accumulate and poison the system.

These facts are coming to be more widely known, and it is important to continue their dissemination. Meanwhile, in many quarters their partial dissemination has so far led mainly to misunderstanding. Any discussion of the possibility of oversaving, however defined, is likely to take on the appearance of an attack upon the undoubted virtue of private thrift. Likewise, any suggestion for the redistribution of income to prevent an excess of money savings is likely to be regarded as a species of argument closely related to robbing Peter to pay Paul.

Nevertheless, the Commission believes that a sober consideration of all of the available facts will bring most people to the conclusions reached by the Brookings Institution in 1935, namely, that in this country under conditions of reasonable prosperity (1) there is a tendency for money savings to grow more rapidly than consumption expenditures, (2) there is a tendency for money savings to outrun the opportunities for remunerative investment in productive capital equipment, and (3) the excess money savings which result are productive of economic maladjustment and unemployment.[1]

Until ten years ago, mainly because the previous analyses of the saving process had been so defective, orthodox economic thought was unanimous in the belief that though some degree of central control might be necessary for other purposes, such as to achieve various objectives of social amelioration, to maintain a free flow of resources into the various industries and occupations, and to organize the banking and monetary system for price stability, central controls were not necessary in order to maintain full employment. According to the economic doctrines which have entered into the training of most government officials, corporation executives, and leading editors, a system of free enterprise will automatically provide full employment, if only it is let alone.

We know now that this is not the case, at least under the conditions of relative price inflexibility which accompany large-scale enterprise. Historically, full employment has occurred in the industrial centers of wage employment only occasionally, and at times when the economic system was riding the crest of a boom. Full employment is not necessarily the position of stable equilibrium; on the contrary, some degree of working adjustment might be attained at a level much below full employment.

This may perhaps be indicated by the following four propositions, which together make up a highly simplified version of the general theory of income, spending, and employment.

1. Of the total flow of money income, a part is spent currently for consumption by the recipients and another part is saved. The part saved may or may not be currently invested by the holders, and if invested, it may or may not be currently expended for the physical production of capital.

2. If at any time the recipients of money income have a tendency to

[1]Harold G. Moulton, *The Formation of Capital* (Washington: The Brookings Institution, 1935), 207 pp.

increase their checkbook balances and holdings of cash by withholding part of their income from expenditure for consumption or investment, there will be a contraction of total production and employment, unless there is some offsetting creation and expenditure of new money elsewhere in the system, as, for example, through private capital formation financed by bank borrowing, or through increased government spending financed in the same way.

3. If at any time the recipients of money income have a tendency to draw down their checkbook balances and holdings of cash by increasing their expenditures for consumption and investments in new capital formation, there will be an expansion of total production and employment, unless full employment has already been reached, or unless offsetting influences are set up elsewhere in the monetary circulation by central banking authorities, government, or business.

4. If the total flow of money income is currently spent in its entirety for consumption and capital formation, without either additions or subtractions elsewhere in the monetary circulation, there will be no resulting tendency toward either a contraction or expansion of employment. The system will be in equilibrium at the existing level of employment and unemployment, whatever that level may be.

The first of these four propositions is necessary merely to remind us that the saving of money and the actual physical production of capital equipment are very far from synonymous economic operations. The other three propositions each define a state of affairs which is capable of existing and which probably has existed historically on various occasions both in the recent and the more distant past.

The fourth proposition, for example, might be designated as the economics of how to get on dead center and stay there. It offers much more than a clue to the explanation of such historical periods of economic stagnation as the one from 1873 to 1879, previously referred to in this chapter.

During most of the time in former years, the tendencies toward optimism were so general and the poverty of capital equipment was so great that strong incentives for investment could usually be provided. A general tendency to hoard cash appeared only under panic conditions, and an excess of money savings over the funds actually used in the formation of capital was possible only in rare instances.

In the last generation, it appears, the situation has changed completely. The large money savings of the late 1920's were not the only cause of the depression which followed, but it seems likely that they played an important part. During the depression years, we succeeded in making ourselves poor enough to prevent any excess of savings in some years, but the lack of understanding of the economic machine on which we rely was so widespread that a confusion of counsel was the prevailing situation.

A sufficient understanding requires much more analysis than is contained in the four propositions which have been stated. Their principal usefulness is in providing a framework for further study; certainly they do not point immediately to any particular panacea or course of action.

It is important to emphasize, however, that they must occupy a key position in any general formulation of the economics of the present day, notwithstanding the fact that at the beginning of the great depression they were no part of the main body of orthodox economic doctrine. On the contrary, they were in part overlooked, in part denied, and in part offset by the vigorous maintenance of older theorems not consistent with them.

The most important such theorem was the time-honored proposition to the effect that total income equals total production, all income is spent for consumption or capital formation, and general overproduction is therefore impossible. For a century this was the bedrock of the main structure of economic doctrine, regardless of the evidence of experience that on occasion a general attempt may be made to turn money income into savings hoarded in cash or checkbook balances, and that when this occurs, underconsumption and unemployment will be general.

Progress in rebuilding the basic tenets of economic doctrine has been rapid in recent years, but is still far from complete. Economic technicians are actively engaged in the necessary researches and controversies. While so engaged, they are scarcely intelligible to each other and still less to the lay public, but it does seem likely that within a few years a relatively complete body of economic doctrine will be available which will be consistent not only internally, but also with the factual situation in a world of advancing technology and large-scale private economic enterprise.

It is of overwhelming importance that this objective be reached, and with all possible speed. It is easy to scoff at theory and to deny the importance of general principles. Yet it is a fact that every economic decision is influenced in some degree by the theoretical concepts imbedded in the minds of the persons who make such decisions. Until theories more sound than those formerly in vogue are so generally accepted that they exercise influence without conscious thought, the economic decisions of legislators, government administrators, and corporation executives will fall short of the statesmanship required for the maintenance of full employment.

Meanwhile, however, we must proceed as best we can on the basis of existing knowledge. Even when there is agreement as to the fundamental economic difficulties of the present era, there is room for wide difference of opinion as to the social and economic policies which may best be pursued to cure those difficulties. But in any event it would seem imperative to find and adopt policies which will accomplish two objectives which are distinct but closely related: (1) the expansion of economic activity up to the level of full employment, and (2) the maintenance thereafter of the flow of income into consumption and capital formation at such rates respectively that a condition of balance will be continuously achieved and purchasing power will be adequate to move all industrial production at a full employment level.

For the present, economic activity is being expanded under the forced draft of expenditures for the war effort, and the problem of controlling the flow of income has highly special characteristics. There is no doubt that the government has or can obtain the powers necessary to deal with the present situation. It is to be hoped that the appropriate powers will be obtained and used in a timely and effective manner.

For the future, there are many ways by which the flow of income may be influenced by governmental action even under peacetime conditions. For a temporary period, large-scale government spending with deficit financing is one of the most powerful means of influence, but it is not the only way in which governmental influence may be exerted. Every form of taxation has some tendency either to expand or curtail the total amount of purchasing power and to affect its distribution, even though present taxation policies have been determined with relatively little consideration for these effects. Every other function of government which affects consumption, investment, or capital formation likewise has its effect, in many cases inconsequential, but in other cases of great importance. The central banking authorities have always been active in this field, and their efforts might become more influential if exercised in conjunction with other governmental activities designed to reach a common objective.

The income flows and the total amount of purchasing power are also influenced by private action in many ways, some obvious, others much less so. The millions of income recipients who have sufficient financial strength to exercise choice between spending, saving, and hoarding exert a profound influence. When, under the impact of mass fear, their collective decisions are adverse to the operation of the system, only the most powerful offsetting influences will suffice to save the situation.

As already indicated, the corporation executives who determine price policy exert a vital influence on the distribution of income. If the benefits of technology are to be distributed and mass industry is to expand, either the prices of manufactured products must be reduced or money incomes, primarily wage payments, must rise. In many ways price reductions would be a smoother road to progress than increases in money wages, since a rising level of real income in the form of goods and services would thereby be more widely distributed.

The distance to which it will be necessary to go in the adoption of special governmental controls will be largely determined by the extent to which private economic behavior can and will assume more desirable forms on a voluntary basis. Certainly every effort should be directed toward the inculcation of personal habits of stability in regard to expenditures for consumption and capital formation. In terms of the necessities of our present system, no form of personal behavior is more dangerous and antisocial than an irresponsible flight from goods into money or from money into goods.

Voluntary measures which stabilize the flow of income by distributing it widely are especially to be commended. The greater development of consumer cooperatives would be a favorable factor because of the effect of such institutions upon the distribution of income, as well as for other reasons. All plans of profit-sharing, whether with wage earners, consumers, or both, are likely to have favorable effects on income distribution and are therefore desirable if sound in other respects. Those in industry who are responsible for price administration should especially accept and emphasize their responsibility for passing on the gains of progress as rapidly as possible through price reductions.

If the need for such measures can become widely understood, we shall reduce the need for governmental intervention and at the same time facilitate governmental action to the extent that it is needed. It is true, however, that individuals are frequently placed in a position where because of their individual necessities they must act in a manner contrary to the general interest. In such cases, there is no solution other than governmental control. The sooner the appropriate controls can be devised and instituted, the better off we shall be.

In general, there are three stages of governmental control for consideration. First of all, virtually every existing activity of government should receive attention from the specific standpoint of its effect upon income distribution, capital formation, and employment. Many government activities, especially those related to taxation and finance, have economic effects of great moment which were overlooked or disregarded when the activities were initially planned. The reconsideration of these activities in relationship to the requirements of full employment is an imperative duty in any form of planning for the post-war future.

Second, it may be desirable to construct a new system of major controls over the flow of income. Such controls, for example, might include a very severe curtailment of the privilege of hoarding money balances without either spending or investing them, as well as restrictions upon the present opportunities of corporate institutions to hold funds in excess of working balances without proceeding to the actual production of additional plant and equipment. Any such system of controls would doubtless include distinctive measures of taxation and income redistribution and of central bank interest rate policy.

Both the feasibility and the desirability of a number of proposed controls of the kind just indicated are at present the subject of extreme controversy among economic technicians. It seems likely that the results which might be obtained from such measures have been exaggerated in some quarters. When and if such controls are desired, they should be created by legislative action, and appropriate standards should be specified in the legislation for the guidance of the executive.

Third, it will probably be desirable to give careful consideration to types of governmental activity which would go directly to the heart of recent difficulties by using the powers of government to assist industry in concerted action for industrial expansion under peacetime conditions. Every individual businessman is under severe limitations in planning for the expansion of his own activities; even if he is skilled in sales promotion and is willing to pursue progressive policies of price reduction to expand his market, the general level of economic activity will finally determine the extent of his opportunities. Likewise, even a whole industry, if permitted to work together, would find that it can affect the size of its market somewhat by price and promotional policies, but that general economic forces are likely to have a dominant influence.

The situation would be different if all of the important industries producing for interstate commerce could join together in carrying on a coordinated program for industrial expansion. The simultaneous expansion of production in all industry would in itself provide the flow of income necessary to move the production; and the problem of income distribution could be taken care of very largely as a part of the program by including appropriate price, wage, and profit policies.

The participation of government in such a program would be required, for several reasons. In the first place, it would be necessary to protect the public interest by making certain that the program was in reality a program for industrial expansion, and not a device to secure monopoly profits by preventing expansion. Second, the powers of government would be necessary to insure the participation of all enterprises affecting interstate commerce enough to exercise a serious unbalancing effect if allowed to remain outside of the program. Third, because it will never be possible completely to anticipate consumer demand in a free country, it would be necessary for government to underwrite the programmed production, and to guarantee the purchase for storage and later sale of the surplus production which would occasionally result from inaccurate estimates in fitting together the various industry programs into the complete program for expanded production in any given period.

### FIRST STEPS TOWARD CONCERTED INDUSTRIAL EXPANSION

The American Youth Commission believes that it would be unwise to attempt any such concerted program of industrial expansion until it is desired by most of the private economic leadership in industry, labor organizations, consumer organizations, and agriculture. No such plan will work until the necessary cooperative effort can be obtained very largely on a voluntary basis. But in the situation with which this country will probably be confronted when victory has finally been achieved and the war is over, it will be imperative to expand manufacturing production for peacetime consumption as rapidly and as smoothly as possible.

That expansion will be greatly facilitated if in the meantime some generally acceptable basis for cooperative activity can be formulated by the groups mainly concerned. At an early date, it would be desirable to set up a continuing economic committee or conference in which representatives of industry, labor, consumers, agriculture, and government would meet informally to carry on the necessary intergroup thinking and discussion. This group might well start with the assumption that, making due allowance for the possibilities of foreign trade, the American people are perfectly capable of consuming profitably and happily the goods and services which can be produced by this country, and that there is therefore no reason for unemployment so far as capacity to consume is concerned. The group should concern itself with general questions of the best balance of productive effort at a full employment level under peacetime conditions, and especially with the questions of relationship between urban wage rates, industrial price policies, and agricultural price and production trends which are involved in the problem of bringing about a distribution of income which would expand the flow of goods and permit a full level of productive activity. The group might well ask: What can the employer do, that is, what should be his attitude toward accomplishing these ends? What can labor do? What can the consumers do? What can agriculture do? Finally, what can government do, both by keeping its hands off and, at the appropriate times and places, by laying on hands?

The proposed conference or committee is suggested, not because there is any magic in a committee, but because the great need is for education and especially for a particular kind of education, that which results from processes of discussion which cross the present great lines of cleavage in the body politic. There are literally thousands of policy committees and organized discussion groups in industry, in labor, among consumers, and in agriculture, but the amount of organized, responsible, and continuing discussion of major national problems which crosses the gulf between any two of these groups is disastrously small. An outstanding national committee is needed to give orientation and leadership to such discussion, and its activities should be supported by similar enterprises on a smaller scale throughout the land.

Since the effort to harmonize conflicting interests would be the major objective of such activities, they should not be delayed until harmony has been established. It would seem, however, that progress in all matters of economic adjustment would be much more rapid at a time when delay is perilous if all discussions start with the premise that labor is to be accepted without question as a full partner. There is no doubt that the whole problem of employment and unemployment has been deeply affected in a negative way by the fact that the most powerful labor unions must continually remain aware that large sections of industry are still quite unreconciled even to their existence. The right atmosphere for harmony and progress will not be established until capital and management are prepared to accept and give unmistakable evidence of their faith that under private enterprise in a democracy, it is to be desired as well as accepted that labor shall be organized. There is a functional interest to be served by such organization without which democracy would be severely handicapped.

During the last fifty years, we have made progress both in a material way and in connection with many social reforms, but our progress was slow because the situation seldom seemed critical. We are now in a situation of crisis which doubtless involves many dangers, seen and unseen, but it is also a fluid situation in which rapid progress is not only possible but imperative if we are not to lose even what we have. The period ahead may be chaotic, but if we press forward with vigor and resolution, we may well find in the end that we have been the beneficiaries of opportunities as great as they were unexpected.

In any event, so far as the specific problem of full employment is concerned, it is the belief of this Commission that in one way or another, this problem can and will be solved under democratic government and without giving up the liberties we prize. The problem is already much farther along the road to a solution than is commonly realized. Progress could be hastened and made less difficult by a general effort on the part of all concerned to understand the economic problems of the present era, and by the rapid and widespread dissemination in usable form of all tested additions to economic knowledge.

To the extent that governmental intervention is necessary even under peacetime conditions, the requisite controls will undoubtedly restrict in some degree the accustomed freedom of some individuals. But the offsetting contribution which full employment can make to individual liberty must never be forgotten. For most young people, true freedom will never exist until we establish conditions which will maintain an abundance of available employment opportunity in a world at peace.

This Commission is convinced that if we come to the end of freedom and of private enterprise in this country, we shall arrive there by default, and because we have failed to make timely use of the knowledge we already have of how to improve the operation of our present system. It will never be possible to take the requisite steps without controversy or by unanimous consent, even when the necessary widespread support is available. But when the time comes, to most people the necessary measures will seem a small price for the economic progress and stability to which they will be directed.

# Part II
## OTHER BASIC PROBLEMS

# CHAPTER
# VI

## THE NEEDS OF YOUTH

---

THE American Youth Commission assumes that the United States will survive as a stronghold of freedom, that in the future we shall eventually solve our problem of peacetime full employment by achieving the right combination of social control and private enterprise, and that until that time we shall be increasingly successful in providing such supplementary employment opportunities under public auspices as may be necessary. If we provide adequate opportunities for employment, private or public, the most difficult problem of youth in the prospective post-war situation will be relieved.

In this part of the report, major questions in the fields of education, occupational adjustment services, use of leisure time, marriage and the home, health and fitness, juvenile delinquency, and preparation for citizenship will be discussed. Before turning to the more specific issues in these fields, however, it seems desirable to review briefly some of the more important needs of young people as they develop from childhood to maturity.

In any population the youth group is composed of those who are in the various stages of transition from the dependency of childhood to membership in the adult community as workers, parents, and citizens.

105

For this group no age limits can be set that will not depart from the facts in individual cases. For many purposes, however, the Commission has defined the period of youth as that extending from 12 to 24 years of age, although its primary concern has been for the period from 16 to 21. Age 12 was selected as the beginning point because it is the age which marks the advent of early adolescence for the largest number of children.

## ADOLESCENT YOUTH

The characteristic feature of the beginning of adolescence is change in the rate and character of physical growth. In the years immediately preceding adolescence, children normally grow at a relatively slow and even rate. The interests of childhood have matured into a sort of stability. Physical growth during childhood promotes the development of those interests without upsetting them. Differences between the sexes in interests and in personal adjustment are not so great that they complicate the problems of home or school.

With the beginning of adolescence, growth in height and weight becomes markedly more rapid. Moreover, the various parts of the body grow at different rates. Most youth pass through a period during which there is a serious lack of balance between bones, muscle, heart, and lungs. This is the basic cause of the "awkward" age.

Individual children reach adolescence at different times and grow at different rates. Differences of as much as two, three, or even four years are relatively common in the ages at which different children reach the same stages of physical development during adolescence.

Sex differences in the rate and timing of physical growth are particularly important. Girls enter adolescence and reach sexual maturity from one to two years earlier than boys. At the ages of 12, 13, and 14, the average girl is likely to be taller, heavier, and more developed physically, mentally, and socially than the average boy of the same age.

As boys and girls grow out of childhood into adolescence, the physiological changes which they undergo naturally awaken a new, inward-looking interest in their own bodies and personalities. During this period almost everyone is attacked by the misgivings expressed in the question, "Am I normal?" Those who obviously depart from the average in the rate and character of their development are almost certain to experience a time of acute strain, with little progress in school and in social relations until some degree of physical and emotional adjustment has been reached.

First experiments in escape from parental control are not always deferred until adolescence, but they take on a new urgency at that time. With the first stirrings of physical maturity, the young person begins to think of himself as "grown up." All about him former associates of childhood are successfully asserting adult prerogatives in the control over much of their time and their social relationships. The young person is fortunate who benefits by parental understanding of the situation, and is neither retarded unduly nor pushed forward too rapidly into the self-direction and self-dependence which are necessary for maturity.

The desire to achieve self-direction is closely related to the desire to attain a satisfactory relationship to other young people, which is one of the most powerful driving forces of youth. All individuals experience need for the friendship and respect of their fellows, but this need is most urgent during the initial adjustment to social life outside the family. At this time it is entirely normal for young adolescents to seek the largest possible number of acquaintances and to search for those who are most congenial. With greater self-reliance there comes later some relaxation in the drive for social activity and social approval. Relationships with other young people become more selective and more adult in type, but continued effort to win and maintain membership in a like-minded group is the normal situation.

This whole process of social adjustment even when proceeding in a perfectly normal way is likely to prove disturbing to many parents. Yet it is a fact that wholesome personality development is largely dependent upon a feeling of belonging to and acceptance by a group of those similar in age and status. From the standpoint of the young person, approval by parents, teachers, or supervisors is a poor substitute for approval by others of the same generation. Failure to achieve such approval is almost certain to result in some degree of mental ill health.

An intense craving for personal achievement, especially achievement along lines highly regarded by associates, is a characteristic aspect of youthful adjustment. For most young people failure is common enough when they first attempt new activities, both in school and out of school. Any failure is disconcerting. Continued failure may have a very adverse effect upon personality, particularly in youth when self-confidence has no firm foundation in prior experience. Young people therefore need to explore constantly their abilities in various fields and to find if possible those fields in which they have aptitude. A reasonable balance of success and failure is essential to the nourishment of healthy personality.

A broad range of experience that is interesting and occasionally exciting is another major craving of youth. It shows itself in all forms of physical activity, in the desire for the friendship of new companions, and in the experimentation in search of achievement. It is also manifested by absorption in all of the media of vicarious experience, including fictional and biographic literature, motion pictures, and the radio.

The search for vicarious experience becomes the more urgent the more youth are sheltered from real dangers, real burdens, and real responsibilities. In the absence of reality, vicarious experience may have some value as a substitute. But it is only by providing real experiences of the most vital sort that young people can be given adequate raw material from which to construct attitudes and build character, or even be given a basis for appraising the immense amount of vicarious experience which now presses in upon many of them.

If experience is limited and inadequate, personality and behavior can hardly fail to be the same. Moreover, if the adjustment of personality to the realities of life does not take place concurrently with the physical and emotional changes of adolescence, adjustment may be impaired for life and a true maturity may never be achieved. This is the great danger which may result from too much protective care in childhood and youth, and from too long a postponement of adult responsibilities and opportunities.

### LATER YOUTH

The needs of youth so far discussed are mainly those which arise in early adolescence, although they develop progressively throughout the period of adolescent growth. For most young people in the United States, these are years of school attendance in the junior and senior high school grades.

As young people approach the time of leaving school, which in most cases occurs at age 16, 17, 18, or 19, their interests and problems begin to shift again in a manner somewhat similar to that at the beginning of adolescence. Their attention begins to focus on the adjustments necessary for satisfactory life in a world of adults, as distinguished from a world of young people in school.

This is not to say that all of the problems of adolescence are left behind with the completion of school attendance. Many young people by necessity or choice leave school considerably before they have completed the physical, mental, and emotional adjustments normal to adolescence, partly because of the wide variation in school-leaving ages, and partly because of the wide range of variation in actual maturity at the same chronological age. Adjustment to the out-of-school environment is doubly difficult for those who have not progressed in maturity beyond early adolescence.

In normal times, the great problem for most individuals on leaving school is that of adaptation to vocational life. This involves much more than the finding of a first job, but even this first step may present great difficulty. Compared to the young people of preceding generations, the youth of recent years suffered conspicuously from the fear that they would not find any suitable employment.

The importance of this problem grips almost every boy as he approaches the time of leaving school. Work and wages loom larger and larger as the necessary prerequisite for nearly every type of desired experience. Most phases of school, home, and social relationships tend for a time to be valued in terms of their possible contribution to the achievement of desirable gainful employment.

For girls, the vocational problem has become very nearly as compelling as it is for boys, although the social pressure to seek work is not as great and there is less stigma attached to failure in the search. Our habits of thought are still influenced by the conditions of former years, in which the typical home was a center of workmanlike activity in the production of clothing, the processing of food at all stages, and a multitude of other basic economic activities. In such a home, the older girls were in every sense contributing members of the social organization and could properly remain in the parental home as full-time workers until they married and became homemakers in homes of their own. Under modern conditions, however, most girls who have left school are as much in need of gainful employment as boys if they are to become useful, well-adjusted, and productive young adults.

Whether young people are employed or unemployed, the problem next in importance for most of them in their day-by-day life is that of how to make satisfactory use of their leisure time. This is not a problem which is confined to the younger generation, but it has special difficulty and special importance for them.

In most communities the young people who have left school but have not yet married are stranded between school and community recreation programs. Neither school nor nonschool community agencies assume sufficient responsibility for this group. Yet the unmarried, out-of-school youth have an acute need for an attractive and suitable recreational program, to use constructively their abundant energy, to fill in the spare time which hangs heavy on their hands, and to facilitate the wholesome relations between young men and young women which will lead to normal courtship and marriage.

Marriage and the establishment of a home are the normal desires of young people who have reached physiological and emotional maturity. In recent years, young people have found many difficulties and complexities in their way. The war will be a major obstacle to marriage for hundreds of thousands of young people. Previously, unemployment and low and insecure incomes, even for those employed, were major factors deferring marriage. In other cases, although the same factors did not prevent marriage, they prevented the establishment of separate homes and retarded parenthood.

Although the period of youth is for most people the time when they experience their greatest health and vitality, health is a matter of serious concern to the young people of today. The current advertising programs of concerns manufacturing real or purported aids to health, greater emphasis on health in the schools, and increasing discussion of health as a social problem have all had an effect upon their thinking.

Nevertheless, the actual health of young people remains much less satisfactory than it should be. Almost every new compilation of data concerning the health of any large group of youth contains a series of unpleasant shocks. This has been especially true of the revelations resulting from the physical examinations for induction into the Army, which have made it abundantly evident that the misfortunes of disease and ill health are not confined to childhood and old age.

Mental health is no less important than physical health. The tragedies associated with mental ill health are shown most vividly in connection with the increasing numbers of persons admitted to mental institutions, of whom a considerable proportion are young people. Many other individuals are suffering from mental illness not serious enough to warrant institutional care. Their difficulties may not be generally recognized even by associates.

Youth is a time of frustration for many because of the nature of the transitions through which young people must pass on their way to maturity. In many cases the trials and tribulations of youth, if they leave any permanent impression in later years, are remembered only as a source of amusement. But in recent years of unemployment and in the period of uncertainty about our foreign policy which followed the outbreak of the war abroad two years ago, hundreds of thousands if not millions of young people who had not been able to find any place of usefulness or satisfaction were being subjected to a degree of frustration and strain which was highly dangerous to mental health and stability.

Young people naturally desire to understand and to feel at home in the world in which they live. They have an inner compulsion to find some degree of meaning and unity in life. Yet a questioning, suspicious attitude of disillusionment was exceedingly common among the youth of recent years, because our failure to develop and use constructively a wealth of human resources was so conspicuous. In the post-war period which we shall eventually reach, young people will again be restless, dissatisfied, and resentful unless at that time the rest of the country accepts the challenge and prepares on the widest scale to reopen permanently the channels of opportunity for youth.

While this country is at war, young people, along with those of other ages, will submerge their individual doubts, frustrations, and misgivings in the necessities of service for a common cause. Before long we shall make a place for everyone to give his best as a part of the total war effort. As long as the war lasts, inability to find an occupation will not be a major factor in the situation of youth.

The problems of mental health and personal stability will not be ended, however, during the present period. They will take a different form, but are likely to be intensified by the strains of war.

In the years of toil and struggle ahead, our former negligence in the preparation of young people for the present situation is likely to rise up to haunt us. For the future, we must redouble our efforts to prepare oncoming youth adequately for the burdens and responsibilities both of war and of peace.

# CHAPTER
# VII

## EDUCATION

---

EDUCATIONAL agencies provide a service which is pre-eminently one with long-time objectives. Some of the benefits are immediate, but most of them are realized over long periods of years. Because this is the case, there is sometimes a tendency during a period of emergency to postpone education to a later period. Pressures in this direction become especially acute if the emergency places large financial demands upon government.

At times such as the present, it therefore becomes important to look beyond the governmental fiscal situation to the actual realities of available human time and energy and other resources. It is imperative to arrange our affairs in such a manner that no resources will be wasted and that all of the people will use their time to the best advantage. What does that mean for education in our present situation?

Among other things, it means that some teachers and some students, especially in colleges and universities, must interrupt their present activities in order to undertake specific war assignments. The number of such teachers and such students will probably grow rapidly, although they will be offset somewhat by other students and teachers who must be brought into the educational system exactly because of the imperative training demands of the war emergency.

It is obvious, however, that we shall not take the children from the lower schools and place them in the Army or the war industries. Moreover, children and adolescent youth will not stop growing merely because we are preoccupied with the war.

In general, the only sensible educational policy for a program of total war is to maintain educational services unimpaired. Where those services appear reasonably adequate by current standards, no great expansion will be possible during the present period. In other cases, our deficiencies are so great that even under present conditions it is urgent to press forward with remedial action.

For many years, we have known that a shocking amount of illiteracy still persisted in some parts of this country, but it has required the revelation of the facts from selective service examinations to awaken us to the importance of the problem in relation to national defense. Those too illiterate for service in the Army are undoubtedly also too illiterate for successful civilian life. Moreover, there are undoubtedly many others who are perhaps literate, but whose educational attainment is far below the level represented by a complete elementary school education. Some of these youth may be found in every state, but they are heavily concentrated among both white and Negro youth in the rural areas of the southern states.

Our most imperative duty in connection with education in the United States is to bring the schools everywhere to the level where all children and youth, regardless of race, will receive at least a sound elementary school education. This is so clearly essential as a contribution to national strength in the months and years ahead that the emergency due to the war makes such action even more necessary than before, not less so.

Other fields of urgent action include all phases of health and physical education for children and youth in school, the expansion of vocational education to supply training for industrial and agricultural occupa-

tions, and a revitalized program of education in the values and practices of democracy for youth both in and out of school. For these tasks
we cannot afford to wait; all of them are of immediate concern. Some
of them, moreover, will require additional expenditures, local, state,
and federal, although the generation of a will to act throughout the
institutions of education is much more important than the provision
of funds.

For a more complete reconstitution of educational standards and
procedures, we must look mainly to the post-war period of reconstruction. A great expansion of educational services with improvement in
their quality throughout the nation would be one of the most desirable
ways of taking up some of the slack during the period of economic
readjustment which we shall eventually face.

We must have our plans in readiness and be prepared to move
rapidly at the proper time. The problem of financing the elementary
schools in the financially less able states will undoubtedly need additional attention, even though we should not wait until the post-war
period to begin our attack on that problem. For the secondary schools,
we shall be compelled not only to face a financial problem which may
be acute in all areas, but also to come to grips with the most basic
problems of philosophy and objectives.

## THE OBJECTIVES OF SECONDARY EDUCATION

In this country we have adopted the ideal of secondary education
for all youth. This is distinctly an American ideal. The rapid and
constant growth of enrollments in high schools during the past forty
years has already taken us a long way toward full realization of that
ideal. In some states and cities, particularly the state of Utah and the
states of the Pacific Coast, approximately nine out of ten youth of
high school age are attending high schools. In some other states, particularly in the South, high school opportunities are as yet much more
restricted for pupils of all races. In some states where the Negro popula-

tion is concentrated, only one Negro youth among ten of high school age is in school.

In every American state and community efforts should be continued toward making secondary schools accessible to all youth. Progress toward this ideal carries with it an imperative necessity that broader, more varied, and more appropriate objectives be adopted for the secondary school.

There should be no weakening of the schools' performance of the function of preparation for higher education, but this function is no longer relevant for even a majority of all high school pupils. The secondary school must also discharge the duty of providing suitable curricular and other experience for many youth who will never attend institutions of higher education, and for a considerable number who will continue to leave school at about the end of the tenth grade. Before his period of schooling is terminated, each pupil must be given the highest possible level of preparation for the social, economic, and cultural problems which will be faced by his generation.

The schools must reconsider the fundamentals of education in terms of the objectives that have become appropriate. These objectives must include the effective preparation of young people for life in all its aspects—for work, for health, for use of leisure time, for home membership, and above all for the obligations of citizenship in a democracy.[1]

The American Youth Commission recommends that American secondary schools adopt these comprehensive and varied objectives, and make such continuing revisions of their curricula and methods as the attainment of these objectives may require.

### THE CURRICULUM OF SECONDARY EDUCATION

The objectives of secondary education necessarily must find their expression through the day-by-day activities which make up the total curriculum. It is much easier to revise objectives than to bring into

[1]For a further discussion of youth needs and educational objectives, see Harl R. Douglass, *Secondary Education for Youth in Modern America* (Washington: American Council on Education, 1937), 137 pp.

existence a curriculum which will actually achieve them. The cardinal objectives of secondary education under modern conditions were stated many years ago. Those objectives were not being achieved by the traditional curriculum of the time. Since then the revision of the curriculum has moved only at a snail's pace in the direction of the requisite objectives.

Because of the changing composition of the high school population, the situation has become so acute during the last ten years that it has become obvious that fundamental reorganization of the secondary school curriculum can no longer be deferred. After several extensive surveys of the problem had been made by various organizations, it appeared that some agreement on major lines of reorganization might be possible. Under the auspices of this Commission, a special committee was called together and the result was the brief report entitled *What the High Schools Ought to Teach*, published in August 1940 with the commendation and approval of this Commission.[2]

In that report the initial emphasis was given to the importance of continued instruction in *reading* as an important and much neglected element in the high school curriculum. Equal emphasis was given to *work* as a factor in general education second in importance to none. Instruction in the *social studies* and instruction to prepare young people to meet major *personal problems* were stressed as essential elements of the reorganized curriculum. The traditional course of study, particularly in the ninth grade, was attacked as inappropriate for many young people, as destructive of pupil interest, and as standing in the way of the curriculum reconstruction which in some manner must take place.

This thumbnail summary can give no adequate conception of the scope of the report. It merits reading in its entirety, as it has been read by many thousands of teachers, school administrators, and laymen. It is already apparent that the report may mark a turning point in the

[2]Ben G. Graham, chairman, Special Committee on the Secondary School Curriculum, *What the High Schools Ought to Teach* (Washington: American Council on Education, 1940), 36 pp.

development of secondary education in the United States and that it will continue to have great influence for many years.

The Commission is not without pride in this accomplishment. It greatly appreciates the many favorable comments which greeted the report, as well as the even more important indications that it is becoming the basis for action in many school systems. In the nature of the case, however, the report has stirred up controversy in some quarters. The Commission therefore desires, first, to reaffirm its belief in the soundness of the major recommendations set forth in the report and, second, to make some brief further comment.

In some of the recent discussion of the curriculum in general education, both at the secondary school and college levels, it has been said that the present disorganization of western civilization is in large part the result of the progressive removal from the curriculum over a period of fifty years of the basic cultural studies. It is these studies, it is said, which gave their characteristic outlook to the men who created the modern democratic state. Without such studies, the argument further holds, we are in grave danger of becoming a nation divided, a people with no agreement on fundamental purposes, unable to maintain the principles of freedom because we do not understand them.

These contentions express a point of view with which this Commission has much sympathy. As applied to the secondary school curriculum, however, it is no simple matter to devise an effective plan for passing on the elements of a great cultural tradition. It does not seem likely that we shall solve this problem merely by clinging in the high schools to the tattered remnants of the ancient curriculum of the academies.

The traditional curriculum did have the purpose of passing on the culture of the past. This much is undisputed. What is forgotten is that the culture of the past, like that of the present, was not undivided in its search for the good, the true, and the beautiful.

As they found expression in the traditional curriculum, the classic studies actually had two objectives. In some cases, they did serve to bring young people to grips with "the deep, disconcerting issues of the nature of the universe, and of man's place in it and of his destiny." This was their great and enduring value. More often, however, the same studies in practice served no purpose more important than to provide mental furniture for the members of the professional and leisure classes in a society which was regarded as justifiably stratified, self-perpetuating, and relatively changeless.

Unfortunately, what is left of the classic studies in the high schools serves the second objective much more than the first. When Latin was retained in the secondary school curriculum as an easier language than Greek, the effect, automatic but unnoticed, was to shift the emphasis away from any valuable consideration of life values and the problems of freedom. Plato's *Republic* contains some essential ideas and material for any curriculum in general education, but values of the same order are not to be attained from a reading of *Caesar's Gallic Wars* in the original or in any other language.

The high schools must face the task of teaching in the field of life values and social ethics, difficult though the task may be. Moreover, if we are to be successful in teaching the principles of a moral order to the youth who crowd the high schools, we must recover the essential values of the traditional curriculum, but we must do so by providing subject matter and teaching methods that come to grips with the really great issues in terms that can be widely understood and appreciated. It is not impossible to deal with the greatest ethical problems in simple terms and with a multitude of homely illustrations. When we are prevented from doing so, it is seldom because of questions of pedagogical technique. More often it is because we fail to muster the necessary courage and resolution.

### THE ORGANIZATION OF SECONDARY EDUCATION

In attempting to provide a program which will achieve its professed objectives, secondary education has burst the bounds of the traditional high school curriculum, not only in content but in years of length. It is now regarded as beginning at the seventh grade and extending through the fourteenth. Eight grades were seen not to be needed by most children for instruction in the so-called tool subjects, and elementary education in many schools has been compressed to six grades. There is now a tendency in some schools to emphasize the first four grades as the period for acquiring basic skills, while further instruction in these skills is regarded as a recurrent need which persists even in the high school grades.

With these developments the distinction between elementary and secondary education has broken down in practice and become of little use in theory. No doubt the nomenclature will persist for many years. The Commission believes, however, that in looking to the future we should think in terms of a unified public school system, beginning with such provision for nursery schools and kindergartens as may be possible, and continuing without special break through the fourteenth grade. Within the fourteen grades, there should be a developing educational program which at each grade level contains subject matter of appropriate difficulty and diversity to meet the individual needs of all youth.

At present for most American youth who wish to continue their schooling through the complete secondary period, it is necessary to leave home after the completion of grade twelve in a four-year high school and to attend a lower division of some college or university. This is financially prohibitive for many capable young people and, furthermore, constitutes an indefensible break in the organization of secondary education.

For the purpose of making the final years of secondary education accessible to all youth who want them and whose records promise that they will put them to good use for individual and social benefit, the Commission recommends that public junior colleges and technical institutes be added to the local school systems in every state. These institutions should be created in sufficient numbers to be accessible to all qualified youth, so far as possible without the necessity of incurring the financial burdens attendant upon moving their residence from their parental homes.

The provision of these facilities as rapidly as possible is amply justified by the promise of enhanced economic and cultural well-being for the nation and its communities. It will be financially feasible and can readily come about with the adoption by the national, state, and local governments of appropriate roles in the financing and organization of public education.

### PROVISION FOR PUPIL FINANCIAL NEEDS

Everywhere there is ample evidence, though not as widely known and pondered as it ought to be, to the effect that attendance at high school and junior college is conditioned very largely upon the economic status of the family from which the pupil comes. Studies of the reasons for leaving school in recent years, made in many places by the American Youth Commission and by other agencies, indicate that among all pupils whose schooling was terminated before they had completed high school, fully half left school because of sheer lack of the financial requisites which would have enabled them to continue.

Our free public high schools are often far from effectively free in a true sense. Not only are they inaccessible to qualified pupils in many rural areas, but even in cities they are encrusted with a number of traditions and customs reflecting their middle-class origin. These customs virtually require some outlay of money by the pupil if he is to obtain the full value of the school experience and maintain his status as a functioning member of the school community.

Many of the most valuable activities of the school are still called extracurricular, and are maintained not out of public funds, but only through more or less obligatory contributions from pupils and such other means as sales of admission tickets. Often, too, it is necessary for the pupil to purchase his own equipment for participation in these activities. Pupils possessing no money for these purposes are generally denied access to many of the most fruitful and stimulating experiences in the school career, and are effectively assigned to a lower social class even by associates of their own age. Not infrequently this deprivation of status contributes to a feeling of dissatisfaction and distaste which is the actual cause for leaving school.

Somewhat fragmentary data indicate that the special cash costs of public high school attendance may range from $30 to $200 per pupil a year, with a marked tendency for these expenditures to rise as the pupil progresses through the grades. These are the costs which would not be incurred if the pupil remained at home unemployed. Such costs are directly related to the extent of extracurricular participation. They are also directly related to the character of the particular school, and to the extent to which a real effort is made by the school administration to promote a democratic atmosphere in which pupils from low-income homes will be embarrassed as seldom as possible. Even with good administration, however, some minimum costs to the pupil are at present unavoidable under any circumstances in most high schools.

The financial problem of the pupil becomes increasingly difficult in grades thirteen and fourteen, the junior college grades, even when instruction in these grades is provided as a part of the local school system. The expansion of public school systems to include the thirteenth and fourteenth grades has been widely urged, and is endorsed by this Commission, but it cannot be brought about on any equitable basis unless very far-reaching measures are adopted to equalize the financial status of competent pupils.

As a step in the direction of a solution, we have had for some years the program of student work which is financed by the federal government and administered by the National Youth Administration. Under this program, pupils from low-income families are given employment a few hours a month under the supervision of the school, and are paid modest wages which they may utilize for the cash expenses of school attendance.

On the whole this program has been effective not only in giving pupils the cash resources they need, but also in giving them some experience in working for wages and occasionally some practical training in specific skills. The employment has not been planned and supervised as carefully by the schools as it should be, but there has been a distinct improvement in this respect and further progress will probably continue.

Two major criticisms of the program have been made. In one case, attention is centered upon the fact that the work done by the student workers tends to set them apart from the rest of the student body. It is felt that this may tend to draw class distinctions between needy pupils and others, and it is further argued that if needy pupils are compelled to work for necessities which other pupils obtain from their parents without personal effort, the services of the school are not equally available to all.

In the other case, attention is centered upon the educational aspects of the work for wages which the needy students perform. It is said that all pupils should be given some training in work under the direction of the school, and that wage employment, even in limited amounts, has especially valuable educational aspects if conscientiously supervised and performed. Therefore, it is argued that all pupils should have the opportunity which is now extended only to a relatively few needy pupils.

From these two sets of contentions, it may readily be seen that there are offsetting aspects in the present situation of the needy students on the student work projects. To the extent that they benefit from special training, they cannot be said to be disadvantaged by special discrimination.

In an ideal situation, however, it is certainly true that the school program would be on a much sounder basis if limited amounts of worth-while wage employment were a part of the standard curriculum for all pupils in the upper secondary school grades. This would extend the advantages to all, and eliminate grounds for charging either favoritism or adverse discrimination in the case of a minority of the pupils.

Some such provision appears to be essential in connection with any part of the public secondary school program which is placed upon a tuition basis. As a matter of principle, the Commission believes that no junior college operated as a part of a public school system should charge tuition fees unless at the same time it makes sufficient provision for wage employment to enable any qualified student to earn his tuition. Furthermore, if this principle is accepted, the Commission believes that all pupils in such tuition-charging institutions should be required to earn personally at least a part of their tuition, in order that financial distinctions among pupils may be minimized and that all may have a desirable form of experience.

This does not mean that all pupils should be required to devote the same amount of time to gainful employment, or that all employment should be under the school. On the contrary, a flexible policy of adjustment to individual circumstances and needs should be followed. In many cases, and not only for financial reasons, pupils in the upper years of high school and in junior colleges should divide their time equally between school attendance and wage employment. Half-time work in private employment, with half time devoted to instruction in the schools, would be an especially appropriate type of program for the twelfth, thirteenth, and fourteenth grades.

### THE PROBLEM OF LOCAL SCHOOL UNITS

In all the forty-eight states the maintenance and control of public schools is legally a function of the state itself, but is in part habitually delegated to local public school districts. These districts vary in population from the 7,500,000 in the district under the jurisdiction of the Board of Education of the City of New York to fewer than fifty people and sometimes fewer than ten pupils of school age in small rural districts. Many of the smaller rural school districts have so few people and such meager taxable resources that it is impossible for them to maintain good modern schools even at the elementary level.

Among the forty-eight states the greatest multiplicity of small school districts is found in Illinois, which in 1941 had more than 10,000. Contrasting situations are exhibited in certain other states, notably in West Virginia, where the number of school districts equals the number of counties, 55, and in Maryland, where the counties and the city of Baltimore provide the basis for 24 school districts.

In some areas, including substantial parts of whole states, a plan of district organization is followed by which autonomous high school districts are laid down over autonomous, small elementary school districts. Each set of districts may have independent power to tax for school purposes, and there is little provision for coordination of either educational or fiscal policies. With the development of the junior college movement, the further danger of a third set of independent and uncoordinated local school units has become real in some areas.

This Commission believes emphatically that no plan of local districting is sound which provides overlapping, independent local units of school administration. Every local school district with governmental powers should include an integrated system of local schools providing instruction beginning in the primary grades and extending through at least the twelfth grade.

In many parts of the country where the population is thickly settled, even though partly rural, the most desirable plan of district organization would provide districts which embrace within their boundaries from seven to twelve thousand pupils of all ages. In such districts it is possible to organize a complete system of elementary and secondary schools, including a junior college organized as a part of the local public school system and offering facilities for general and technical education to those who should continue in school to the end of the fourteenth grade.

In stressing a plan of district organization which is necessary if suitable educational opportunities are to be provided for adolescent youth, the Commission is not unmindful of the values which have attached to rural community life around the small district school. Every effort should be made to retain and strengthen these values. This can be done by continuing to provide schools close to the homes of the pupils in the first four to six grades, by carefully observing community boundaries in laying out the school attendance areas, and by continuing to give parents in the various communities an advisory relationship to the administration of the neighborhood school. In some states consolidation of attendance areas as well as governing districts has proceeded so vigorously under the financial pressure of recent years that small children are now being transported long distances and real damage has been done to rural community life.

In every plan of district reorganization, desirable conditions for school administration should be adjusted so far as possible to the structure of local government. In many states of the central and southern parts of the country, as well as in the Far West, the county or the parish is the most feasible unit for the operation of a complete, modern local school system. In the northeastern states, the true focus of local government is found in the town or township, which should frequently be adopted as the local unit of school administration. Where it is possible to parallel other major units of local government in laying out school district boundaries, advantage comes from the facilitation of cooperative relations between the schools and other governmental services.

The Commission recommends that all possible steps be taken to move promptly toward a situation in which all local school units are adequate in size and harmoniously adjusted to local conditions of government and community life. Except in the most sparsely settled areas, the smallest local school district should be large enough to permit the organization of at least one high school with no fewer than 100 pupils in the tenth grade, and a proportionate distribution of pupils in the other grades.

### THE PROBLEM OF STATE SCHOOL ADMINISTRATION

In every state, efforts to improve public education must confront the fact sooner or later that action at the state government level is essential. If the school districts are to be reorganized, the state must act. If an adequate basis of financial support is to be provided, the state must act. If assistance, supervision, and leadership are to be provided for the improvement of schools in rural areas throughout the state, the state must act.

For all of these and many other reasons, the quality of the state agencies dealing with education is of the utmost importance. Unfortunately, the situation in most states is very unsatisfactory.

In thirty-two states the state commissioner or superintendent of schools is an elective official, frequently under state constitutional provisions defining his status which have not been revised for many years. In eight states he is appointed by the governor, and in eight by a board of education. In salary, tenure of office, and qualifications of the incumbent, the position of chief school officer in most state governments compares very unfavorably with that of a superintendent of schools in any one of the two or three largest cities of the same state. The cities should not be reproached for obtaining the best educational leadership they can find, but it would seem that rural areas which must look mainly to the state government are also entitled to competent leadership.

The chief state school officer is assisted by the staff of the state department of education, which he heads, and in some cases is responsible to a state board of education. When the head of the state department of education is himself incompetent or politically minded, the staff he assembles is not likely to be highly qualified. In other cases, state commissioners of education suffer from a lack of assistance because they are unable to obtain adequate financial support for their departments.

Most states have a number of boards exercising educational powers, but the states which have established boards of education with effective responsibility for the general determination of school policy are much in the minority. If the chief state school officer is elective, it is difficult, although perhaps not impossible, to organize a state board of education which can function in a desirable relationship to the state superintendent or commissioner and the department of education.

On the basis of recent surveys, it seems fair to conclude that there are not more than six or eight states in which the state agencies dealing with public education are working effectively to provide reasonably adequate educational leadership on a state-wide basis. In at least ten or twelve states, at the opposite extreme, the existing officers and staffs are hopelessly incompetent. In the remaining states, some good work is being done under such severe limitations that the results cannot be regarded as at all sufficient.

The present situation is no worse than that of former years, but it is also no better. The facts just summarized have been widely known for a long time without giving any apparent impetus to action. In many states the necessary legislation and administrative action could take place only with the support of the state education association, which for one reason or another has not been sufficiently active.

Ideally, in every state there should be a board of education of well-qualified laymen, in which should be vested general authority for the supervision of the elementary and secondary schools of the state. The chief state school officer should be appointed by the board and should be responsible to it. The department of education should be staffed, financed, and equipped to give effective attention to every major problem of the school system in the state.

State constitutional provisions are notoriously an impediment to the attainment of these objectives in many states. In most cases, however, the exercise of some ingenuity would find ways to improve the situation materially even within the present constitutional provisions. Moreover, we should never accept the point of view that revision of the constitutions of the various states by democratic processes is a hopeless undertaking. Most of the states have modified their state constitutions many times in the past, and will continue to do so in the future.

The American Youth Commission urges all citizens and all agencies and organizations concerned with education to give major emphasis in the immediate future to campaigns for the improved organization and functioning of the state departments of education. Those who are concerned for the conditions of rural education and of rural life should be especially active in such campaigns.

With every year that passes, action to improve educational administration in the forty-eight state governments becomes more imperatively necessary if educational progress is to continue under state and local control.

### SCHOOL FINANCE

Because the schools have been left so completely to local initiative and responsibility, the educational situation of this country is one of great variety. The best schools are very good. The average schools are creditable. The poorest schools are so bad that the conditions are almost beyond the belief of those who have not seen them. The poorest schools are also the ones in which the rate of progress is the slowest, with little discernible improvement and often some retrogression over a period of a generation. Moreover, in the more poverty-stricken and isolated parts of the country, there are hundreds of thousands of children whose school attendance is very irregular, and many children of elementary school age who are not even enrolled in any school.

These conditions are the result of dependence upon local property taxation for school support. Some school districts have taxable values a hundred times as great for each child as those of other districts even within the same state. States as a whole differ widely in their financial ability; the wealthier states are eight or ten times as able to raise school funds for each child as the least able. In proportion to their means, the poorest states make the greatest effort to support schools. Despite great sacrifice, they are unable to provide good schools for all the children.

The principle is well established that states should equalize educational opportunities within their borders by state aid to schools, but the amounts and the method of distribution are in urgent need of improvement. Some states must increase their aid to the local school districts, and others must distribute their present state-aid funds in a manner better designed to decrease educational inequalities.

In view of the marked inequality in tax resources among the several states, it is now widely recognized that federal aid to the states for educational purposes, safeguarded against federal interference, is essential and should be expanded as rapidly as possible. In general, the agricultural states have the smallest ability to raise money for education. In most of the predominantly rural states, the resources taxable by the state and by the communities are entirely insufficient to support good schools and other educational facilities, such as libraries, for all of their children and youth. Yet these are the states that have the largest proportion of children of school age in their populations and so are contributing most heavily to the future citizenry of the United States.

One outstanding illustration of the necessity for federal aid results from the obligation to provide equal or equivalent educational opportunities for the children of minority races. The segregated schools for Negroes in some seventeen states are generally characterized by markedly shorter terms, grossly inferior housing and equipment, substantially lower salaries for teachers, and distinctly inequitable financing in all respects as compared with schools for white children in the same states. The fact that there are occasional local exceptions serves only to emphasize the general condition.

As compared with the support and quality of schools in more fortunate states, the schools for both races in the states requiring segregation are on the whole at an inferior level, though most of these states devote larger proportions of their local revenues to schools than the average state. The combination in these states of relatively small taxable resources with relatively large proportions of children and youth of both races renders it impossible for these states to improve their schools to a point where they even approach the national average if they must depend solely on their own state and local revenues.

The gravity of the situation is accentuated by decisions of the federal courts which have enunciated the eminently sound and just principle that if there is in fact discrimination solely because of race or color between the salaries of white and Negro teachers who are required to possess the same minimum professional qualifications and who are doing substantially equivalent work, then there is a violation of that part of the Fourteenth Amendment to the Constitution of the United States which forbids any state to deny any person within its jurisdiction the equal protection of the law.

This principle has been declared in separate cases by a United States District Court in Maryland and by a United States Circuit Court of Appeals in Virginia. The Supreme Court of the United States has refused to review the latter case. It may be said that the principle has become a part of the law of the land, marking a step forward which must be implemented by suitable fiscal measures.

These decisions are recent and their repercussions are being widely felt throughout a large part of the country. In these areas a financial situation which had been difficult for many years has suddenly been made far more acute than formerly.

Preoccupied as we are with the military activities of the war, it is not easy to secure action by the federal government in regard to even the most urgent problems of educational finance for which only federal action will suffice. Yet education is established in public policy not as a secondary interest but as the first line of true defense against that internal breakdown which in many nations has proved to be even more dangerous than external attack.

The Commission believes that financial support must be provided by the federal government if an adequate educational system is to be developed throughout the country, and that even under war conditions it is essential that some financial support for the removal of educational inequalities be provided without further delay. The Commission is in agreement in principle with the recommendations of the Advisory Committee on Education.[3] Federal funds for school support should be distributed in such a way that they will go to the states and school

[3]Floyd W. Reeves, chairman, The Advisory Committee on Education, *Report of the Committee* (Washington: U. S. Government Printing Office, 1938), 243 pp.

districts where needed most. The plan of administration should guard with all possible care against the intrusion of federal control over the instructional process in the schools, but should include adequate provisions to protect minority groups from discrimination in the distribution of federal support for schools.

Equalization of educational opportunity should be regarded realistically, not as charity from wealthy cities and states to their poorer brethren, but as a necessary provision for national security. The children born on poor land are as much citizens as those born in richer areas. Their obligations of citizenship as adults will be the same, and their need for adequate preparation as great. Their education is a national concern which is in no way lessened because they happen to have been born where real estate is of low assessed value.[4]

The Commission is fully aware of the dangers involved in bringing the federal government into the general field of school support. It has debated this problem over a period of six years and has become convinced that federal aid is urgently required. It was never more important than it is now if we are to maintain and defend the ways of democracy.

### LIBRARIES AND OTHER EDUCATIONAL SERVICES FOR YOUTH

Education is a process which does not cease at the termination of formal schooling or upon the attainment of any specific age. There is a continuing public responsibility to afford facilities whereby adults of all ages can improve their mastery of language and other tools of learning, their cultural insights, and their vocational knowledge.

Young people who have left school have special need for a wide variety of educational services. Often this need is not realized immediately after leaving school, when a time of letdown in intellectual interests is common. As they measure themselves against adult requirements, however, ambitious young people very soon find the need for some means of further education.

[4]Newton Edwards, *Equal Educational Opportunity for Youth* (Washington: American Council on Education, 1939), 189 pp.

In order to care for these needs of out-of-school young people and of adults generally, every local school system should include provision for part-time educational services for adults and for other activities to further the cultural interests of the community. The special requirements of young people, especially of those who have left school prematurely, should be the object of unusually careful attention.

Many school systems are handicapped by limitations of size and financial resources in providing more than the rudiments of a program for children. The importance for democratic progress of having functioning institutions of adult education is another weighty reason for pushing onward with the reforms in school administration and finance already recommended in this report.

The public library is an institution of primary importance for adult educational service. In many cases, libraries have been major instrumentalities in the education of young people whose talents were later of the greatest importance to their country.

The free public library is pre-eminently an American institution, but even in this country adequate library services have not been developed. As one of the less conspicuous public services and one which was originally supported to a large extent by private contributions, libraries in most cities have never been given sufficient financial support. Some American cities and many towns have not yet mustered enough intelligent public spirit even to provide a public library. Throughout the country, libraries were starved during the depression years, although they served more patrons than ever before.

For many years it did not seem possible to provide an effective public library service in the rural parts of the country. More recently, suitable methods of administration for library service in rural areas have been developed. So much progress has occurred that in some states it may now truly be said that every inhabitant of those states has access to the storehouse of riches in books.

In most states, however, rural library service is still undeveloped or lacking entirely. Some time ago, the Advisory Committee on Education recommended a modest plan of federal aid for rural library service through grants to the states. The American Youth Commission believes that some such plan to provide small federal grants for rural library service should be revived and carried through at the earliest possible date.

Persons who are able to read and who have access to books have within their grasp the means for a complete self-education. If they are unable to read, almost no other method of instruction can be fully effective until this deficiency has been repaired.

Defective reading ability is a major handicap to citizenship and to personal success throughout life. Usually it can be remedied by relatively simple training. Remedial training should therefore be made accessible to all who need it, and it should be especially emphasized in all training programs for out-of-school youth. If such training is provided in an adult setting and under sympathetic auspices, it is usually welcomed by the youth and adults who need it most.

CHAPTER

# VIII

## OCCUPATIONAL ADJUSTMENT

---

Each year in the United States about 1,750,000 young men and women usually seek employment as beginning workers. About half are town and city youth; the other half have grown up in villages or on farms. Some of these young people have attended colleges and professional schools. Many others are graduates of high schools or of vocational schools or classes. In the country as a whole, perhaps 40 percent have dropped out of school without going beyond the second year of high school. In a few states more than half have dropped out without going beyond the elementary schools.

Each member of this annual crop of beginning workers must face the problem of understanding his employment prospects and of attempting to make the most of them under the conditions prevailing at the time. In recent years of youth unemployment, young people in the last years of school and the early out-of-school period were primarily concerned with techniques and services through which they might become members of the fortunate elect who were able to secure jobs. Under present conditions, with the rapid development of war industries, young people mainly need help in selecting the most appropriate types of work, securing training for them, and, in many cases, adjusting their personal vocational plans to the necessities of compulsory military training and service.

Whatever the character of the economic and political situation, the need is perennial for occupational adjustment services of guidance, training, and placement. The services are provided by schools, public employment offices, personnel offices of employing establishments, and various agencies of other types. The need for services of occupational adjustment has been widely recognized for a long time, but it is only within recent years that plans have begun to emerge for services adequate in scope and organized for effective administrative relationships.[1]

## VOCATIONAL GUIDANCE AND EDUCATION IN SCHOOLS

The school reaches more children than any other agency and is in a position to give constructive guidance in connection with occupations, training, and placement. Unfortunately much less is accomplished than is desirable, mainly because of deficiencies in the curriculum.

As already noted in this report, the curriculum of most secondary schools should be drastically reorganized. Among other changes, the amount of occupational information and training which is included should be greatly enlarged. In some cases this may be done by organizing special courses, but in all cases the occupational implications of the regular courses of instruction in social science, geography, and history should be fully developed. If this is done, there is no valid financial reason why material dealing with occupations, of great practical interest to youth, could not be offered even in small schools.

Moreover, beginning at about the seventh grade and continuing as long as they remain in school, every pupil needs some individual advice in regard to his future occupation and to desirable courses of study as preparation. Cumulative records of the student's work and characteristics should be started in the early grades and should be maintained

[1]For a full discussion of community services of occupational adjustment and their organization, see Howard M. Bell, *Matching Youth and Jobs* (Washington: American Council on Education, 1940), 277 pp.

throughout the school career as a basis for further guidance. Full-time counselors are to be found at present in fewer than 6 percent of all secondary schools; the number should be increased in larger schools as rapidly as possible, and similar part-time service should be provided in smaller schools. Small high schools are necessarily at a disadvantage, but should give all possible emphasis to guidance activities, and should seek to improve the qualifications of their personnel for such service.

For many years, city school systems have offered vocational education courses to prepare pupils to enter specific trade and industrial occupations. Since 1917, such courses have been assisted by federal grants under the Smith-Hughes Act and later supplementary legislation, and there has also been provision for vocational courses in agriculture and home economics in rural high schools.

As a part of the conduct of the war, federal funds in large amounts are being provided for (1) vocational courses of less than college grade for workers already engaged in or preparing for war industry occupations, (2) short courses in colleges and universities to meet shortages of technical specialists, (3) vocational courses and "related or other necessary instruction" for youth employed on NYA work projects, and (4) vocational courses and "related or other necessary instruction" for out-of-school rural youth and for other similarly situated youth.

Activities of this sort will probably continue, perhaps with increasing emphasis, for the duration of the war, and their influence on the structure of school programs will undoubtedly be evident for many years to come. The contribution which the schools can make to industrial efficiency is being demonstrated so impressively that it will never again be possible to relegate vocational education to a position of minor importance.

The present experience is emphasizing the need for more vocational education in rural areas, and is facilitating the experimentation necessary to find solutions for the difficult problems of rural vocational education. To give rural young people some preliminary preparation for work in the war industries, general shop courses are being organized in the larger rural high schools throughout the country. It has been demonstrated that these courses give rural young people a useful preliminary orientation for industrial work, as well as materially increasing their skill for the miscellaneous work activities of rural areas.

In rural schools, it is seldom possible to give the specialized types of vocational education which prepare for entrance into specific trade and industrial occupations. The need of rural young people for such training is now being met to a considerable extent by the resident centers for work and training which are operated jointly by the state boards for vocational education and the National Youth Administration. In these centers, rural young people with limited financial resources are enabled to obtain training which could be provided in their home communities only with the greatest difficulty, if at all.

In urban areas, the new programs of vocational education for the war industries are proving highly successful as means through which to "upgrade" the vocational competence of those already at work. Most of the youth who have found beginning employment in recent years have started in jobs which required at most a single specialized skill which could be quickly developed. By securing related training at vocational schools, youth and adults have been able to broaden their knowledge and skills, thus preparing themselves for new opportunities.

Other special programs of vocational education have included intensive short courses operated on a full-time basis for a few weeks each. These courses have been used to train or retrain workers for the rapidly expanding semiskilled occupations in the war industries. These courses have demonstrated how rapidly large groups of workers can be retrained. A special need for such programs may recur in connection with the prospective industrial readjustments of the post-war period.

Young people who until recently were pursuing typical high school programs have participated in all of the various types of vocational training just mentioned. In addition, the vocational courses which have been carried on as regular parts of the full-time secondary school curriculum have been greatly strengthened and revitalized. They have been brought into closer relationship with the available employment opportunities of the present period. In the planning of such programs, there is increasing recognition that highly specialized types of vocational education should be reserved until the period immediately prior to the time when the pupil leaves the full-time school, and that in many cases the young person can better come back for specialized vocational courses after he has made a beginning in some suitable occupation.

The American Youth Commission believes that in the future we shall wish to provide much more vocational training as a part of secondary education than we have in the past, particularly in grades twelve, thirteen, and fourteen. In many cases, the so-called terminal programs in the junior college grades should include a large amount of vocational education.

The place of vocational education in the total curriculum should receive increasing attention, particularly during the period of readjustment when the present federal emergency grants for vocational training are being replaced by some other provision for financial support. An expansion of general federal aid for education on a long-term basis would greatly facilitate the problem of readjustment in local school systems.

### EMPLOYMENT COUNSELING AND PLACEMENT

The responsibility of the school for educational and vocational guidance for pupils in school is clear and undisputed, although frequently much neglected. When young people begin to seek employment, however, they need something much more specific than vocational guidance. They need counseling in terms of the available employment opportunities. To be effective, employment counseling must be carried on in connection with placement service.

Public employment offices are required by law to provide placement service for all who apply. All of the offices provide a minimum amount of service for juniors and a growing number provide special services of employment counseling. On the other hand, a number of large city school systems have organized junior placement services and many secondary and vocational schools provide some assistance for graduates seeking work.

In an effort to determine the most workable plan of relationships between schools and employment offices, the Commission has carefully studied several different patterns of organization. Notwithstanding the legal and other responsibilities of each agency, in actual practice it appears to be possible to centralize the major operating responsibility for junior placement in either agency, at least in large cities. If the central placement office for juniors is located in the school system, the public employment service can fulfill its legal obligations by entering into an agreement with the school system and referring juniors, including those trained in other school systems, to the school placement office for service. Likewise, if an adequate service is centralized in the public employment office, the school system can discharge its responsibility to graduates and withdrawals by referring them to the public employment office and by transferring vocationally significant information concerning them for use in employment counseling.

Each of these plans of operation is now in existence and operating successfully in a number of American cities. Probably no two of these cities have plans of organization identical in all respects, but as a group they are all characterized by the fact that school system and public employment service have recognized their mutual interests and have entered into definite agreements by which they regularly exchange information and frequently share the financial burdens of junior placement service operation.

Regardless of which agency accepts the major administrative responsibility, the Commission is convinced that any plan of organization based on joint action will have merit. In the end, constructive results will come not so much from insistence on any one plan of organization as from such universally essential things as competent professional leadership, sympathetic public support, and recognition of the need for practical interagency cooperation under any system.

When duplicate and unrelated services are provided by the two public agencies, waste, friction, and inferior service are inevitable. A smooth coordination of relations with employers is impossible, community support is likely to be endangered by antagonism among professional workers who should be united in their objectives, and resources which are usually inadequate in any event are used at less than full effectiveness.

In many parts of the United States, a realistic study of the local labor markets will show that most of them include from six to twenty secondary schools operated by almost as many autonomous school districts. It would be futile and hopeless for most school systems to attempt the independent organization of junior placement services. On the other hand, by working closely with the public employment service in the development of itinerant employment counseling and placement services, even small country high schools could do much to improve the employment opportunities of local young people and to provide them with guidance concerning the problems of migration.

### THE BASIC NEED FOR OCCUPATIONAL OUTLOOK INFORMATION

Services of occupational adjustment are basically dependent upon information which is accurate and up-to-date, and which forecasts the future so far as possible. The general employment situation is constantly changing. Individual occupations are affected in special ways by technological change, as well as by changes in general economic conditions. Regions, states, and localities differ widely from one another in the character of available employment and in developmental trends.

All of these complexities have been enhanced in the present period by the exigencies of a total war effort. The war has brought a new, powerful influence upon occupational trends in all areas while intensifying the demand for vocational training and placement service. Fortunately, the shifts resulting from the war have been so conspicuous that the need for accurate information has been recognized more widely than ever before.

To obtain and organize the needed occupational outlook information, provision should be made for continuous studies at all levels and by all of the agencies concerned. Local public employment offices are the agencies most directly in contact with hiring for industry, and they must provide a very large part of the basic information for planning emergency programs of vocational training. In the revision of their regular vocational programs, schools can obtain much of the needed information by making follow-up studies of pupils who have left the schools in recent years. Such studies not only reveal current facts but have a certain predictive value. There is no substitute for follow-up studies organized on the basis of individual schools, since every school population has its own characteristic vocational outlets which ought to be determined as a basis for curriculum planning.

In addition to school follow-up studies and the information which currently becomes available as the result of employment office operations, in many communities there is a continuing need for other types of surveys designed to produce information concerning youth migration into the community and concerning the basic economic, industrial, and occupational trends of the community. Every large junior placement office should therefore include a specialist in occupational research. Where this is not possible, other means of carrying on a local occupational research program should be developed.

Local research programs are closest to the point of action and are most likely to bring tangible results if competently conducted. But since no locality is immune to general economic influences, local research must be fitted into a framework of state and national data. Data on a state-wide basis are now being provided increasingly by occupational information divisions of state boards of vocational education and by the state headquarters offices of the public employment service. At the national level, a number of different agencies provide important information services.

For some years the United States Office of Education has devoted attention to the problem of the occupational adjustment of youth. It has distributed information concerning occupations and has encouraged local programs of occupational adjustment. Recently it has expanded its plans to include cooperation with other national agencies, public and private, for the collation, interpretation, and dissemination of the facts useful in guidance that are gathered by these agencies. In the promotion of state programs of occupational information and guidance, which now exist in about one-third of the states, the Office of Education has developed an important new attack on some of the problems that are difficult to solve on either a national or a strictly local basis. As an agency for the dissemination of vocational information and the promotion of state and local programs, the Office of Education is in a position of central importance.

National statistics of employment service operations are compiled by the Bureau of Employment Security in the Federal Security Agency. In addition, the Bureau makes many special studies. It is responsible for keeping up to date the *Dictionary of Occupational Titles*, a working tool needed by every counselor. The analysis of job requirements and of worker characteristics is a continuing function of this bureau.

In order that the resources of the federal government for economic research may be brought to bear upon the problem of occupational trends and outlook, an occupational outlook service was established two years ago in the Bureau of Labor Statistics of the United States Department of Labor. This service was in process of organization in 1940 when the emerging requirements of the war made it necessary for it to focus its attention upon the prediction of occupational requirements in the war industries. The new service has made a creditable record in this field and is at present beginning an expanded program of studies of the occupational realignments which will be necessary in the prospective period of readjustment at the end of the war. The American Youth Commission urges the rapid development of the occupational outlook service and recommends that its analyses be made widely available to schools, public employment offices, and other agencies dealing with youth.

Although it is not a function of government to guarantee a satisfactory living to everyone who may choose to follow a given occupation without regard to the measure of his skill and activity, government should help to remove the barriers which impede a more balanced distribution of labor and capital among the several occupations and industries. Government agencies should therefore disseminate widely the facts concerning the various occupations and should seek to find and to make known the way in which, under the existing legal and social order, every individual may have an opportunity equal to his ability, skill, and energy.

### OCCUPATIONAL ADJUSTMENT IN PRIVATE EMPLOYMENT

Occupational adjustment is not a completed process when the young worker has been placed on his first job. On the contrary, in this day when the requirements of employment are constantly shifting, occupational adjustment must continue throughout the working life of most employed persons.

Public employment offices have a recurring function in connection with placement whenever the individual is unemployed, and schools can render great service by providing training for entrance into a new vocation or for advancement in an old one. But the major aspects of occupational adjustment must be worked out between the individual and his employer. In so far as services of training, counseling, and transfer between jobs within the establishment are provided, these services are mainly the responsibility of industry.

The art of personnel management is being rapidly developed by large employers who have found it profitable to select and assign young workers with every possible care for placing the right persons in the right kinds of jobs. Small employers often make up for lack of scientific personnel management by more intimate acquaintance with their workers and the use of personal judgment. Further development in the public employment offices of scientific personnel classification, and of corresponding job classification, will doubtless be of assistance to many small employers in their hiring problems.

Employers have a special responsibility for vocational training. Most occupations require some special training that can be gained only through actual experience. Schools can sometimes provide such training under practice conditions, but for a large majority of the 18,000 occupations currently found in the United States, training on the job through productive work under supervision is at once the most effective and most economical method of developing vocational skills.

It is especially important that the channels through which inexperienced young workers can learn skilled trades through apprenticeship be kept open. Otherwise the shortage of skilled workers will be very acute during every period of industrial activity. This consideration has a vital bearing upon the nation's industrial capacity at any time. Its importance is especially apparent in a time of war.

The Commission notes with commendation the efforts in recent years of the Federal Committee on Apprenticeship in the United States Department of Labor, through which modern standards of apprentice training have been developed and put into operation in many places with the cooperation of employers and unions. This activity is not yet on a scale sufficient to approach the magnitude of the numbers of youth who would benefit from such training, or the size of the prospective need for skilled workers. It should continue to be expanded.

Apprenticeship is only a part of the total program of "on-the-job" training. Many occupations in industry require some training, but of a character less intensive, less extended, and less formal than apprenticeship. The nature of this need is well expressed in the statement of the purpose of the Training within Industry Branch of the Office of Production Management: "To assist defense industries to meet their manpower needs by training within industry each worker to make the fullest use of his best skill up to the maximum of his individual ability, thereby enabling production to keep pace with defense demands."

The Commission commends the acceptance by employers and by

unions of increased responsibility for job training, believing that this tendency will operate to the advantage of young workers and of industry and labor as a whole. The accompanying tendency toward more minute division of labor, by reducing skilled crafts to a series of single operations performed by semiskilled workers, indicates a need for judicious shifting of efficient workers in order to broaden their training, diversify their skills, and equip them for suitable advancement. The "upgrading" of workers should also be facilitated by programs of "related training" in classes or schools within or without the industrial establishment.

### OCCUPATIONAL ADJUSTMENT IN YOUTH WORK PROGRAMS

The public youth work programs of the CCC and NYA have functioned to no small degree as institutions providing occupational adjustment services. These programs have accepted young people of no more than average employability, and in most cases have been able to improve their qualifications for private employment.

The function of the work programs in occupational adjustment is substantially the same as that of private employment. Month for month, most youth probably gain in occupational adjustment as rapidly in typical forms of beginning private employment as they do on the work programs. In this respect, the work programs are a substitute for private employment, just as they are in providing work and an income for self-support.

Because they are public agencies and are free from the immediate necessities of profit-making, the work programs can and should go somewhat farther than the typical employer in giving attention to factors of occupational adjustment. In selection for employment, they can employ first the youth who are most in need of beginning work experience, rather than those who have already gained extensive experience in employment. In assignment of tasks, they can afford to rotate young workers more rapidly from task to task in order to give a variety of experience and to develop well-rounded ability. In the appointment of supervisors, they have a special obligation to select persons who not only are technically competent in the supervision of productive activity, but also have qualities of leadership and some ability to inspire youthful initiative. Finally, in terminating the employment of young people they are able to give consideration to their prospects for other employment and their readiness for it.

All of these considerations are important and help to explain why the work programs are able to improve the employability of young persons who have been unable to secure other employment. Private employment, however, has its special advantages for occupational adjustment in the constant drive for production under the spur of the profit motive and in the discipline of a relationship under which wages must be earned if employment is to continue. The public work programs can probably never be more than a partial substitute for private employment even in the field of occupational adjustment. Our situation will not be wholly satisfactory until young people leaving school can obtain regular employment without any preliminary necessity of passing through a special youth work program, although it may be a considerable number of years before this desirable state of affairs can be established on a permanent basis for all youth.[2]

## RURAL YOUTH AND THE PROBLEM OF MIGRATION

The population balance between country and city has been such for generations that a constant flow of youth toward the city is the normal state of affairs. In the decade of the 1920's, for example, about 40 percent of the youth reared on farms moved to towns and cities. During the early years of the great depression, this flow was interrupted and even briefly reversed, but by 1935 rural youth were again moving cityward in considerable numbers. Recently the employment opportunities for footloose young workers in the war industries have been so attractive that migration has been redoubled. It is quite likely that

[2]For additional discussion of the youth work programs, see Part I of this report.

the number of youth in many farming areas has been reduced to the lowest point in twenty years or more.

The migration which has been going on has been largely unguided and has had many unfortunate aspects. Some excellent farming areas have been almost depopulated for the time being, while numerous submarginal farming areas still have their stranded populations.

The period of migration arising out of the war effort is still far from completed. On the contrary, if production for the war and for civilian needs is expanded up to the limits of full employment as rapidly as possible, it will be necessary to decentralize many industries, to establish plants in areas not previously industrialized, to emphasize maximum subcontracting of work to existing smaller factories in rural areas, and to shift several million workers from the places where they are now to places where employment can go forward.

The public employment offices and the emergency programs of vocational training for the war industries are being used so far as possible to facilitate and to guide the necessary migration. The fact that the employment offices have been organized under state administration has reduced their effectiveness in dealing with the requirements of migration from a national point of view. State officials are frequently subject to embarrassment when it becomes their duty either to bring any considerable number of workmen into the state or to send them out. Inevitably local interests and attitudes enter into the operation of employment services under state administration. In view of the pressure for production growing out of the intensification of the war effort, it may possibly become necessary to place the public employment offices under federal administration.

In the post-war period, the problem of migration may be no less acute than it is at present, but it probably will be different in character. More than likely there will be a tendency for many workers to return from the war industries and the military services to the areas where they formerly lived, regardless of the capacity of those areas to provide employment in peacetime occupations.

For another two or three decades, at least, existing population trends indicate that there will be a continued necessity for the migration of about half of all oncoming farm youth away from the farm. The quality of the occupational adjustment eventually achieved by migrant rural youth will continue to be largely dependent upon the training they receive before they migrate. It is therefore of great importance that increased emphasis be placed upon vocational guidance and general occupational training in the rural schools.[3]

In the future, it will be essential to plan a long-term program to deal in a comprehensive way with the needs of migrant rural youth. Public vocational schools on a residential basis and NYA resident centers for work and training are two types of public institutions which offer much hope. These institutions seem destined to play a prominent part in any solution of the problems of migration which will be effective.[4]

## SPECIAL PROBLEMS OF NEGRO YOUTH

Negro youth have all of the occupational adjustment problems of white youth, with the additional complication of discrimination based on race.[5] Most occupations above the unskilled level can be entered by Negroes only with great difficulty. Notwithstanding the handicaps placed in their way, however, Negroes have been successful in virtually all occupations which they have been able to enter.

During the depression years of unemployment and of great surpluses of all types of labor, Negroes found themselves more and more restricted in the amount and kinds of available employment. White workers were hired for work formerly reserved for Negroes, while such relatively

[3]For practical suggestions, see E. L. Kirkpatrick, *Guideposts for Rural Youth* (Washington: American Council on Education, 1940), 167 pp.

[4]For a discussion of the resident centers, see pp. 36-37 and 67-70.

[5]Racial discrimination as a factor in the occupational adjustment of Negro youth is considered in all of the Negro youth studies prepared for the American Youth Commission and published by the American Council on Education. Especially pertinent material will be found in the following: Ira DeA. Reid, *In a Minor Key* (1940), 134 pp.; E. Franklin Frazier, *Negro Youth at the Crossways* (1940), 301 pp.; and Robert L. Sutherland, *Color, Class, and Personality* (1942), 135 pp.

new and expanding industries as airplane manufacturing excluded Negroes entirely or hired them only for limited kinds of unskilled labor.

With the recent expansion of employment, Negroes have benefited, but not in proportion to their numbers. The situation has been dramatized by the widespread discrimination which has been practiced against Negroes in many of the war industries. For a considerable period many employers enjoying substantial contracts for armaments production were blatant and unashamed in their outright refusal to hire Negroes, regardless of training or competence. Because of difficulty in securing placement for them, public employment offices in many areas were not active in referring Negroes, and they were frequently refused admittance to the emergency programs of vocational training for war industry occupations.

Within recent months, energetic and commendable efforts have been made to remedy the situation. The responsibility of the federal government in connection with private employment for war purposes and in governmental service has been officially recognized by an executive order of the President, reaffirming "the policy of the United States that there shall be no discrimination in the employment of workers in defense industries or government because of race, creed, color, or national origin," and providing for the establishment of a federal Committee on Fair Employment Practice, with powers of investigation, persuasion, and recommendation.[6] This committee has been actively at work and has undoubtedly brought about some change in the attitudes of many government officials, corporation executives, and labor union leaders. Public employment offices are making special efforts to place Negroes, and they are entering the training programs in increasing numbers.

All of this is helpful, but the Negro people generally are still deeply discouraged over the situation because the current expansion of employment so far has seemed to confirm their previous disadvantages more than to relieve them. All public expressions indicating a change

[6]Executive Order No. 8802, June 25, 1941.

in the attitudes of influential white citizens are cordially welcomed, but no small amount of skepticism will remain until professions of good will are followed by a commensurate degree of actual performance. Negroes who are best able to assess the progress which is taking place feel strongly that there is some tendency in white official circles to acquire a strong feeling of self-conscious virtue from a very limited exercise of the precepts of religion in regard to race relations. In quantitative terms, the problem of racial discrimination in employment is so large that much more than a token beginning must be made before a cure can be claimed.

As labor shortages become acute in many areas, employers find it easier to reconsider their previous ideas as to the employability of Negroes in semiskilled, skilled, and professional occupations. The present efforts to break down discriminatory practices therefore work in an unusually favorable situation.

Nevertheless, the problem is one which will remain acute for many years. It should continue to receive the attention and assistance of all men of good will. Employers and unions have the greatest responsibility, and should be made aware of their obligations to pursue policies of justice in making decisions as to employment. Schools and public employment offices are in strategic positions and should bend every effort toward securing opportunities for Negro youth on an equitable basis.

One youth in every ten is a Negro. If opportunity continues to be denied, the frustration and bitterness of Negro youth will be no small element of weakness at a time when we wish to be strong. If given opportunity, Negro youth will add to the strength of the nation of which they are a part. They will demonstrate with enthusiasm that they are American citizens of whom the nation can justly be proud.

# CHAPTER
# IX

## THE USE OF LEISURE TIME

---

The quality of an individual or a civilization becomes most starkly apparent in the use of leisure time. When people can do what they please, we find out what they please to do.

If they are eager to use their time in the development and use of creative skill, in active sports and games, in social activities that can unite a whole community, and in all the various forms of mutual assistance, we can be moderately certain that their civilization will have a tone of vigorous optimism even under conditions of adversity. On the other hand, if there is a disposition to decline the toil necessary to bring any skill to perfection, to prefer the passive participation of a spectator, to withdraw from neighborhood types of social activity, and to consult personal convenience when others need help, the tendency to become soft, selfish, and lazy may become so general in a civilization that only a rotten shell remains.[1]

Of the two sets of characteristics just outlined for contrast, the first was typical of the United States under frontier conditions. The second, in the opinion of some people, was representative of the United States before the war. If they were right, our position was indeed desperate.

[1] For an exposition of this theme, see Henry C. Link, *The Return to Religion* (New York: Macmillan Co., 1936), 181 pp.

It is true that strong tendencies had been carrying us in the direction of the second set of characteristics. The causes for this drift were deeply imbedded in the progress of material wealth, in the conditions of urban life, and in the weakening of religious faith. The relations between these matters are given some further discussion in Part IV, the concluding part of this report.

For this chapter, however, it must be noted that the use of leisure is a problem that has been increasing in importance for decades. There has been an obvious growth in the actual amount of relatively free time under the control of most individuals. Over the same period, a satisfying use of leisure time has become more difficult as more and more people have been dispossessed of any unifying purpose in life. Throughout the ages the mere struggle for existence supplied driving purpose for most individuals, while many found a more complete basis for personal integration in religious practice. In recent years, the situation changed in both respects.

Our present preoccupation with the prosecution of the war is minimizing the problem of leisure time in some ways, in others intensifying it. In terms of leisure hours available, the problem becomes smaller as more people secure employment, work longer hours, and engage in civilian defense activities. The need for suitable means of relaxation, however, may become more acute.

The factor of purpose in life is vitally affected by the war. The reports from England on the behavior of that people under stress indicate graphically the effect of a purpose so compelling that it can unite a nation and release the full energy of every individual. Now that this country is completely in the war, we are beginning to experience much of the same effect.

It is a reproach to our way of life that only in a time of war do we achieve the level of national effort necessary to bring a united citizenry to the heights of great accomplishment. Our habits in the use of leisure time are far from being the only factor to blame. Those habits are in part the result of conditions we have not troubled to remedy, but the habits themselves are important because they will be a major influence in the development of the future.

The presence of an enormous vested interest in the form of the commercialized amusements is an aspect of the situation that cannot be neglected. In most cases where selfish, self-indulgent, or even merely passive uses of leisure are in competition with alternative uses of an active, outgoing, and unselfish sort, the commercial amusements are a heavy weight in the balance on the side of the former. It is easier to watch a baseball game than to play in it, easier to go to the movies than to help organize a little theater, easier to listen to the radio than to take part in a community sing, easier to sit at home than to help a neighbor. But the continued choice of that which is easier will in the end lead to a life of futility, not of satisfaction.

Of all the ages of life, youth is the time when energy, idealism, and interest in other people can be captured most readily for constructive purposes. It is accordingly the period when the greatest effort should be invested in facilitating the best use of leisure time.

### COMMUNITY RECREATION PROGRAMS

Young people and other individuals who find that time hangs heavy on their hands have a number of alternatives. If they have enough energy, imagination, and initiative, they may be able to devise some form of self-sufficing activity for themselves. This may or may not be constructive; most forms of juvenile delinquency are the result of one kind of youthful initiative, coupled with a lack of other opportunities.

If they have money, the various forms of commercial recreation are available, some desirable, others much less so. If they do not have money, services of one kind or another may be available from some public recreational agency or from the voluntary agencies which provide leisure-time services for children and young people.[2]

---

[2]For a comprehensive report on the problems of leisure, recreation, and young people, see C. Gilbert Wrenn and D. L. Harley, *Time on Their Hands* (Washington: American Council on Education, 1941), 266 pp.

The availability of public or nonprofit leisure-time services is much less general than may be supposed. In only a few cases are the needs of youth adequately met by existing community programs, which appeal mainly to children under 16 and to adults who have become established in the community. In most cases, the local public recreational agency, if it exists at all, is primarily concerned with park and playground administration, and often has no other functions. A few cities have developed comprehensive public recreational departments in their municipal governments. Such departments may operate community centers, promote craft and hobby clubs with voluntary leadership, and provide facilities for various types of social recreation and cultural activity, as well as organizing athletic programs and managing the parks and playgrounds.

At present, all of the community leisure-time and recreational agencies have become preoccupied with problems arising out of the emergencies of the war effort. These problems are especially acute in the areas adjacent to the military training camps and in the centers of industrial activity for defense. The available trained recreational leaders are rapidly being absorbed into military service, industry, and the emergency programs in expanding war industry communities. The regular community programs elsewhere are meanwhile being drained of qualified personnel. They are also in danger of reduced financial support, although they have never been very well financed.

The American Youth Commission believes that community recreation programs are an essential social service and one needed even more at present than in times of less stress and strain. The existing community programs should be vigorously maintained and where possible expanded. In many cases new community programs should be organized, in part because of the requirements of the present emergency. In all cases local defense councils and voluntary civilian defense organizations should give attention to community organization for recreational service, because of its evident close relationship to all factors of morale and community solidarity.

Wherever it is possible to think in terms of long-time needs, the effort should usually begin with a community survey of recreational needs, existing programs and facilities, and available resources of material and personnel. Whether or not a formal survey is made, usually there is need for greater coordination of the activities of the public and private agencies of the community which deal with recreation and the use of leisure time. In many cases a representative community council will be found helpful as the means through which to organize the collaboration necessary for a survey, and as a continuing agency for planning after the survey has been completed.

Public recreational agencies should expand their conception of their responsibilities and provide increasing facilities both for recreation in the form of physical sports and for the social types of recreation. The voluntary leisure-time agencies should seek to overcome present limitations and should especially seek to find means by which they can extend their services to the great mass of children and young people in the underprivileged sections of the population, with whom they have had insufficient contact.

Both public and private agencies should give renewed attention to two groups in the population for whom their services have been particularly deficient. One such group consists of the rural people generally and of rural youth in particular. In many rural areas the social organization of former times has disintegrated with the coming of the automobile and effective agencies have not yet been established to promote suitable forms of social recreation for rural young people under modern conditions. This is a problem to be taken into account in all forms of rural social planning, including planning for the reorganization of school districts.

Whether rural or urban, Negro youth are usually compelled to live in a slum environment.[3] The wholesome use of leisure time is literally impossible within the four walls of many Negro dwellings, and ac-

---

[3]Charles S. Johnson, *Growing Up in the Black Belt* (Washington: American Council on Education, 1941), 360 pp.; W. Lloyd Warner, Buford H. Junker, and Walter A. Adams, *Color and Human Nature* (Washington: American Council on Education, 1941), 301 pp.

cordingly there is a need, seldom met, for socially provided facilities. As they become aware of what it means to be Negro in a white man's world, most Negro adolescents experience their share of feelings of inferiority, resentment, and aggression. For these youth, attractive facilities for active sports and for social types of recreation would have much of the potential healing and corrective power which they have for unemployed youth of all races.

Assistance in the operation of community leisure-time enterprises should be recognized as a form of service especially appropriate for youth. Definite efforts should be made on as permanent a basis as possible to mobilize youth effort for the mutual benefit of youth and the community, and young people should share in the planning of programs.

In times of severe youth unemployment and of consequent heavy demand for community recreational services, it would seem especially appropriate to use the youth work programs for the improvement of recreational services. Work projects should be organized for the construction of recreational facilities of all kinds, and youth project workers should be assigned in increasing numbers to the nonprofit leisure-time agencies, both public and private, as staff assistants.

Public inertia in dealing with the problem of youth recreation results mainly from a common habit of thought which regards any recreation program as something extra, a luxury to be provided if convenient and to be dispensed with when not. Nothing could be further from the truth. Soundly conceived and properly administered, the community recreation program provides not only an indispensable service in itself but also the key to character training and to the general development of morale and patriotic citizenship.

#### PROBLEMS OF VOLUNTARY LEISURE-TIME ORGANIZATIONS

Voluntary community services, such as the YMCA, YWCA, and the Scouting organizations, do an immense amount of good and perform a unique function. But they have various limitations. Reliance upon much voluntary leadership is at once their greatest strength and greatest weakness. Since they depend upon contributions both of time and money for their maintenance, frequently their development is arrested before they have begun to serve more than a fraction of their appropriate constituency. In most cases they find it necessary to charge fees; in some cases their clientele is so restricted by the fees charged that they become very inadequate as institutions of social welfare. Because of these limitations, not more than one young person in four has an active and effective connection with any one of the major voluntary agencies. In general, the youth who are not reached by these agencies probably have greater needs than those who are.

The voluntary organizations have difficulty in reaching or holding youth in the age range from 16 to 20. Membership in the Scouting and other organizations for adolescents drops off rapidly after 16 years of age, and at 18 only a small percentage remain. Some of the youth organizations are successful in their work with young adults, but much less successful in reaching youth during their first three or four years out of school. Yet it would seem that the services of voluntary agencies are most needed in the years when youth are most unsettled.[4]

It may be that one cause of difficulty in program building for youth in the late adolescent years is the general tendency toward too much management by adult leaders. When young people have developed to the point where they refuse to be treated as children, particularly when they are no longer under the tutelage of the school, they are likely to lose interest in a program which is not yet ready to accept them as adults. All of the character-building organizations give a prominent place among their aims to the development of personal initiative and responsibility, but competent observers report that rather frequently the intended development miscarries. It is evident that many of the organizations must reconstruct their programs if they are to be effective in reaching older youth.

[4]M. M. Chambers, *Youth-Serving Organizations* (Washington: American Council on Education, 1941), 237 pp.

Fortunately, under the impact of the depression years the voluntary character-building agencies developed a new capacity for self-criticism which is having far-reaching results. Almost every one of the major organizations has recently subjected its work to a searching inquiry. There is a growing appreciation of the importance of evaluative studies and of basic research. The concept of group work as the basic educational technique underlying a variety of activity programs continues to be clarified and increasingly accepted, and there are many evidences of a growing professional solidarity among the workers on the staffs of the various leisure-time agencies. All of this is helpful and indicates that even those organizations most encrusted by a wealth of tradition may be on the threshold of a period of renewed vitality. In the future they may achieve much greater usefulness than at any time in the past.

The Commission believes that it is of major importance to find some solution for the financial problem of the private character-building and leisure-time agencies. It would be unfortunate if such organizations as the Boy Scouts and Girl Scouts, as well as the similar organizations with more definite forms of religious sponsorship, were to be supplanted by public organizations of young people, governmentally administered, supported, and controlled. As long as the private organizations are doing only a fraction of their job, however, there will be a tendency and a need for expansion of the organizations of young people under the auspices of police departments, agricultural agencies, and schools.

Those responsible for community chest policy in the various cities, as well as private individuals who make contributions, may well give thought to this problem. Certain of the welfare functions which were formerly carried on as a form of private charity are obviously in process of becoming public functions supported through taxation. Regardless of its merits, this trend seems certain to continue. The Commission recommends, therefore, that available private resources be reserved with increasing care for types of activity which should not be turned over to public administration, with special emphasis on the private voluntary agencies for youth.

### RELATIONS BETWEEN RECREATION AND EDUCATION

All wholesome recreation is in a sense educative. The schools have a responsibility to equip their pupils for fruitful use of leisure which is equal to their responsibility to equip them for useful work. Upon this, much of the quality of our local and national culture in the future depends. The Commission recommends that facilities and opportunities for participation in creative leisure arts and crafts, in health-building recreative sports and athletics, in leisure reading for enjoyment and culture, and in personality-developing social activities be made available for all youth in the schools. Furthermore, schools should extend these opportunities to youth out of school when the leisure needs of such youth are not otherwise being adequately met.

Schools should encourage pupils to form recreational interests that will carry over into adult life. Schools have an especially heavy obligation to provide appropriate training for the intelligent use of the three great forms of commercial recreation: the newspaper and periodical press, radio, and motion pictures. Schools should make some provision for the vacation-time activities of youth, especially by keeping school playgrounds open during the summer and by conducting summer camps.

In communities which have public recreation departments as going concerns, and in which nongovernmental recreational agencies are functioning, there should be maximum cooperation and joint use of personnel and facilities among all these agencies and the schools. In rural communities and small towns where the schools constitute the major existing public recreational agency, the school authorities should assume leadership for public education in a broad sense, embracing public recreation.

In the expansion of useful work as a part of the secondary school curriculum, schools have an opportunity to establish an effective new relationship to community recreation programs. Since the typical secondary school offers only limited opportunities to provide pupils with wage employment, high schools and junior colleges should use student labor made available by the NYA student work program to strengthen community services outside the school in all feasible ways. Undoubtedly there are significant opportunities for the assignment of students as staff assistants in the community recreation agencies. Where the school is itself the major community recreation agency, pupils can be used with special effectiveness as assistants on the program.

Moreover, there is a need in the curriculum for useful work other than work for wages. Voluntary service in the assistance of worthwhile objectives is one of the life-long obligations of the citizen. Young people should be trained for this obligation by devoting stated periods of time while attending school and college to various forms of community service. Community recreation services would benefit greatly from the general adoption of this principle in the administration of secondary schools and colleges throughout the country. The benefits would not be confined to the assistance offered directly by the students. Within a few years, much greater benefits might become apparent in the larger amount of available voluntary service from qualified adults.

### RECREATIONAL USE OF PUBLIC LANDS

Many highly desirable forms of outdoor recreation require the use of considerable areas of land. The extent to which mere space is an essential is emphasized by its absence or scarcity in congested areas. For many recreational uses, moreover, land not only must be available but must also be developed for the purpose.

These considerations indicate the important relationship between recreation and the ownership and administration of land. Fortunately, in this country large areas are publicly owned. A considerable part of the total land area of the United States is owned and administered by the federal government. Cities, counties, and states also have substantial holdings. In many cases the states could rapidly increase their holdings of land which would have desirable public recreational and other uses by taking title to lands which become tax delinquent.

The Commission recommends that the lands available for public recreational use be increased in extent in the more densely populated parts of the country; that their recreational potentialities be more effectively developed, especially by providing leadership for activities; and that consideration be given to ways by which the use of recreational lands may be facilitated for the groups which are at a disadvantage in using them.

It should be possible to make the state and national recreational lands more readily available to youth than to any other section of the population. The energy, enthusiasm, and love of the outdoors that are characteristic of youth mark them out as the most natural clientele for the large recreational areas. Moreover, when the spirit of adventure is aroused, the simplest facilities will suffice. The vitality of young people will carry them through experiences that would be hardships to older people.

Yet, of all age groups, young people have the most difficulty in making use appropriate to their age of the opportunities that the larger parks and forests offer. In many cases they are able to reach the areas only as members of family parties traveling by automobile. Family recreation is desirable, but the family unit is often not the one best suited to the rugged forms of recreation for which the larger public parks and forests are especially appropriate. It would therefore seem that young people have a special need for leadership and facilities that will enable them to make effective use of the state and national parks and forests.

The Commission commends the National Park Service and the United States Forest Service for recent activities designed to promote organized camping in the national parks and forests. It recommends that both the federal government and the state governments go much farther in the organization of activities especially intended to increase the recreational use of public lands by youth. Low-cost transportation to the areas and simple overnight shelters would be necessary. In some cases the transportation might be provided in school busses and the shelters might be built by the ccc. Even more important is the indispensable factor of able and vigorous leadership for the program. Group participation should be organized with the assistance of schools, churches, and the private leisure-time organizations for youth.

To make the outdoor recreational resources of America effectively available to the youth of America is an effort we owe our young people. There is every reason to suppose that the response to such a program would be gratifying.

# CHAPTER

# X

## MARRIAGE AND THE HOME

---

EVERYONE who has any concern for American youth realizes that many of their difficulties arise out of the conditions of home and family life in this country today. Likewise, every study of youth attitudes and interests makes plain the fact that young people themselves are deeply troubled by questions concerning family and marital relationships. In setting up any series of problem areas for planning in regard to youth and the future, obviously a place must be made for the problems of marriage and the home.

The field with which we are here concerned, however, is not easy to define and is difficult to organize in terms of solutions acceptable to any representative group. The area is not one which is dominated by any great social service, existing or prospective, as in the cases of education, recreation, and health. Rather it is a diffuse and, in part, a highly emotional sector of human life.

In terms of the preparation of youth for family life, the area seems to contain one set of problems. In terms of the responsibilities of parents, certainly a major aspect, it is something else, and different problems appear. In terms of the social responsibilities of the whole people as expressed in the functions of the state, still other problems are revealed and other considerations are relevant.

With the present heightened national consciousness and the increased interest in national stability and progress, there has been an increasing tendency to take a national view of the problems of family life. Obviously national stability will be endangered if family life is generally unstable and insecure. Desirable conditions of family life seem much less assured in the present era of urbanization and of wage employment than they were in a former day.

### POPULATION TRENDS AFFECTING FAMILY LIFE

We have recently begun to be conscious of some of the effects on family life of the spreading practice of family limitation. Whether or not family limitation in its various forms is good or evil from the standpoint of religion and morals, a matter on which there is not likely to be agreement in the near future, we must reckon with the social consequences of the existing state of affairs. In the present situation there are two new facts of major importance, each of which may well be cause for social concern.

The first fact is the distortion in the size of the family unit which has come about as the result of the way in which practices of family limitation have spread. In colonial America, there was such a thing as a typical family; when completed, it usually included from six to twelve children, averaging possibly eight. We now talk in terms of a typical family of two or three children, but actually there is no longer any typical family size. In an average sample of five families, taken at random from all social groups and all parts of the country, it appears that when these families have been completed, one family probably will never have children, one will have one child, one will have two children, one will have either three or four children, and the other, when completed, may include anywhere from five to fifteen. The large families of five or more children are distinctly in the minority, but they are responsible for a very large part of the future population.

On the basis of available evidence, it seems probable that at least 40 percent of all youth come from families of five or more children, and over 20 percent from families of seven or more.

Whatever the income group to which the family belongs, unless the position is one of wealth, large numbers of children tend to depress the family living standard far below that of smaller families whose situation is otherwise similar. Moreover, the large families are heavily concentrated in the lowest income groups and are frequently forced onto public relief rolls simply by the pressure of family needs even when the primary wage earner has continuous employment.

In the past, assistance has often been given in these cases, but it has been given grudgingly. The feeling has been common that parents of large families have only themselves to blame for any difficulties which later develop, and that family limitation is the only policy consistent with a proper feeling of parental responsibility toward children.

Regardless of the merits of this point of view, it has served in practice mainly as an excuse to evade social responsibility. Certainly it has done nothing to lessen the disadvantages of the children in the large families.

The second fact of major importance is closely related to the first. Mainly because of the effectiveness with which family limitation is being practiced by a part of the population, the rate of population increase has been slowing down. We are now confronted with a further development, which is the prospect of an actual decline in the total population of the United States. This will begin within two or three decades unless there is a change in trends recently evident.

At any given time, it is possible for the current generation of childbearing age to fail to reproduce itself even though the total population may be growing because large numbers born in the past have not yet reached the age at which the death rate is high. That has been the situation in the United States in recent years. In the period from 1935 to 1940, the current generation of childbearing age was reproducing itself only to the extent of 96 percent. The rate for urban people was 76 percent; for rural nonfarm, 116; and for rural farm, 136.

In the period since the census of 1940 was taken, the birth rate has risen and the net reproduction rate for the country as a whole may be above 100 at present. The birth rate has always been subject to fluctuations from year to year and especially so in times of war. The present rise in the birth rate therefore seems likely to be no more than an interruption in the downward trend which has been irregular but persistent for decades. How far the decline for the country as a whole may go, no one can say. But the available evidence suggests that in California in 1940 reproduction rates were becoming stabilized at a level where each successive generation would be smaller by about one-sixth than the generation preceding it, while in New York State the net reproduction rate was considerably below that in California and the long-term trend apparently was still downward.

The American Youth Commission does not wish to engage in a general discussion of population policy, which would lead far afield from youth problems; but it seems obvious that the situation of the children and youth who grow up in large families cannot be considered entirely apart from the facts of population trends.[1] The Commission assumes that it is desirable to prevent or at least to retard any large decrease in the population of the United States. It is likely that the number of very large families will continue to decline, and it does not seem likely that this factor will be offset by any large increase in the number of births in the families which are now childless or which have only one or two children. Accordingly, if the impending population decline is to be arrested, it would seem necessary to make it easier for a considerable number of families to continue to have substantial numbers of children.

If all of the families which in former times would have had five or

[1]Although the conclusions and recommendations are not endorsed, the following is suggested as an especially illuminating discussion of population policy: Gunnar Myrdal, *Population, A Problem for Democracy* (Cambridge: Harvard University Press, 1940), 237 pp.

more children were now to stop with four, the decline in the total population of the United States would begin very quickly and would proceed very rapidly. On the other hand, many of the parents in these groups prefer large families and would make a good home for the children if it were not for the financial pressure which continues to drive them in the direction of family limitation.

The Commission believes that as a matter of social justice, steps must be taken to relieve the difficult situation of the families with large numbers of children. Considerations of justice should be sufficient by themselves to bring about such steps, but if other motivation is needed, it may well be found in the present population situation of the United States. When there is general public understanding of the population trends which are already far advanced, and when there is realization of the extent to which the citizens of the future are being reared under conditions of extreme poverty, there will be an insistent public demand for measures of family assistance of the most far-reaching character.

### ASSISTANCE FOR CHILDREN IN LARGE FAMILIES

The means by which assistance for children in large families may best be provided will be a matter for consideration and development for many years. In the present period of rising living costs, however, it would seem urgent to assure as soon as possible a decent minimum level of subsistence for the millions of children and youth for whom it is not now provided. The need for assistance on some regular basis that will avoid the stigma of public relief is particularly urgent for children in large families in the low-income group. Assistance for this group should be provided, not in any way as a reduction in the responsibilities of parents, but in simple recognition of the fact that there are also social obligations in the matter.

In some cases it will not be desirable to distinguish between the children in large families and those in small; instead the policy may be adopted of providing services directly for all children. This is the policy which has been followed for many years in regard to the cost of school operation, one of the expenses of parenthood which has already been taken over by the state to a considerable degree. Schools may be used with increasing frequency as a convenient means of providing services for all children and thereby relieving family budgets of some of the special expenses of caring for children and adolescent youth. Provision for school lunches as a standard, universally available school service is an obvious next step.

In other cases where the school cannot readily serve, but where it is determined that assistance for children is necessary, assistance should be provided so far as possible by furnishing goods and services of direct usefulness rather than by money payments. This will give assurance that basic essentials are provided for the children. Moreover, it will be continuously evident to all concerned that aid to children is the public purpose justifying the assistance, and that it is no mere gratuity to private individuals.

One measure which would commend itself would be special provision for the distribution of food to families with children in the income levels where food is a major financial problem. Such provision might take the form of a newly created food stamp plan distinctly different from the one in operation at present. As a part of the new stamp plan which is suggested for consideration, upon purchase of stamps sufficient for an adequate minimum diet for the adult members of the family, free stamps sufficient for an adequate minimum diet for the children would be made available. There should also be provision for dietary instruction to accompany use of the stamps, since ignorance concerning food values is greatest in the very places where food resources are most limited.

It should be noted that the present proposal is not a plan for the distribution of surplus foods; it is a proposal for the distribution of the food that is needed by children. It would undoubtedly have a very favorable effect upon the market for farm products, but the primary objective would be benefits to children rather than benefits to agriculture. The present highly commendable system for the distribution of surplus foods should not be abandoned, however, but should be integrated with the proposed new plan if it is established. Surplus foods could still be used to great advantage to supplement what would otherwise be minimum diets.

The problem of adequate food for children in large families is somewhat less acute on farms than in cities. Farm families usually have or can obtain access to food sufficient in quantity, although there is frequently a deficiency in the quality and variety of the available food. In many cases where the situation is unsatisfactory, the best solution may be found in the promotion of improved live-at-home practices through which farm families may produce a larger part of their own immediate necessities. It should be remembered, however, that many low-income families in cotton farming and in some other forms of agriculture are compelled to purchase most of their food. The children in these families are as much in need of assistance through some provision for food distribution as the children in low-income families in cities.

In any case, the Commission desires to stress the fact that any general effort to provide assistance for children in large families should start with the elemental question of food. Most low-income families do not get enough food; those with three or four children or more are often not far above the starvation level in actual fact. Yet they are compelled by sheer hunger to spend so much of their incomes for food that they are forced into the lowest grades of slum housing for shelter, and have virtually nothing left for clothing and the other essentials.

In the future, public housing on a subsidized basis should be provided preferentially for families with children. The objective should be to make it possible for large families in the low-income groups to obtain adequate housing without paying more for housing than the amounts spent by small families in the same income groups.

A clothing-stamp plan to secure the distribution and use of surplus cotton already exists on an experimental scale. This suggests the possibility that special clothing stamps negotiable only for children's clothing might be distributed for children in low-income families.

Recommendations made elsewhere in this report concerning health and medical service should have special emphasis in connection with maternal and child care.

## THE RESPONSIBILITIES OF PARENTS

One of the most important results of many recent studies of the development of personality from birth through adulthood is the finding that the earliest years of childhood are much more influential in shaping subsequent character than was formerly supposed. The implications of this discovery for parents are many and important.

Good nutrition and other health care during the prenatal period and during early infancy are important to the best development of human personality. There may also be a direct relationship between a life marred throughout by emotional storms and neuroses, and an early childhood beset by fears and unhappy experience in the home. These conditions are perhaps more likely to exist among the economically submerged elements of the population, but they also exist elsewhere to a surprising extent.

Parents at every economic level bear a responsibility to apply modern scientific knowledge to child-rearing as completely as their limitations permit. They should encourage and support the agencies through which this knowledge is discovered and disseminated, such as the United States Children's Bureau and the federal and state public health services and similar agencies at the community level. The more fortunate parents should assume leadership in seeing that these facilities are made available to all parents in their communities.

Despite great progress in public appreciation of the necessity of putting a stop to oppressive child labor, there are nevertheless many thousands of instances where children of tender ages are subjected to long hours of harmful drudgery. In many cases irreparable injustice is being done, especially when the labor of the child interferes with regular school attendance. Likewise, when parents compel children to engage in near-mendicant pursuits on the streets, the damage done to childhood may easily outweigh any possible pecuniary advantage. The Commission believes that these abuses can be lessened in part by the education of parents regarding their duty to their children, and in part by improvement in the drafting and administration of state laws touching child labor and school attendance.

The Commission recognizes that every parent owes his child not only protection against oppressive child labor, but also a chance to learn to work at an early age at tasks of a kind that will contribute to his physical well-being and to his knowledge of the practical world. By this means the child acquires habits, both motor and mental, which fit him to look after himself, to assume responsibility, and to become a useful member of society.

On family farms and in other family-operated enterprises, the children usually have these opportunities at hand. In urban localities where housing facilities are greatly restricted and where parents are employed in large industrial or commercial establishments, the opportunity for parents and children to work together has largely vanished. In this situation parents have a responsibility to exercise ingenuity in finding for their children suitable ways of engaging in handcrafts under parental tutelage. They also have a responsibility as citizens to encourage and support the development of community facilities where children and youth can learn to work under able guidance.

Parents who are alert and intelligent have learned much in recent years from the new scientific knowledge of infancy. Adolescence is in general a formative period which is second in importance only to infancy, and of far more decisive importance in character formation and the development of personality than the years of childhood between the ages of 6 and 12. Yet this is a fact with which relatively few parents are prepared to cope, although they are conscious enough that their problems multiply when their children begin to go through the physical, emotional, and social changes of adolescence.

Under the impact of modern conditions of living brought about by the automobile, the radio, the motion picture, and other factors, as well as the upward trend in the age of school-leaving and of beginning employment, the social organization of life in the adolescent years has changed since the time before the first World War. Those who spent their own adolescent years in the old order have had great difficulty in adjusting to the new situation when confronted with their responsibilities as parents.

Fortunately, this particular period of difficulty will soon be past. The "flaming youth" of the early 1920's have now become themselves the parents of adolescent youth. The psychological distance between the generations is undoubtedly becoming shorter, with an advantageous reduction in the amount of strain within the family. But a sound philosophy of relations between parents and adolescents is still only in process of formulation.

As in the case of the scientific knowledge of infancy, parents will do well to become familiar with the available scientific knowledge concerning the problems of adolescence. The amount of such knowledge is not as great as it should be, but it is beginning to grow rapidly. In the future it will undoubtedly become much more available to parents than it is at present. Certainly every parent should be made aware of such basic facts as those summarized in Chapter VI of this report. If every parent were aware of those facts and would act accordingly, the situation of young people would be very greatly improved.

### PREPARATION FOR FAMILY LIVING

Young people are conscious of the increasing number of homes broken through divorce. They have before them the spectacle of many cases of frustrated and unhappy home life. In view of all the circumstances of present-day life as they relate to marriage and the home, it is not strange that young people are troubled and confused about their marital problems. They feel a need which they often express for some sort of special preparation for marriage, a need which is seldom met to their satisfaction.[2]

The Commission recognizes the need for both group instruction and individual counseling for the purpose of equipping youth for the responsibilities of family living, and regrets that this need is so inadequately met. In most of the cases where extensive services of these kinds are being provided at present, there may well be misgivings as to the wisdom of the activities. But the Commission hopes that in time, class instruction may be developed on an impersonal level, and individuals may be found who are wise enough to help solve immediate personal perplexities by individual counseling.

To be effective and relatively free of risk to the pupil, both class instruction and individual counseling on the more difficult topics will require syntheses of knowledge from the professions of medicine, social work, education, and the ministry. It will be many years before such syntheses can be developed to a point warranting general adoption of programs of the kind advocated in some quarters.

Meanwhile, there are some things which can and should be done. Many practical and valuable aspects of home management are being effectively taught in home economics classes in secondary schools throughout the country. Such classes for girls should be made universally available, and the home economics classes for boys which exist in a few school systems should be widely emulated and further developed. Child care has become a major part of the home economics curriculum; this is one of the soundest and most valuable elements of training for home and family life, and training in child care should be made increasingly available to boys as well as girls. Sex hygiene is a subject on which young people need specific instruction, but one not easy to handle in an appropriate manner. Progress may be made by giving it special attention in connection with health and physical education.

[2]Joseph K. Folsom, *Youth, Family, and Education* (Washington: American Council on Education, 1941), 299 pp.

Finally, in regard to many of those topics which are not suitable for classroom instruction and in connection with which the competence of many teachers may well be called in question, the Commission endorses the suggestion made in *What the High Schools Ought to Teach:* The best solution may be simply the use of good reading materials which are put in the hands of young people without ever being made the subject of recitation, examination, or discussion between teachers and pupils. The unaided printed word is a universal means of communication and instruction. The secondary school should not be afraid to prepare and use such instructional materials.

# CHAPTER
## XI

## HEALTH AND FITNESS

---

Throughout its field investigations of youth problems, the American Youth Commission has been continuously concerned with youth health. It has found that a comprehensive investigation of almost any particular group of youth will reveal that most of them have specific health problems of greater or less consequence which are not receiving attention, while at least a few are suffering under such major handicaps from bad health that progress in other aspects of their development is difficult or impossible.

Even among college youth, in general an economically favored group, bad health habits are frequent and impaired health is common. Many of them secure adequate amounts of exercise and of sleep only under compulsion, are careless about securing medical and dental attention even when they are aware that they need it, and are quite unable to select for themselves a diet which is conducive to high vitality. In a study of the health of college students, the Commission found abundant evidence that many physical deficiencies are common among such youth. The study also revealed that the colleges and universities with reasonably complete health facilities and good health programs were the exceptions.[1]

[1] Harold S. Diehl and Charles E. Shepard, *The Health of College Students* (Washington: American Council on Education, 1939), 169 pp.

176

The opportunities to train for better health at any educational institution are so great that failure to take advantage of them is a major
form of social waste. It is difficult to excuse the delinquency of many
institutions of higher education in matters of health care and training.
Yet the fact is that college students, in general, are at least as well off
in regard to health as the young people of the same age who are
employed in stores, offices, and factories, while these young people
in turn are probably healthier than most of the working population,
simply because youth is normally the healthiest period of life.

A few forms of physical disaster are especially common in youth—
rheumatic heart disease, venereal diseases, tuberculosis, and appendi-
citis. Even under modern methods of control, diabetes is a much more
serious condition in youth than in later years. Other less acute dis-
orders that are common in youth include dental decay, postural
defects, infections of nose and throat, allergies, vitamin deficiencies,
and other nutritional disturbances.

Yet health is not a special problem of youth in the same way that
occupational adjustment, for example, is primarily a youth problem.
All of the causes of bad health that are especially common in the age
group from 16 to 25 may attack those of other ages, while young children, mature adults, and aged persons each have health problems
somewhat peculiar to their respective age groups. Health is a major
problem of youth, but for exactly the same reasons that it is a major
problem for all.

In planning ways to improve youth health, therefore, the Commission has found it necessary to consider programs, existing and proposed,
and to make recommendations which have as their objective the improvement of the health of the whole population. In addition, special
programs for youth are needed. Such programs are recommended not
so much because youth has special needs as because the period of youth
offers special opportunities to carry on health training and to attack
health problems which otherwise might persist throughout life. Youth
is a period in which the foundations of future strength or weakness are

laid, and in which habits of adult life are formed that will later result in health or sickness.

## THE BASIC PROBLEM OF NUTRITION

Some time around the turn of the last century, the dietary practices of the American people probably reached their lowest level from the point of view of health. Food was ample in quantity and no more lacking in variety than in previous years. But foods and food habits had felt the impact of the machine age without yet having benefited to any appreciable extent from the scientific study of nutrition.

For centuries, mankind has been steadily developing a food culture which has little in common with the natural foods and which finally reached an apex of a sort in the production of white flour, granulated sugar, and refined lard—the last item being important because it is used as a substitute for butter on bread by many low-income families. At the same time that the tendency toward the production of denatured foods was reaching its peak, urban life was making it difficult for millions to obtain pure milk, fresh eggs, and green vegetables. The result was the development on a wide scale of dietary practices built around the combination of white bread, meat, potatoes, sugar, and lard—a basic diet unlike any previous standard diet.

The results of this diet, though not immediately apparent, were certainly far from good. Eventually, however, some processes of improvement set in. A rising level of income facilitated purchases of milk, eggs, fruits, and vegetables, and with improvements in transportation and refrigeration these foods became increasingly accessible. Nutritional science and education began to develop, and with the general modification of food habits during the first World War, progress toward a better diet became more rapid.

Within the last few years, the study of nutrition has made spectacular progress. We now know that nutritional deficiency diseases may constitute the greatest medical problem of our time, that more than a third of the families of this country are living on diets that are generally inadequate for their basic needs, and that the health and vitality of a very large part of the population could be greatly improved by the general adoption of better dietary practices.

The problem of improving health through better nutrition must be attacked in three ways. First, there is still room for an intensification of research. We need more knowledge concerning the food needs of human beings of all ages and under various conditions of life. We need to know more about the nutritive values of particular foods under different conditions of processing and supply. We need to know how to organize economical combinations of food which will provide an adequate diet at low cost. The recent advances in nutritional research are greatly to be commended; such research should be continued and expanded.

The second attack must take place on the level of education. Much of what is already known by food scientists is not known by the greater part of the population. Deficiency diseases can result quite as much from wrong eating habits as from poverty. One of the problems in the Army, in migrant worker camps, and in campaigns of health improvement is to induce people to eat a properly balanced diet, properly prepared, whether they buy it or it is furnished free. In many parts of the country, teaching the people to eat protective foods which they could readily obtain if they wanted them is a major health problem.

Recently some aspects of the newer knowledge of nutrition have been widely disseminated through the press, and undoubtedly much of the further dissemination must take place through newspapers, magazines, and radio if it is to go on rapidly. In rural areas, a thriving program of adult education through the Agricultural Extension Service and the Farm Security Administration is having an effect upon the food habits of several million white and Negro farm families. In towns and cities, a similar program for adults is greatly needed and should be provided by the schools and other public agencies. In the regular school programs for children and youth, both rural and urban, detailed instruction in regard to nutrition is being provided in many home economics classes, and should be made universally available.

In the third place, to improve faulty nutrition, attention must be given to family income levels. For millions of families research and education alone will not have much effect upon faulty nutrition because most of these families do not have income enough to purchase an adequate diet. At prices recently current, only the most expert buying would produce even a fair diet at an expenditure level of $2.00 a week per person for food at retail. This is considerably less than the Army has spent for food on a mass purchasing basis, yet it is more than millions of urban families have been able to spend. Moreover, families with several children are especially at a disadvantage in securing an adequate amount of food.

Because of the combination in recent years of a widespread need for relief and of surpluses in many food crops, the federal government has experimented with a number of methods for distributing surplus foods to needy consumers. The plans have included the direct distribution of surplus food to relief clients, the relief milk program, the surplus food stamp plan, and the school lunch program.

The Commission endorses the objectives of all of these programs and recommends particularly that the surplus food stamp plan and the school lunch program be expanded as rapidly as possible until the benefits of these activities are universally available throughout the country. Moreover, the Commission repeats the recommendation presented in the last chapter, that special attention be given to plans through which adequate quantities of food may be provided for the children and youth in large, low-income families.

## PUBLIC HEALTH AND MEDICAL CARE
### FOR THE WHOLE POPULATION

This Commission is concerned specifically with young people, who are in a comparatively healthy period of life. But the problem of health affects all ages and is always important. It should not have to wait for the emergency of war to bring it to public attention, since the efficiency and soundness of the nation are weakened at all times by any failure to bring the physical condition of the people to the highest practicable level.

The problems involved in improving the health of the whole population may be grouped roughly into three classes, which are, however, interrelated: (1) public health engineering, (2) health education, and (3) individual medical care.

What may be called public health engineering covers those preventive and protective measures which can be administered by the public health authorities collectively to the whole community.

These include provisions for safe water and milk, pure food, sanitation, and sewage disposal; quarantine in emergencies; mosquito and fly control; rodent control where bubonic plague is threatened; and precautions against the spread of hookworm and amoebic dysentery, undulant fever, trichinosis, typhoid, and other food-, water-, or milk-borne diseases. The knowledge exists to control all these diseases; all that is needed is the appropriation of sufficient public funds for adequate staff and equipment in public health departments.

In the control of contagious diseases this health engineering approaches the borders of individual treatment. Vaccination against smallpox, for instance, must be administered to the individual. But the individual is not ill when it is administered, and its purpose is not to "cure" him of anything from which he is already suffering. The primary purpose is to protect others against him, and it is therefore a measure of public rather than of private health. The same is true of quarantine and other measures against the spread of infectious diseases.

The schooling part of health education, like that of all education, is primarily a concern of youth and of the school authorities. But there is no department of life in which broad services of adult education are more needed than in matters of health. Children and young people are frequently the victims of the ignorance of their parents and of the false traditions of their communities.

Public health authorities inevitably find it necessary to engage in educational activities in the performance of their protective and preventive functions. The explanation of public regulations dealing with health and sanitation is an essential form of educational activity. Effective public health programs require a positive approach to health education, in which officials consciously plan continuing educational campaigns and seek to utilize all of the available educational forces of the community: press, radio, motion pictures, schools, churches, community organizations, employing and labor organizations, and all other possible channels for the dissemination of information and the mobilization of community effort.

No amount of public health engineering or of health education can abolish all illness nor alter the fact that when people are sick they are sick individually and need individual care. The problems of illness are medical, economic, and social. Unless all three aspects are met, the omitted ones may nullify the benefit of the others. The sick person needs a doctor, and perhaps a hospital. He also needs food and shelter for himself and family at the very time when the illness may have cut off his income. And he needs these things by methods not demoralizing to himself nor to the community, not unfair to the medical profession, and not incompatible with the essentially individual nature of medical care.

It has become a platitude that these needs are now measurably met at the two ends of the economic scale in most urban communities. Those in the upper-income groups can and do provide for themselves. As to them, there is no problem which they cannot meet, and no suggestions are made as to any change in the present system.

In principle, the same thing is true of the indigent. Their care is recognized, at least in theory, as an obligation of society. To be sure, in the past much of the care has been met by what amounts to charity by the medical profession. Such charity has been recognized by the medical profession as its duty from time immemorial, and is still practiced to a considerable extent. But modern conditions have made it a disproportionate burden which the profession should not be called upon to bear alone. The patient must have medical care, but the physician is also worthy of his hire. Moreover, to an increasing extent he is receiving payment from the society whose interests he protects in caring for the needy. The only question as to service for the indigent economic group, so long as society otherwise permits it to exist, concerns the manner of compensating the members of the medical profession for their services. The Commission believes that this particular public service may properly be performed by salaried public physicians, on full or part time.

The problem of medical economics thus remains for that large group of persons in the intermediate income levels—those who are normally self-supporting, and who would be able to meet the average cost of average illness if it came in average amounts, but who may be individually unable, out of current income, savings, or available credit, to meet the emergency cost of serious or protracted illness.

Among these normally self-supporting persons, there is in fact a large group of "medical indigents," who ordinarily are able to meet their other expenses, but who are frequently compelled to get along without medical care unless they can obtain it free. In many rural areas, this group includes almost the entire population, since few farmers have much ready cash for the doctor, while in every rural area there are families that somehow exist and stay off of relief at an income level markedly below the relief income level in cities.

Since so much of the rural population is unable to meet the full cost of medical service as it is organized at present, few young doctors who have made the investment required for a present-day medical education are willing to settle in rural areas. The older doctors who are there already are steadily reaching the age of retirement, while those who continue to practice are overworked and normally collect only a fraction of the fees they charge, which in turn are usually low by urban standards.

In some of the western provinces of Canada, an even more acute situation has existed in the form of large, sparsely populated rural areas, where in some cases in the years since the first World War it has become impossible to obtain or retain any competent physician on the usual basis of independent practice. In these cases necessity compelled the expedient of employing a doctor as an officer of local government to provide medical care for the entire rural population of the area, the doctor receiving his salary from public funds.

This plan of medical care is certainly not ideal, but it is so much better than no medical care or the inadequate care which would otherwise prevail that in some rural areas, both in this country and in Canada, it is probably the best solution. The practice of providing medical care as a normal function of local rural government has become firmly entrenched in Saskatchewan and Manitoba, appears to be satisfactory to the farm population and to the physicians, and is spreading steadily to additional areas throughout those provinces.

Because the provision for medical care in rural areas in this country has been so inadequate, the Farm Security Administration discovered some years ago that when its rehabilitation clients failed to repay their loans, bad health was the cause in many of the cases. The FSA therefore began to develop a plan for medical care which, with some variations, is now in effect in more than 850 counties in 35 states. Medical care is being provided for more than 100,000 low-income farm families, a population group of more than half a million, a majority of whom are children. In areas where Negroes form a part of the rural population, they have been included, and Negro physicians have taken part in providing the service. In view of the inadequacy of the previous provision of medical care for the rural Negro population, the benefits in the case of Negroes have been especially notable.

In every case, these medical care agreements have been approved by the state and county medical associations in the areas covered. At the beginning of a twelve-month period, each participating family pays a fixed sum into a pooled fund, and thereafter is entitled to such medical care as may be needed during the period. Each month, the participating doctors bill the trustee or treasurer of the fund for services rendered. If the month's allotment in the pooled fund is sufficient, the doctors are paid in full. If not, the available funds are prorated against the bills. Any surplus is carried forward for application against deficits in later months.

So far, in most parts of the country, the FSA medical care plans have been open only to the rehabilitation clients. In the same counties where these plans are in operation, however, there are hundreds of thousands of other "medically indigent" farm families. In many of these counties, if the plans were enlarged to include these families on some appropriate basis, it is possible that at least a minimum program of medical care could be provided for most of them on a self-supporting basis, with great benefit both to the families and to the doctors practicing in those areas. Moreover, the increase in effective medical purchasing power which would result would in many cases make it easier to attract the additional young doctors who are so greatly needed.

In urban places, the proportion of "medical indigency" is perhaps not as high as in rural areas, but there are many normally self-supporting persons who habitually pay their other bills but receive much of their medical care free. This suggests that for those in ordinary wage employment the problem of self-support to meet the costs of illness may differ fundamentally from the problem of meeting the cost of food, shelter, clothing, and other primary needs.

For other risks which increase living costs and which do not strike individuals in average amounts, the established remedy is insurance. We use insurance universally for the risks of death, of fire, of traffic accidents, and for a multitude of other vicissitudes which may be estimated for the group but not for the individual. We have long done the same as to disabilities resulting from industrial accidents or occupational diseases. For many of those in wage employment we now have insurance for unemployment and old age. This leaves illness as the only similar risk not generally so covered. And the United States is virtually the only advanced nation in the world which has not done this also. That there is demand for it here is shown by the large number of private health insurance plans, never adequate and frequently unsatisfactory, which find eager customers.

Current discussion of this problem among urban groups in America has generally proceeded as if it were a new one, with no benefit of experience behind it, or as if the only lessons to be learned from experience abroad were the warnings from various failures and inadequacies. On the contrary, there is no branch of social insurance on which such a wealth of instructive experience is available.

The warnings of experience are important, but the one lesson from all experience abroad, on which there is no division whatever, is that in no country which ever adopted general health insurance is there any movement to cure its evils by abolishing it. No country which started with a partial or voluntary system has ever changed it except in the direction of a complete and obligatory one. This consensus of human experience at least challenges America to examine and consider it.

Much of the health program which has been advocated by the present federal administration will probably require federal aid in the districts unable to provide an adequate program from local revenues. But this does not necessarily apply to health insurance. Workmen's compensation for industrial accidents is now self-supporting. The cost of the medical part of health insurance, confined as it should be to those who are normally self-supporting in other respects, is within the financial capacity of its beneficiaries and their employers (who also benefit), with a contribution from the state which may or may not be limited to the costs of administration. Cash payments to beneficiaries in lieu of wages lost may well be assimilated into the present unemployment insurance system by adding unemployment due to illness as an insurable risk and making a separate charge for it. None of these problems presents any question to which existing experience does not offer an answer.

There remain the more controversial questions. Although there is violent opposition in some quarters, authorities on the subject of health insurance are generally agreed on certain points. Among these are:

1. Any system of health insurance should include free choice of physician by the patient (subject, of course, to the consent of the physician) and the same individuality of relation between patient and physician that now exists, with the single exception of the manner of paying the bills.

2. Cash benefits, to cover a part of wages lost by employed persons, should be an integral and inseparable part of the system. This is the case now with workmen's compensation and is universal in the health insurance systems of the world. Considering illness as a social problem, and not merely as a medical one, it is as vital to provide shelter and food as it is to pay for the doctor and medicines.

3. The cost should be assessed and collected, as other social insurance costs are met, from the beneficiaries, from the employing industry, and from the state.

4. The medical part of the administration should be conducted as far as possible by medical men, with only such oversight by them of the individual physician as universal experience has found necessary and acceptable. The whole system should be divorced from politics, partisan or medical, and should be open to all legally qualified physicians wishing to practice under it.

5. Physicians should be paid from the insurance fund, either by separate fees for each service rendered or by an annual sum for each patient choosing that physician. Though American physicians at present generally would prefer the fee system, the other system has been found more satisfactory in most countries.

6. The system should be obligatory for approximately the same group for which workmen's compensation and other social insurance are now compulsory.

It is unnecessary to discuss here other details, such as the services of specialists and consultants, the relation of the system to existing medical groups, maternity care, the inclusion of the family of the insured in the benefits, and the provision of hospitalization, drugs, and dental care, all of which are important and difficult, but are secondary to the six essentials just specified.

It is of major importance to recognize, however, that special administrative difficulties will be involved in extending health insurance to rural areas, and that the system will be incomplete unless those difficulties are surmounted in some way. In some states, it may be necessary initially to omit farmers and farm workers from any general health insurance legislation. On the other hand, the Canadian experience and the present experience of the Farm Security Administration may suggest ways by which they can be included in legislation for a general program of medical care. In any case, the farm population is so large a part of the total population of the United States that it must not be overlooked.

If the United States is to be the last country in the world to adopt health insurance, it should also be the one to do it best. It has the experience of other countries to guide and to warn it, and it has a general level of living adequate to provide a standard in this respect which others have had to forego by reason of the inability of their citizens to pay for it.

The American Youth Commission recommends, if not present action, at least earnest study of health insurance, the only remaining important omission in our system of social insurance. In any event, the Commission is convinced that ways must be found, and without undue delay, to bring adequate medical care within the reach of all of the millions of families, urban and rural, who cannot afford to pay the whole cost under the present organization of medical service. This is a problem for the medical profession and it is also a problem for the public. It seems evident that the public will not long remain patient if constructive programs of action in the field of health and medical care are not put in operation in the very near future.

## SPECIAL PROGRAMS FOR YOUTH HEALTH AND FITNESS

With adequate provision for nutrition, for public health services, and for medical care on a scale to meet the needs of the entire population, the special health problems of children and youth might become relatively inconsequential. But even if the obstructions which now stand in the way of early action can be overcome, it will take many years, a generation at least, for the full effect of the proposed programs to be felt. Meanwhile, all of the larger programs depend at every step upon education and training that are much easier to arrange for children and youth than they are for adults. Moreover, there are many things that might be done more quickly and more directly for children and youth, simply because social responsibilities for them are more widely recognized and more readily accepted.

At present there is a greatly renewed interest in youth health because most people have been startled and shocked by the results of the physical examinations for military service. According to a recent statement by the Director of Selective Service, "About 50 percent of the approximately two million registrants who have been examined for induction into the Army of the United States under the Selective Training and Service Act of 1940 have been disqualified because of physical, mental, or educational reasons. Of the approximately one million rejected, 900,000, or about 90 percent, were found to be physically or mentally unfit." The reasons for rejection resulting from the physical examinations were distributed as follows:

| Cause | Number of cases | Percentage |
|---|---|---|
| Dental defects | 188,000 | 20.9 |
| Defective eyes | 123,000 | 13.7 |
| Cardiovascular diseases | 96,000 | 10.6 |
| Musculo-skeletal defects | 61,000 | 6.8 |
| Venereal diseases | 57,000 | 6.3 |
| Mental and nervous diseases | 57,000 | 6.3 |
| Hernia | 56,000 | 6.2 |
| Defects of ears | 41,000 | 4.6 |
| Defects of feet | 36,000 | 4.0 |
| Defective lungs, including tuberculosis | 26,000 | 2.9 |
| Miscellaneous | 159,000 | 17.7 |
| | 900,000 | 100.0 |

A special rehabilitation program is being organized by which it is hoped that about 22 percent of those rejected on physical examinations can be prepared for general military service at small cost and within a reasonably short period. Most of those capable of easy rehabilitation are already classified in the group fit for limited military service, a group which includes about one-half of those rejected for general military service, or one-quarter of all those examined. Apparently most of those classified as unfit even for limited military service, another one-quarter of the entire group examined, are not capable of easy rehabilitation even for limited service. Many of those not fit for limited military service can continue to be useful in civilian life, but their usefulness is undeniably subject to severe restrictions, and especially so as long as no improvement is made in their physical condition.

On the basis of this experience, it would seem safe to conclude that from 20 to 40 percent of the young men and women who stand on the threshold of adult life suffer from physical handicaps which have an important effect on their usefulness. Some of these handicaps are not remediable. The afflicted young person must work out the best possible adjustment under the circumstances and go ahead. Such youth, however, are entitled to accurate information concerning their handicaps and to the best possible counseling and assistance in organizing their life for the future. In other cases, the handicaps are remediable, sometimes easily, but often only through a carefully worked out plan of rehabilitation and physical development which is continued under supervision and with some assistance over a period of months or years.

Within the last two years, there have been exploratory efforts to promote new programs of physical examination and health care for out-of-school young people in need of such service. These efforts have been met with the reply in some quarters that it would be unfair to the remainder of the population to provide a special health program for youth.

Nevertheless, we are at present providing exactly such a special program—the rehabilitation program for the rejected selectees who can be prepared for general military service. In view of the fact that we shall inevitably look to young people, both young men and young women, to carry the major burdens of many aspects of the prosecution of the war, it would surely seem appropriate to provide an adequate program to increase the health and physical fitness of all youth, and to do so without waiting for some of them to be rejected in physical examinations for the Army. Even if we are not ready for a general health program for the whole nation, we might well begin our attack on this fundamental problem by giving special attention to the physical preparation of young people for adult life during the period immediately prior to the attainment of some appropriate age.

As a practical recommendation for discussion and possible adoption, the Commission proposes that a thorough physical examination be made available, free of charge, to every young American immediately after his or her eighteenth birthday, that the year between the eighteenth and nineteenth birthdays be observed as youth health year, and that special effort be made by all governmental, school, and community agencies to see that young people receive during that year such medical, dental, and other health assistance as they need. Under present conditions, physical examinations and follow-up for young people 18 years old might well be provided as an important contribution to national defense. If such a program is at all successful, however, it should be continued permanently.

In recent years, an important contribution to youth health has been made by the youth work agencies, the Civilian Conservation Corps and the National Youth Administration. The ccc has provided the most comprehensive health program, a program including all of the following elements: (1) physical examinations, (2) remedial attention and care for specific defects, (3) food adequate in abundance, quality, and variety, (4) physical work and exercise, (5) adequate amounts of sound sleep, (6) good environmental conditions, (7) recreation, and (8) health education for self-directed health habits.

The Commission believes that the ccc work camps and the nya

resident centers should be utilized as the means through which to provide an intensive health program for the out-of-school youth between 16 and 21 who are in greatest need of such a program. The physical standards for enrollment should be reduced, greater provision should be made for remedial attention and care, and some of the camps should be designated as preliminary conditioning centers for enrollees who are not fit to begin work on the projects when first enrolled.

The use of some CCC camps or NYA centers as physical rehabilitation camps, or the establishment of special camps for the purpose, will undoubtedly present some administrative problems and may require revision of the provisions under which the CCC and NYA have been operating. The Commission believes, however, that the establishment of such camps would be an important public service and that they might appropriately be administered by a youth work agency combining the present functions of the CCC and NYA.

The National Youth Administration has given special attention to the health needs of the youth workers on the out-of-school program who remain at home, and has sought to secure the correction of health defects by promoting the use of available community facilities and by stimulating the efforts of the individual youth. The Commission commends these activities, and recommends that they be broadened in scope to include provision for medical and dental care in cases of need where other resources are lacking. It also recommends that a comprehensive responsibility be accepted for the development of the physical fitness of the youth workers through health counseling and adequate provision for work and recreation. In the further development of all youth work programs, health benefits should be regarded as an objective coordinate in importance with work experience.

The youth work programs for unemployed, out-of-school youth necessarily will continue to reach only a part of all youth. Their contribution to the health of youth can be significant mainly because so many health deficiencies are concentrated among the youth groups which they do reach. But to reach the great mass of all youth with measures of prevention and cure at as early an age as possible, the schools must play their part.

It has always been difficult to secure adequate attention to health by many schools, since they are mainly preoccupied with the responsibilities of classroom instruction. Nevertheless, they have an essential duty to perform in any long-range program of national preparedness. Their unmet responsibilities in the field of health are sufficiently important and urgent to warrant a drastic revision of their activities in this field.

The perfunctory annual physical examinations given pupils in many elementary schools should be replaced by thorough examinations every second or third year, and should be maintained throughout the periods of secondary and higher education for the youth who continue in school. Follow-up work after the examinations should be given the attention it deserves, even though medical and dental services are not the direct responsibility of the school. The results of the physical examinations should be utilized as basic data for individual guidance, for special attention to nutrition, and for the general adaptation of the educational activities, as well as for the suggestion of medical and dental consultation, when indicated. Health instruction should be given a major place in the classroom curriculum at all grade levels, including the high school and junior college grades.

Physical education should be improved and greatly extended. In order that physical education personnel and facilities may be devoted to the development of an effective program for all pupils, there should be no reluctance to curtail or eliminate interscholastic athletics in times such as these. Intramural sports and games, however, should be emphasized in order to develop among all pupils qualities of initiative, teamwork, courage, and endurance.

Special attention should be given to the great part the schools can play in combating the scourge of malnutrition among children and youth. Schools should accept nutrition as a major permanent responsibility to be shared with parents.

The present school lunch program reaches only about 5,000,000 children, although it has been in operation for several years. Almost all those reached are in the elementary grades. If this program were made universal throughout elementary and secondary schools with federal assistance, as the Commission believes it should be, it would reach 28,000,000 children and youth. The effect upon child and youth health throughout the nation would be commensurate.

Putting the school lunch program on a universal basis for all children in all schools should be regarded as an essential step for health education as well as for the immediate nutrition requirements of the children. As a means of carrying on the learning process, no amount of classroom instruction about new and unaccustomed foods is a substitute for eating them. One of the greatest obstacles to improving the dietary habits of millions of Americans results from the simple fact that most people dislike experimentation with unfamiliar foods. Children share in full measure the food prejudices of their parents. In some localities a frontal attack on such prejudices might endanger the school lunch program. Over a period of time, however, the most stubborn food prejudices are likely to yield when confronted with actual foods that are attractively presented as parts of well-cooked meals.

In the operation of the community school lunch program, older pupils in school and other young people should be used so far as possible in order that youth may obtain work experience and may share in the actual labor of providing a social service from which they benefit. The program should also be used as a further means of instruction by explaining the planning of the meals in terms of nutritional standards to the youth workers who participate, and by securing their assistance in the planning of subsequent meals.

# CHAPTER
# XII

## DELINQUENCY AND YOUTHFUL CRIME

---

ANTISOCIAL conduct in its more serious forms is not evident among any large proportion of young people and has perhaps been overemphasized as a youth problem. It nevertheless deserves careful consideration, both because of the loss it brings to society in human and material resources and because it is symptomatic of deep-seated social maladjustments which ought for every reason to be corrected.

Though crime may not bulk large among youth, young people are a disturbingly large element in crime. Half of the persons arrested for known or suspected offenses are under 30 years of age, and one-third are less than 25. More are 19 than any other single age. Criminologists believe that three-quarters of all confirmed criminals may have begun their antisocial careers during their childhood or youth.

The annual cost of crime to the nation cannot be accurately assessed, but it is certainly very large. Crimes committed by youth are chiefly against property, theft predominating. It is thus probable that they comprise more than a proportionate share of the total pecuniary loss entailed by all criminal acts, large as that share would in any event be.

### CAUSES OF DELINQUENCY

It is often difficult to determine the origins of a particular act of juvenile delinquency, but it is clear that delinquency is the product of definite circumstances. The belief that crime represents a spontaneous outburst of malignant human nature now hardly merits the effort to controvert it. Social maladjustment of such intensity that it leads to conflict with the law can seldom be traced to a single cause. It is contributed to by all the imperfect adjustments of our complex society. Every major element in the environment of a child or youth can add and in many instances has added its quota.

Faulty home life often generates a rebellious attitude toward authority that eventually leads a youth into an open infraction of the law. This can result from either too much or too little parental control. It can also arise from many other factors in the home. Strained emotional relations between parents may rob the youth of the sense of security he requires and cause him to seek recognition among his contemporaries by conspicuous behavior involving some breach of social customs or codes of law. Persistent economic difficulties in the family generate a feeling of insecurity and can lead to a similar result. Lack of space for home recreation or failure of parents to understand the youth's needs and interests will drive him out into the streets and expose him to temptations and bad examples.

There is ample evidence that schools are sometimes an important factor in producing delinquents. A misreading of the capacities of young persons is not infrequent among teachers. In a considerable number of schools, relations between groups of pupils and between pupils, teachers, and administrators are such as to promote the growth of frustrations, grudges, and antagonisms. There has been a frequent failure to provide the mental, emotional, and moral development that participation in constructive citizenship activities would afford.

The public health program, too, must bear a share of the responsibility. There has been failure to attend to nutrition, to other physical safeguards needed by the growing adolescent, and to give visual, dental, and other types of remedial care. Youth to whom this neglect has been a handicap are unable to do justice to themselves either in school or in the search for employment. It is not unnatural that some of them should be drawn into a state of conflict with society.

There are many other respects in which our failure to surround young people with the conditions necessary for normal growth and development has encouraged a rebellious attitude toward society's formal codes. Youth able and willing to work often have not succeeded in finding employment that would provide them even with pocket money. The lack of facilities for public recreation has rendered young people susceptible to the excitement involved in any infraction of the law. The absence of helpful contacts with older youth and adults, such as an intelligently planned social organization would insure to all out-of-school youth, has been a particularly serious deprivation, since it denies young people assistance invaluable in the formation of character.

### PRESENT TREATMENT OF YOUNG OFFENDERS

The problem of delinquency and youthful crime has been created mainly through faults of omission. But there have also been grave faults of commission. These relate to our handling of young people who come into conflict with the law.

Common sense would suggest that when youthful maladjustment reaches so advanced a stage that it expresses itself in some overt act against society, a special and determined effort should be made to salvage the young person and repair his character before it becomes irretrievably fixed in degenerate ways. To an impartial observer it must often seem that our course of action in such a situation would be the same if it were deliberately calculated to have the opposite effect. Certainly the result is frequently to lead the youth on to the next false step and eventually to confirm him in a life of crime. We do not allow a young person to vote or sign a civil contract until he is 21, but we punish him for his indiscretions much earlier. In no other civilized country are young men and women given so much latitude of conduct, and in none are they punished more severely when they misuse that latitude.

A youth suspected of an offense may be arrested and detained overnight in jail before he obtains a magistrate's hearing. If held for appearance before the grand jury or a higher court, he will, if unable to furnish bail, be compelled to remain in this environment for days, weeks, or even months. If remanded for trial by the grand jury, his detention will continue for a further indefinite period. During all this time he lives in a world peopled with jailers, guards, and the various unsavory characters found in a county jail. Finally he appears before the judge and receives a formal trial. Even if he is found innocent, he has gone through emotional experiences which may leave their mark upon his mind and character. If convicted, he is sent to a reformatory where a longer and hardly less degrading course of detention awaits him. Frequently he is compelled to associate with confirmed criminals and learns from them the only trade that society seems willing to afford him an opportunity to practice—the trade of the professional lawbreaker.

If the offender is fortunate enough to commit his offense in a community that has a juvenile court and if he is young enough, he will get different and wiser treatment. But many communities have no special provision for dealing with youthful offenders, and in the majority of instances the jurisdiction of the juvenile court goes no further than the age of 17 or 18 years. Even in those few instances where it extends to 21 the result is not wholly satisfactory. Juvenile courts are usually overworked, and there is also serious doubt whether they can deal effectively with the more mature psychology of the older youth of both sexes as long as their services are primarily designed to meet the needs of children.

## POLICIES FOR THE FUTURE

There are two parallel lines of approach to the problem of antisocial conduct among young people. On the one hand we must reduce to a minimum the deficiencies in the social environment that predispose to delinquency. On the other hand we must extend an intelligent, sympathetic understanding to youth who become enmeshed with the law, carefully avoid anything that might increase or confirm their rebellious tendencies, and seek to restore them to a useful place in society.

The measures necessary to avoid the maladjustments that are a major factor in leading youth into crime are the broad measures of social improvement advocated throughout this report. They are desirable and indeed essential for other and more fundamental reasons than the reduction of delinquency and youthful crime, for they are requisites of a social order that will afford all people the opportunity to live full lives and make their maximum contribution to the common good. Crime is simply one of the end products resulting from a deficiency in the essential elements of an effective society. It offers an additional reason why every effort should be made to supply them.

To reduce delinquency to a minimum we need especially to correct the environmental defects known to be causative factors in crime. We need to give stability to the economic basis of family life, to build homes with space enough for healthy living and for family recreation, to provide parks and playgrounds sufficient for the needs of our population, to place medical care within the reach of all, to ensure an adequate food supply to everyone and to give them the nutritional knowledge that will enable them to employ it effectively. We need adult education that will help parents to avoid the emotional pitfalls of married life and to guide their children safely through the difficult and crucial periods of infancy and of adolescence. We need school teachers with a better understanding of child psychology, and a curriculum better adapted to the real needs and abilities of young people.

The various agencies working with youth in an effort to guide the formation of character deserve commendation and support as an aid in the reduction of delinquency. Various levels may be distinguished with regard to their relationship to antisocial behavior. Agencies such as the Big Brother and Big Sister organizations work mainly with youth who have already manifested delinquent or predelinquent tendencies. Agencies such as the Salvation Army, settlement houses, and police and other boys' clubs, while not so immediately concerned with delinquency, concentrate their efforts in social strata where the conditions which produce delinquency are especially prevalent. General character-building agencies with a predominantly middle-class clientele, such as the Scouting organizations and the Young Men's and Young Women's Christian Associations, probably have some effect in keeping delinquency within bounds, since the problem is not confined to any one class but occurs at all levels of society, intelligence, and income. All of the character-building or group-work agencies perform a valuable service in giving young people the benefit of helpful adult contacts outside of home and school.

Concurrently with the effort to eliminate unsocial conduct among young people by distributing opportunities more widely and more equitably, we should energetically follow the second major line of approach—intelligent and sympathetic treatment of youthful offenders. The United States is known abroad for enunciation of the principle that the state is the ultimate guardian and protector of children whose parents are unable or unwilling to give them proper education and moral guidance. The juvenile court implements this principle for the benefit of all children, as the old court of chancery did for children who were placed under its guardianship when their parents were unfit and the estate was administered by the crown.

The contribution of the United States has been to apply the child-saving power of the community to those who are poor and unfriended. We need now to reaffirm and implement the principle that immature youth cannot be in conflict with the state. They have, it is true, obligations and responsibilities toward society; but their immaturity confers on them certain privileges and immunities. A youth who finds himself in difficulty with the law should not be proceeded against as a public enemy; he should be taken in hand and re-educated as a public asset, the state supplying the parental care and discipline which has been lacking.

An important step toward an appropriate handling of young offenders has recently been taken. The American Law Institute has made a two-year study of our system of criminal justice in so far as it deals with young people. It has issued recommendations for major changes in our methods of handling young offenders and suspected offenders. It proposes that each state create a Youth Correction Authority to handle the cases of convicted young persons above juvenile court age. This agency would consist of three or more members with terms of nine years and it would function through district units. It would employ social workers, psychologists, and educators, whose duty it would be to investigate the background of youthful criminals, estimate in each case the capacity for improvement, apply scientific measures of rehabilitation, and determine when these have so far succeeded that the youth may safely be returned to society. The proved techniques of correction and social treatment which now exist in scattered form throughout the nation would be integrated in the proposed new agency. The chief effort would be to save those youth who can be regenerated, and at the same time to protect society more effectively by attacking recidivism at its source.

The Youth Correction Authority would have power to establish places of detention where youth awaiting trial could be separated from older criminals. A judge who tries the case of a young person would retain his usual discretion as regards acquittal, fines, and life imprisonment. For any other appropriate degree of discipline intermediate between the payment of a fine and life imprisonment he would turn the youth over, on indefinite sentence, to the Youth Correction Authority which would then undertake rehabilitation through one or more of the various types of institution for the treatment of young offenders which it would be empowered to establish. Throughout its work, the proposed agency would cooperate closely with all the state's established youth services and welfare and correctional agencies, utilizing their facilities wherever possible.

Clearly this plan, representing the considered judgment of the nation's leading professional association of jurists, is a notable advance in penology. It should not be assumed that the plan will work miracles, and other plans emanating from other quarters are not unworthy of attention. Nevertheless, at this time the proposal of the American Law Institute is the one which may best be used as the basis for constructive action throughout the nation. It is already being put into effect in California, and other states are giving it serious consideration. The American Youth Commission endorses the plan for Youth Correction Authorities and urges that it be widely adopted.

# CHAPTER
# XIII

## CITIZENSHIP

---

$I$n this country the task of preparing the young for citizenship must be viewed against the height of our conception. We have an ideal, the ideal of democracy. In practice we frequently fall far below the ideal, but it serves its function nonetheless.

The assumption upon which the democratic ideal is founded is that human personality is sacred and therefore endowed with prerogatives that are inviolable. Democracy is a form of social organization that accepts the dignity of the individual as an act of faith.

If democracy is true to itself, it exercises constant vigilance lest any force develop that would invade or even threaten to invade the fundamental rights that belong to every man, woman, and child because they are human beings. At the same time it labors to create the conditions that are necessary if individuals are to have resources for achieving their full human stature.

Democracy's ultimate safeguard is the enlightened conscience of the citizen. Being a government of the people, by the people, and for the people, it must depend for perpetuation upon the moral integrity of the people. If they lack the intelligence necessary to make decisions in line with right reason or the morality required to conduct their lives in accordance with such decisions, sooner or later the necessities of public order will demand resort to force and coercion—and democracy will cease to exist.

Through the Northwest Ordinance of 1787 our government made provisions for schools and means of education because it believed "religion, morality, and knowledge . . . necessary to good government and the happiness of mankind." The framers of the Ordinance envisaged a commonwealth in which people are happy because they are governed well. To be well governed in a democratic way, they must be intellectually enlightened. But enlightenment will prove beneficial only as it is translated into moral action.

It is significant that every attack by contemporary tyrannical governments on human rights has begun with an assault on religion. Those who see human beings as nothing more than creatures of the state begin their attempt to break down human dignity by seeking to destroy all contact with the Divine. Yet it is everlastingly true that man does not live by bread alone. Bread is only a means to an end, the end being the progressive improvement of that which in men and women is truly human: their competence in the realm of the ultimate values of life.

National survival and progress look inevitably to the future and must be concerned primarily with the young people who will be the America of the future. If our democracy is to continue, it is the young especially who must have a true conception of democracy, of its moral basis, and of the results that attend its successful operation. To them democracy must seem to be worth every sacrifice and to offer the brightest opportunities for happiness and the good life. Otherwise, any effort to preserve it will be a waste of time.

### EDUCATION FOR CITIZENSHIP IN SCHOOLS

Parents obviously have the first and heaviest responsibilities for citizenship training, and especially so during the transitional periods of early infancy and of adolescence. All agencies of religious education have a unique function in this area, in view of the moral aspects of training for a democratic social order. The voluntary character-building agencies have great importance, although they reach only a fraction of all youth. The juvenile courts and other welfare agencies are frequently called upon to provide training for citizenship after parents and all other social institutions have obviously failed.

Nevertheless, the school is the one social agency which has extensive contact with all young people. Its responsibility for training for citizenship is proportionate. Moreover, the responsibility of the school is not limited to classroom instruction on the intellectual level. Good citizenship is only in part a matter of knowledge and of intellect. It is also made up very largely of the right kind of basic habits, personal attitudes, and emotional reactions. The school must be concerned with all of these.[1]

Different individuals differ widely in the value that they attach to some of the virtues that enter into the composite of qualities that we call good citizenship. There is, for example, the virtue of obedience. Unquestioning obedience under all circumstances is not the supreme virtue in a democracy. On the other hand, obedience under appropriate conditions is essential to coordinated group activity, without which civilization could not exist. Most people would agree to these statements as a matter of principle. Yet many extreme points of view on both sides of a sensible middle ground find expression when obedience is under discussion as a virtue to be inculcated by programs of training for youth.

The Commission believes that much confusion of thought can be avoided if a distinction is made between two levels of citizenship. The lower, minimum level consists of those habits, attitudes, and activities of the individual which are essential for the maintenance of an orderly society under any form of government, democratic or

[1]For a discussion of the relation of schools to the inculcation of democratic habits in regard to social stratification and race relations, see the following: Allison Davis and John Dollard, *Children of Bondage* (Washington: American Council on Education, 1940), 299 pp., and Robert L. Sutherland, *Color, Class, and Personality* (Washington: American Council on Education, 1942), 135 pp.

otherwise. The second level of citizenship includes all of the requirements of the first level and in addition the characteristics of individual citizens that are required for the successful functioning of the democratic form of government, in which the citizen is expected to participate. The first level might be designated as conforming citizenship, the second as contributing citizenship. It should be noted, however, that the conforming citizenship with which we are here concerned is not the total conformity of the totalitarian state, but rather the irreducible minimum of conformity that is necessary even in a democracy under the complex and crowded conditions of modern life.

The essentials of conforming citizenship are elementary in character and are very important. They include health habits and vocational competence by which the individual will ordinarily avoid becoming a burden to society; sufficient ability to observe the moral code and to live and work with others in order to avoid becoming a public nuisance under the conditions of civilized life; and ability and willingness to understand and carry out simple instructions, both oral and written, under circumstances when coordinated action is required for the public health, safety, and welfare.

The essentials of contributing citizenship in a democracy are different in character, more difficult to define, and much harder to bring about through any training process. They include respect for the opinions and civil rights of others; awareness of the concept of the general welfare and a disposition to be guided by it; ability to participate effectively in the activities of a variety of self-governing groups; ability to take responsibility in accordance with one's capacity for leadership; a sound working knowledge of the operation of government in relation to the duties and obligations of citizenship; familiarity with major social problems and issues which must ultimately be solved through informed public opinion; and finally an understanding of the basic principles of democracy and a deep loyalty to it both in principle and in practice.

Schools must train for both levels of citizenship. In most cases present school performance is much more nearly adequate in connection with the simpler requirements of conforming citizenship than it is in preparing young people for contributing citizenship. In a few schools, somewhat experimental in character, so much emphasis has been placed upon contributing citizenship that the even more basic requirements of conforming citizenship have been partially forgotten.

Many different types of technique are available to schools in connection with the function of training for citizenship. Most schools use only one or two of these possible techniques, and only a few schools have balanced programs which use a combination of all of the tested methods. The American Youth Commission therefore commends to all school boards and school administrators the report of the Educational Policies Commission, *Learning the Ways of Democracy*.[2] It is one of the most valuable books on educational method in a generation, precisely because it is based on a search of the country for the most illuminating examples of effective ways to assist young people in learning the ways of democracy.

### ORGANIZATION AND DISCUSSION BY YOUNG PEOPLE

In America, where the forming of organizations is a universal habit, young people for many years have naturally insisted on having their own clubs, fraternities, and associations, free from adult interference. It is equally natural that older people have often been critical of these youthful activities, and in many cases have taken measures to control or suppress them.

Healthy young people are prone to rebel against the world as they find it. They gain some little freedom and in due time settle down to defending the *status quo* against the following generation. We may recognize this normal and immemorial conflict of the generations as a fact of human nature without being obliged to accept it as the sole basis of judgment on present-day youth organizations.

[2]Alexander J. Stoddard, chairman, Educational Policies Commission, *Learning the Ways of Democracy* (Washington: Educational Policies Commission, 1940), 486 pp.

The current organizations of young people, it is important to remember, are not so universally devoted to public questions as might be supposed. Actually a very large number of them are still the familiar social clubs and fraternities devoted mainly to personal enjoyment and campus politics. Their existence presents no problems that have not been equally pressing, in one form or another, for the past fifty years. An active interest in economic and political problems is not the most general characteristic of American young people, even at the present time.

Depressed economic conditions, however, brought an increasing number of youth associations devoted to the discussion of public affairs. Many organizations for this specific purpose are found in the colleges, though it is true that the membership is usually relatively small. In addition, local youth councils have been formed in a number of cities, with membership drawn from a wide variety of other organizations.

The main service of the local youth councils has been to provide a forum for the discussion of community problems as they affect youth. Education, recreation, and employment questions can often be handled most effectively at the community level, where most of the pertinent facts are available to those participating in discussion. Young people coming from different backgrounds of experience can gain a balanced knowledge of community affairs, which is of great value as a preparation for their duties as citizens.

The Commission recognizes that youth organizations for discussion of public questions form a small part of the total number, and that social, religious, athletic, and other associations are of great importance and value. A problem of immediate interest, however, is the attitude that should be taken by adults and by youth toward these discussion organizations.

In the Commission's opinion, there is no effective way to train large numbers of competent citizens for participation in public affairs which does not include actual practice in the discussion of public questions. The tendency for such discussions to be one-sided and ill-informed is not a peculiarity of youth. This tendency is equally apparent and far more dangerous among adults who have, or may acquire, actual power over public policy. It is therefore highly desirable that young people who are not yet in a position to exert any great influence on the adult world should occupy themselves in learning how to lead their contemporaries and how to choose and reject leadership. This process is not different from other educational activities which are best carried on at an age and under circumstances that minimize the dangers involved in mistakes or false starts.

Because of the importance of the educational processes to which youth organizations can contribute, the Commission believes that they can have major values. It is imperative for each of us to recognize that the principle of free speech and assembly is established as a safeguard of democracy. It should not be mistaken for a menace. If events similar to those in the dictatorships were to happen here, they would not be the result of discussion or propaganda. They would be the end product of uncontrolled monopoly, unemployment, poverty, and economic paralysis. To distract attention from the real and dangerous diseases that can threaten democracy by hysterical rejection of the curative though irritating processes of public discussion is un-American and might be suicidal.

## CITIZENSHIP AND NATIONAL DEFENSE

Among other responsibilities, the citizen has the obligation to serve in the common defense in time of need. As the Commission pointed out in July 1940, this is an elementary duty of citizenship, older than civilization, and not absent from any form of government, democratic or otherwise. It is a universal responsibility, although one which may be discharged in more than one way.

For the long-term future our necessities in regard to compulsory military training seem completely unpredictable. The Commission recognizes that in the post-war period, it is possible that conditions may arise under which it will seem necessary to establish a continuing system of military training through which annual classes of young men will be called to the colors each year for a period of compulsory military training. In that event, many adjustments in the institutions of education and youth welfare will be necessary or desirable.

For the duration of the present war, our temporary system of compulsory military service, with selection to a considerable extent by lot, is undoubtedly to be preferred. Meanwhile, the Commission continues to hope that the time may come when permanent measures of international collective security will be organized which will justify a considerable degree of disarmament in this country. In that event, it may be possible to dispense with compulsory military training.

In any case, schools and other agencies concerned with the training of youth for citizenship should take a realistic view of the world situation. Even with more good fortune than we have any right to expect, a period of more than one generation may be required for the attainment of a stable world order in which war and violent change are things of the past. During this period, we as a nation may be compelled to pass through decades characterized by revolutionary unrest in one country after another, by explosive population pressures in some parts of the globe, and by further rapid advance in military technology. For safety and survival, the United States must protect itself during this period, by force of arms if necessary.

At the same time, the schools and other agencies concerned with youth should continue with equal realism to hold up the ideals of freedom, international cooperation, and peace. In Europe for centuries it did not seem possible to organize peace with any stability even for brief periods on a local basis. The requirements for the organization of peace on a world scale are not hopeless of achievement. Young people should always be encouraged to give their utmost energy to the cause of organizing a just and permanent peace on a world-wide basis.

Before such a peace is possible, it will be necessary to bring about in all countries a great increase in understanding and tolerance for peoples of other customs, languages, and races. In this connection, the schools of this country might well make more extensive use of reading materials which would convey to pupils a truthful but appreciative conception of the geography, daily life, and history of other peoples.

The Commission believes that at present the great majority of schools in this country fall far short of affording their pupils sufficient opportunity to comprehend the background of the different races which form the composite American people. Young people should be enabled to gain an understanding of what have been some of the outstanding contributions of the different races to the development of world civilization in the past and to the development of our American commonwealth. They should learn that a people made up of a composite of races cannot well go forward if much of its energy is wasted in antagonism among its racial elements, or in efforts by one race to oppress others. The same principle applies to a world of composite races. The dignity of humanity, one of the essential concepts of democracy, requires that racial antagonisms be minimized.

*Part III*

RESPONSIBILITY FOR ACTION
FOR YOUTH

# CHAPTER
# XIV

## ACTION IN COMMUNITIES

---

In this part of the report, questions of responsibility for action are discussed in terms of patterns of organization and responsibility at the various levels: local, state, and national. Before taking up the more specific problems, however, some general comments may be appropriate in regard to the measure of responsibility for youth services which rests upon the public schools.

In many localities the schools make little or no effort to provide any further assistance for the pupils who drop out of school, if such pupils have completed the period of compulsory school attendance. Even the graduates are often bidden an "emphatic farewell." On the other hand, many teachers and administrators have displayed increasing concern for the problems of out-of-school youth. For ten years these problems have been the subject of frequent pronouncements of educational groups and commissions.

Most of these pronouncements have been such as to encourage any friend of young people. It has been evident that the leaders in the schools have been steadily expanding their horizons and that their attitude toward the care and education of youth under modern conditions is becoming increasingly realistic.

215

It is equally evident, however, that those who have grappled most deeply with the really acute difficulties involved in providing a program for out-of-school youth have found themselves face to face with fundamental problems which require no little searching of souls. At times educators show signs of frustration when discussing programs for out-of-school youth which indicate basic conflicts of attitude. The American Youth Commission would like to submit for discussion the thesis that sometimes public school administrators have been unhappy in recent years primarily because they have been attempting to reconcile the irreconcilable: a conception of education as broad as life and a tendency to think of the public school as responsible for all education. This latter tendency sometimes takes the form of objection when other agencies begin to carry on educational activities incidental to their major purposes.

Consider for a moment some of the other agencies which have important responsibilities for that education which is as broad as life.[1] Religious education is primarily the responsibility of parents and of churches. Private organizations carry on essential functions in regard to character development. Occupational adjustment is a process in which responsibilities are shared by several public agencies, as well as by various nonprofit agencies in many communities, and by employers and labor organizations. Public recreational service is in part a function of the schools, but also in part a municipal function and in part a function of state and federal governments. Health and fitness are not the primary responsibility of the schools, although they should participate in the organization of services for children and youth in this field; agencies of public health necessarily must carry on important educational activities, especially for adults. Citizenship training is a concern of all agencies of government and, indeed, of virtually all social institutions.

[1]For a treatment of the relations between schools and other social services which involve educational activities and functions, see Alexander J. Stoddard, chairman, Educational Policies Commission, *Social Services and the Schools* (Washington: Educational Policies Commission, 1939), 147 pp. This report is of major importance in regard to services for children, although not intended to be fully adequate in regard to services for youth.

When education is viewed in the broadest sense, obviously the schools cannot be given responsibility for all aspects of youth education. On the other hand, there is great need for some integrating influence upon the educational aspects of all elements of youth experience. That influence can best be exerted by teachers and by other leaders of youth who have the greatest insight into the educational process during the adolescent years.

In the last analysis, public schools have been organized as a separate governmental service in order that they may be specially responsive to the democratic formulation of school policy. The processes of democracy are now at work in the determination of the extent to which schools shall be invited to enlarge permanently their services for youth beyond the limits of traditional school functions. Obviously the result should and will be affected by the extent to which the schools demonstrate vision and capacity for functions which go far beyond the school routine of an earlier day.

This Commission hopes earnestly that all educators will rise to their responsibilities in regard to the education of out-of-school youth. This field of service is predominantly one in which no program will long be able to operate which cannot appeal successfully to youth on a voluntary basis. In this free field of activity, the educator can find new satisfaction in testing his qualities of leadership in voluntary relationships which must be based upon trust and confidence. When leadership is transferred to him, he will know that it is on the basis of his own merit.

At this time, however, no one can claim or disclaim an exclusive right to the position of community leadership in making known the needs of youth and in presenting the attractiveness and importance of this great new task of community service. In the work of community enlightenment, the help of everyone must be more than welcome. Regardless of where the original impulse arises, when the community reaches the point of action, an important battle for youth has been won.

To be effective, community leadership in regard to the problems of youth requires first of all an awareness of the great changes in the situation of young people which have come about in the last generation. Also it requires insight into the special problems of out-of-school youth in the particular community, an ability to think in community-wide terms, and a willingness to submerge personal or agency interests in a cooperative effort.

The community is fortunate which finds these qualities in its board of education, its council of social agencies, its federation of churches, or its local defense council. These are the places where one might most reasonably expect to find community leadership for the problems of youth. But if these central resources all fail, one of the voluntary youth-serving agencies, a local service club, the chamber of commerce, the central labor union, or some other business or social organization concerned with community well-being may provide the initial channel for action.

In most American communities, leadership is available to take the initiative and to act when need arises. The American Youth Commission is confident that when the individual community sees the part it should play in meeting the problems of youth, responsible community leadership will come to the fore.

### USE OF LOCAL RESOURCES AND LEADERSHIP

The first step in a community program is to find the facts through some sort of local survey.[2] This should seek the answer to such questions as: Are local schools providing realistic vocational guidance and training to prepare boys and girls to fill employment needs? What provision is being made to provide adequate health and recreation facilities for youth? Is delinquency and youthful crime on the increase? What can youth do for civilian defense?

In a metropolitan area, such a study calls for a trained staff, although it would mainly involve the coordination of factual information already available. In a small community the task would be relatively simple,

[2]M. M. Chambers and Howard M. Bell, *How to Make a Community Youth Survey* (Washington: American Council on Education, 1939), 45 pp.

requiring little, if any, outlay of money. Municipal or state placement services and various federal agencies are all in a position to provide information which will throw some light on the economic and occupational peculiarities of local labor markets.

Action for youth by our self-governing American communities can take many forms, depending on the local situation. In some cases a vigorous program of civic education for national defense is an urgent need of out-of-school youth. A constructive program to help youth in securing employment is still likely to be the greatest single need in some parts of the country. Such a program may require community courage and resolution, but for that very reason it presents a challenge. This challenge may be met at least in part by launching a cooperative effort by local employers and organized labor to develop apprenticeship standards and programs to assure the continued training of skilled workers, and by developing the community services of vocational guidance, training, and job placement.

Such activities may not completely eliminate youth unemployment in some communities even under present conditions, but if vigorously pursued they will improve the situation. To care for the remaining youth unemployment in a constructive manner, work projects should be developed to enable idle youth to obtain employment experience and at the same time to carry on community activities of most use.

Undertakings for youth are so intimately connected with all aspects of community public welfare that they are of direct concern to local governmental authorities. Consistent and active attention should therefore be given by the mayors or city managers of municipalities and by the chief executive officers of comparable local government units in rural territory. By spirited action in this field the mayor or manager can bring home to all the people of his municipality a full realization of the extent and gravity of their own local youth problems, particularly in this period of general mobilization of all resources for the war effort. He can lead his municipal council to an understanding of the situation, and stimulate the council to enact measures providing for fact-finding and for public action based on the facts.

The Commission therefore recommends that American mayors and city managers take immediate steps to inform themselves and their constituencies concerning local conditions as to employment and unemployment among youth, educational opportunities and the lack of them, recreational facilities and their use, and the status and need of health services for the youthful population.

As a means of collecting and disseminating valuable preliminary information, and as a means of implementing the findings of technical studies and surveys, the Commission recommends that heads of local government, urban and rural, initiate continuing periodic conferences of local government officers, school administrators, leaders of private organizations and other influential citizens, and representative young people, for the purpose of considering all aspects of the needs of the community's youth and all possible contributions of young people to the community welfare.

In all cases, the essential requirement for action is not the creation of new bureaucratic institutions, but the awakening of a spirit of self-help among the older members of the community, as well as among youth. We need a rebirth of the frontier spirit of self-reliance in every corner of America. Every community has *some* resources for youth which are not being fully utilized. They may not be adequate, they may need supplementation, but first of all every community has the responsibility of seeing to it that its own resources are being used effectively and to the full.

### COMMUNITY RELATIONS WITH STATE AND NATION

The importance of local action in behalf of youth by the use of local leadership and local resources has just been emphasized. It is equally important that these efforts be not made wholly in isolation, especially in this period when every activity for out-of-school youth must be related to the requirements of civilian defense and the war effort.

Community leaders should find means of keeping constantly informed concerning the numerous forms of stimulation and assistance, financial and otherwise, that are available from state and national sources. In planning and executing local surveys of youth, invaluable advice and consultation can often be obtained from such agencies as the departments of sociology and of education in nearby universities or colleges. Similar cooperation is sometimes obtainable from state departments of education, from the United States Office of Education, from the United States Employment Service Division, from the Cooperative Agricultural Extension Service, from federal, state, and local agencies for civilian defense, and from other state and federal agencies.

The planning of local public improvement projects of various kinds can often advantageously be shaped to accomplish eligibility for financial assistance from such agencies as the National Youth Administration and the Work Projects Administration. It is only by keeping alert to all the possibilities of cooperation with the federal and state governments that local communities can fully discharge their obligation and their desire to take their appropriate places in a great national effort to build up the national strength.

The Commission recommends that community leaders everywhere take vigorous steps to keep themselves and their neighbors informed constantly of all possibilities whereby the community may fully enter into its place as a working unit in the large-scale programs on the state and national levels which are designed to utilize the energies of youth in the interest of the war effort and long-run national welfare.

### COORDINATION AT THE COMMUNITY LEVEL

For the purpose of affording needed facilities to the considerable number of out-of-school youth under the age of 25, and of coordinating the services of the schools and other community agencies for the utmost effectiveness in the guidance of all young people, in school and out, some organization for the coalescing of community forces is essential.[3]

Ideally every community would have a regularly functioning association of its people of all ages, pointed toward cooperative conserva-

[3]Kenneth S. Beam, *A Guide to Community Coordination* (Los Angeles: Coordinating Councils, 1941), 21 pp.

tion, improvement, and optimum use of the community's material and human resources. Such an association would necessarily operate in part through smaller representative bodies giving specific attention to particular needs. For example, there might well be a community-wide committee or council concerned with the total problem of youth. There might be subcommittees concerned respectively with civic education, occupational adjustment, health, recreation, or other related essentials.

It is quite possible that the genesis of an effective movement toward the coalescing of community forces might at first be restricted to a special field such as one of those just mentioned. In any event it is futile to argue as to whether an organization should come into being full-blown or whether it should grow gradually by accretion. In either case the lesson of community cooperation can be learned, and in either case progress can be made by concentrating attention at appropriate times upon one or a few outstanding spheres of need.

Some simple principles are of universal applicability. The community should start where it is and build upon what it already has. The coordinating organization, of whatever form and for whatever specific or general purpose, should aim to be representative of the agencies of local government as well as of all reputable nongovernmental societies functioning in the community. Especially should it include delegates from existing clubs for youth. It may well embrace influential citizens of mature age, as well as outstanding young men and women, in addition to those serving as representatives of existing youth organizations.

A most important factor in the guidance of youth is an imponderable element—call it the spiritual element, call it morale, *esprit de corps*, or what you will. It is fostered by working together and achieving palpable results for the common good. Every community and every person concerned with the guidance of youth has a supreme obligation to help boys and girls to catch and hold the vision of a finer American culture, and to fire them with a will to play their parts in an indomitable advance toward it.[4]

[4]For a further discussion of community action for youth, see M. M. Chambers, *The Community and Its Young People* (Washington: American Council on Education, 1940), 36 pp.

# CHAPTER
# XV

## ACTION IN STATE GOVERNMENTS

---

$I_N$ the American federal system the relative role of the state governments, as compared with that of the federal government, has continually declined. Again and again, and with increasing force in recent decades, grave new nation-wide problems have arisen with which the inability of the states to cope alone has been demonstrated.

For example, the problem of unemployment which has been chronic in recent years, as well as the many acute problems of the war today, make it inevitable that direct relations between the people of the United States and their federal government will increase in number and significance. Under modern conditions, the federal government necessarily and rightly assumes new roles in such great fields of service as public health, public welfare, public works, and social security.

This does not mean that state and local initiative and responsibility are to be destroyed. The principle of federalism is not impaired by changes in the relative roles of the states and the nation. Indeed, the amount of state governmental action increases in volume while it decreases in relative importance. The American Youth Commission recommends that attention be given to maintaining and increasing the vitality of state governments in all their branches: legislative,

223

executive, and judicial. Efforts to improve state government in most states have unwisely been confined mainly to reorganization of the executive branch.

The Commission does not recommend that any new state administrative agency solely concerned with the coordination of services for youth be created and added to the existing administrative structure. It is aware that in all state governments there are numerous departments and institutions concerned with important public functions which bear upon the welfare of young people in its various aspects. Unfortunately sometimes some of these agencies work at cross-purposes with others, and the coordination of all their efforts is a difficult problem.

In this situation the Commission proposes two general principles in accordance with which action should be taken. First, uncoordinated agencies whose chief or exclusive activities lie clearly within a well-recognized major public function should be grouped into a single administrative department. This is the principle of administrative consolidation. Second, means should be devised to effect a continuing and active liaison among the many agencies whose principal functions make it impracticable to consolidate them in one department, but whose activities necessarily embrace as indispensable subsidiaries certain matters which touch upon the welfare of young people. This is the principle of interdepartmental coordination, as applied to youth services in state government.

## ADMINISTRATIVE CONSOLIDATION

As the functions of state governments change in scope to fit new conditions, constant attention must be given to the principle of grouping into major departments all agencies whose primary purposes lie clearly within the respective major departmental fields. Often there has existed the spectacle of several state agencies operating in closely related or nearly identical functional fields, in a spirit of competition such that any form of cooperative activity has been difficult or impossible. Under such conditions, the concept of the efficient development of the state's activities within the whole major governmental function to which the rivals plainly belong is largely or wholly lost.

In many states this unfortunate condition exists in varying degrees in the organization for the state function of public education. State activities relating to the lower schools may be divided between an elected superintendent of public instruction, a state board of education, a separate state board for vocational education, a textbook commission, and various other agencies. In the field of higher education, most states support more than one state college or university, frequently with little provision for joint planning of their programs in the interest of wise use of resources.

In Chapter VII, the Commission strongly urged the creation in every state of a state department of education which is properly organized and suitably operated to provide adequate leadership for the lower schools throughout the state. Action of the kind proposed would go far to improve the functioning of most state governments in regard to the schools.

So far as higher education is concerned, it has become accepted in principle that all state institutions of higher education, including teacher training institutions of college grade but not including junior colleges which are parts of local school systems, should be administered under a unified state board of regents and a single chancellor of higher education, to whom the executive officers of the various institutions would be responsible. Within recent years a number of states have shifted part or all of the way toward this pattern of organization for higher education. The Commission recommends that other states follow this example in moving, when appropriate, toward the unification of control over state institutions of higher education.

In some states, it will soon be desirable to take the further step by which the state education department and the state institutions of higher and special education will all be brought together administratively in a greater state education department, a department whose scope and organization will enable it to develop an integrated state system of education at all levels for all children and youth of the state, with appropriate provision for adult educational services. Such a state education department should be headed by a lay board of members chosen for long and overlapping terms to guard against the possibility of partisan domination. Authority to choose the chief administrative officer of the department should be vested in the board.

This chief administrative officer should be an individual of high professional and personal qualifications. In him should be combined the duties which are in some states designated under the respective titles of Superintendent of Public Instruction and Chancellor of Higher Education. With the aid of appropriate staff assistance he should initiate and develop continuing plans and policies for presentation to the board, enabling it to perform the important function of educational policy-making for the entire state and for all levels of education from the nursery school through the university.

Reorganization to unify action at the state level in regard to elementary, secondary, and higher education as here proposed will not be possible or desirable in any state as long as it retains state constitutional provisions requiring the election by popular ballot of the superintendent of public instruction. In the sixteen states where the chief state school officer is appointed by the state board of education or the governor, a more rapid rate of progress will probably be possible. Indeed, in some of these states, notably New York, the general pattern of organization in the state government in regard to the function of education is not far from the one advocated by this Commission as ultimately desirable in every state.

Whether or not it is given a unified responsibility for the state institutions of higher education at any early date, the state department of education when organized for effective performance of the state's function of public education would be subject as a matter of course to the general policy-making power of the legislature and the governor. It would fit into the picture of executive budgeting and

legislative revenue-raising for the state as a whole. It would be subject
to the determination of the state legislative authority (the legislature
and the governor) as to what proportion of the fiscal resources should
go to education as a whole, and what proportions to other governmental services.

Within its own sphere, however, the education department so far
as possible should have full authority and responsibility for all details
of management within the broad limits of the department. Thus would
be reduced or eliminated two unfortunate but widely current characteristics of present-day state educational administration: (1) un-
seemly rivalry among different educational groups and institutions
at the doorstep of the governor and the legislature, and (2) piecemeal
transfer of educational budgeting, and with it inseparable aspects of
educational policy-making, to short-term political officers of the state
or to their appointees in central fiscal posts. Such officers or appointees
seldom have professional competency in dealing with problems of
education, often lack continuity of tenure, and are unable to provide
a substitute for the broadly representative lay interest in education
which could be achieved by a state board of education properly set
up for educational policy-making at the quasi-legislative level.

Education is not the only state function of importance to children
and youth for which many of the state governments are not well
organized at present. Attention to problems of reorganization and
consolidation is also needed in connection with each of the other youth-
serving divisions of state government.

In many cases, the reorganization which is indicated would have
the effect, among other changes, of strengthening the authority of
the governor of the state, and is being impeded in some states precisely
because the people of those states have little confidence in the type of
governor they have been electing. To this it can only be said that in
the short run it may be desirable to protect some particular aspect of
state government by building a wall between it and the governor.
In the long run, it will not be possible to make great progress in the

administration of any department of government, including education, in any state where the people persistently fail to elect governors
who are competent, forward-looking, and devoted to the public
interest.

In some states, it is even more important to look to the legislature
than to the executive branch of state government. Legislative reforms
are sometimes assessed primarily in terms of the quality of legislative
action which thereafter eventuates. But the important relationships
between the quality of the legislature and the quality of administration
throughout the state government should never be forgotten. As long
as the legislature is a chaos of incompetency and futility, as it is in more
than one state, reform in the executive branch of that state will not
be productive of the fullest benefits until major reforms in the legislature have also been carried through.

Efforts to improve state government must, therefore, go forward
on many fronts. Those efforts necessarily face difficulties greater in
some states than in others, but the cause is not hopeless in any state.
In some states, however, the utmost in fearless and vigorous action is
necessary if representative government at the state level is to survive
and retain important responsibilities.

### TECHNIQUES OF INTERDEPARTMENTAL COORDINATION

In every state the relationships between governmental activities
can be improved only in part by reorganization and consolidation
along functional lines. There must also be provision for coordination
wherever the various functional activities impinge upon each other.
In connection with services for youth, principal attention needs to be
directed to the departments, divisions, and institutions in each state
that are concerned with education, health, welfare, recreation, and
employment. Improved coordination among these services is of major
importance at the state government level, as well as in every community.

Coordination is not an objective to be attained by the organization
of a campaign and the beating of drums. It is much more likely to

result initially from efforts that are unpublicized but persistent and which come from some centrally influential source. Usually the best way to begin is by taking up some specific problem which needs attention and action and which is of interest to more than one governmental agency. If a successful technique can be developed for dealing with one such problem, the coordinative activities can then be expanded to include a larger range of subjects.

A frequently useful and sometimes indispensable technique is the organization of an interdepartmental committee. Such a committee may come together on a temporary basis to deal only with a single problem; or it may be created on a continuing basis to consider a wide range of activities of interest to several departments.

Because of the importance of cooperation between youth-serving agencies, the Commission recommends that in every state where a favorable situation can be created, the heads of all state departments and institutions having to do with education, health, welfare, recreation, and employment for youth should carry on interdepartmental conferences on a continuing, periodic basis.

The principal representatives in the state of the relevant federal agencies, such as the National Youth Administration, the Civilian Conservation Corps, the Federal Committee on Apprenticeship, the Children's Bureau of the United States Department of Labor, and others, should also be invited to participate. These conferences would have the purpose of considering the bearings of the work of all departments upon the welfare of the youth of the state as a whole, and of considering the improved services which might be provided through the cooperation of the several agencies.

Another technique of interdepartmental coordination is the device of designating or adding a staff member in each department having important concern with youth, and charging him with the duty of maintaining liaison with other youth-serving departments, bureaus, or institutions. This technique should be used much more widely than at present in all of the state governments.

Coordination of the state's services for the care and education of youth can be influenced materially by state budget officers, state personnel agencies, and state planning boards, within the limits of their respective powers where such agencies exist. With the important reservation that neither state budget officers nor state personnel agencies should be empowered to dictate the minutiae of departmental or institutional management nor allowed to usurp authority, and with the observation that the functions of state planning boards are advisory only, it can be said that all three of these state agencies should be carefully and consistently developed. They can each perform coordinative functions for which there are no satisfactory substitutes.

# CHAPTER
# XVI

## THE PLACE OF
## THE FEDERAL GOVERNMENT

---

MUCH of the recent unhappy division and confusion of thought in regard to the place of the federal government in the total scheme of social institutions grew out of the history of our attitudes toward poverty. This country was settled, parts of it within the memory of living man, by persons who were quite prepared to take their lives and their fortunes in their own hands, to stake their claims in the unappropriated wilderness, and to ask no aid from government or any man. In any country where the frontier attitude still lives, the feeling toward dependent poverty, especially dependency upon the part of an able-bodied man, is almost certain to be an attitude of robust contempt.

Yet in the present stage of our economic, political, and social development, that attitude is almost wholly irrational. Personal weakness is still a factor to be reckoned with. But most poverty is caused in the present day by forces as impersonal as a hurricane, and as difficult to control when once they have been unloosed. The general dependence upon money income, if not upon actual wage employment, puts almost everyone in an extremely vulnerable position. The distribution

231

of income is such that, in combination with the urgent pressures for expenditure in modern life, most families never have any reserve resources and many are below the poverty line even when most fortunate. The fluctuations of economic conditions, moreover, are so rapid, so severe, and so unpredictable that most of the population has lived in fear of want even when in no immediate actual danger.

All of this is an old story, but it needs remembering in any discussion of the present-day functions of the federal government in connection with the social services and the problems of poverty. Until ten years ago, the federal government was almost completely unprepared for any responsibility in regard to these problems other than in connection with the pricing of the public land for distribution. Many people have since become convinced that the federal government must accept major responsibilities in the solution of the problems of poverty, but there remain some irreconcilable differences of opinion on the subject, as well as much room for the development of sound principles and procedures even when there is general agreement as to responsibility.

The social services exist for two reasons. Partly they are an attack on poverty. They provide people with services they need, regardless, or with only limited regard, for their ability to pay the cost of the services. Partly, however, the services are merely a method of providing something needed on a collective basis. For reasons of economy or convenience, the service is provided jointly through the mechanism of the state, without any necessary relation to the relief of poverty or the redistribution of real income.

It is probably true that the social services have been most popular when they seemed most in the nature of joint services, and most controversial when they became primarily an attack on poverty. The public schools, for example, which in many areas began with much bitter controversy as pauper schools, became popular and respectable when they became community services for all children.

To a considerable extent, it is unnecessary for the federal government to be concerned with social services that are merely joint services for those who can afford to pay the cost in any event. To the extent that social services are needed to meet the problems of poverty, however, the federal government inevitably must be concerned because much poverty results directly or indirectly from the operations of an economic system which is nation-wide in scope. Moreover, in many cases the problems of poverty can be treated adequately only through the use of federal fiscal powers. Undoubtedly the part to be played by the federal government in this area will remain highly controversial, but the basic necessities of the case must be faced with realism if there is to be any constructive discussion of specific problems.

### FEDERAL AND STATE ADMINISTRATION

In early days when our society was largely agrarian, and when the social services performed by governmental units were relatively few and simple, these services were financed almost exclusively by property taxes levied by small local units. This was appropriate to that era because the wealth of the nation consisted in large part of homes and farms and other real estate.

In the present day of urbanization and industrialization, with large-scale organization of commerce and industry, it has come about that control over a large part of the nation's economic power is represented by intangible property. Income has become a much more important measure of taxpaying ability than the ownership of real estate. New forms of taxation, such as income, inheritance, and estate taxes, most of which can be levied and administered far more equitably and effectively by the federal government than by any smaller unit, must therefore play greater parts in providing revenue for the support of the social services required for the welfare of all the people.

The necessity for a continued shift of the exercise of the taxing power toward larger governmental units seems apparent. This is resulting in a relatively expanded role for the federal government as a fiscal agency for the whole nation. The American Youth Commission observes, however, that the use of federal tax funds for the welfare of all the people may be accomplished in two major ways: by direct federal administration of some social services, and by federal appropriations to the states or to their local subdivisions for the support of some social services under the direct administration of the state and local governments.

The Commission believes that both of these methods should be increasingly used for appropriate purposes, the selection of the method in each case to depend upon the following principles:

1. In dealing with a problem, such as severe unemployment, which is nation-wide in the sense that it creates pressing needs in all states with which the states are unable to cope promptly and effectively, or in dealing with a problem sometimes requiring emergency action on regional or national bases, direct federal administration is the appropriate method. It is well established that this method is essential in matters directly affecting the national safety, and in other nation-wide or regional emergencies imperatively calling for measures which can be put into operation with the necessary promptness and inclusiveness only by federal administration.

2. In dealing with a problem, such as the operation of public schools, in which the states have had a tradition of reasonably successful administrative experience, and for which the states have in operation administrative organizations actually serving the need on a virtually inclusive basis within the states, the use of federal grants is the appropriate method. It can be used to better the condition of the least fortunate states and localities while at the same time preserving the vitality of state and local self-government and encouraging the improvement of local initiative and control. By requiring the use of state and local revenues and state and local administration, this method tends to promote the flexibility and variety which conduce to general progress.

Whichever method is adopted in regard to any particular problem, the interests of Negroes and other minority groups are likely to be neglected unless care is exercised. In either case, therefore, appropriate safeguards should be provided.

Let the federal government act directly through its own administrative organization in dealing with all nation-wide emergency situations, including those likely to continue subject to sharp nation-wide fluctuations. Let it subsidize the state and local administrative units in dealing with problems which are essentially of a continuing, nonfluctuating, nonemergency character, in whose long-term planning the representatives of the people of the particular states should have a major voice. This is essential if state government is to retain its vitality in some spheres of social service broader in scope than the limited range of activities which can be wholly financed from state and local resources in all states.

### ORGANIZATION OF FEDERAL AGENCIES

Continued improvement should be made in perfecting the organization of the federal administrative agencies in accordance with the principle of grouping under a single departmental or other major administrative head the bureaus and divisions whose principal functions are closely related.

The creation in 1939 of the Federal Security Agency, embracing the Social Security Board, the Office of Education, the Public Health Service, the National Youth Administration, and the Civilian Conservation Corps, with the consolidation of the Employment Service and the Bureau of Unemployment Compensation into a single Bureau of Employment Security in the Federal Security Agency, was a commendable step of considerable importance.

Constant observation of the federal administrative structure should go on with a view toward further desirable reorganization. For example, a study should be made of the functions of the Children's Bureau, now in the Department of Labor, to determine whether some or all of its activities should be administratively integrated with other parts of the Department of Labor or with divisions of the Federal Security Agency, or both.

The Commission again recommends the consolidation of the National

Youth Administration and the Civilian Conservation Corps into a single major subdivision of the Federal Security Agency, charged with the administration of federal activities in behalf of youth who need public facilities for wage employment and for training on the job such as are not available in public schools.[1]

### THE UNITED STATES OFFICE OF EDUCATION

The educational agencies which provide the most extensive and in some ways the most important of the social services for children and youth are represented at the federal level by the United States Office of Education. The Office has been located administratively in the Federal Security Agency since 1939. It is headed by a commissioner who is appointed by the President, subject to the confirmation of the Senate.

The Office was established in 1867 by a brief statute which authorized it to collect educational statistics, to disseminate information, and to "promote the cause of education throughout the country." For many years it existed as a minor bureau in the Department of the Interior, with occasional periods of activity under the leadership of able commissioners, but without ever becoming a major influence on the course of American education. Recently the Office has become better known, but still remains less influential than it should.

The oldest function of the Office is that of collecting and analyzing educational statistics from all parts of the United States. The results of this activity are indispensable for any study of educational development, and, in general, the work has been well done.

Other types of educational research have been increasingly developed. The objective has been to make the Office of Education not only a clearinghouse for information about the best methods and procedures in all aspects of education, but also to conduct original research which will add to the total store of knowledge available for the improvement of education.

[1]See pages 41 and 54 of this report.

New procedures based on tested research are needed in almost every aspect of education. The areas in which relatively conclusive research findings are available, such as in connection with reading and some aspects of child development, are the exception. Most educational procedures, including many of those which appear most firmly established, are based on opinion rather than on definitive research.

Progress is slow because there are only a few places where educational research is proceeding continuously under favorable auspices. The type of cooperative research activity, with federal, state, and local participation, which has been so conspicuously successful in the field of agriculture is notably lacking in the field of education. The Office of Education has been moving in the direction of such a system, but because of inadequate funds has been able to make only a beginning.

For the last generation or more, many different agencies of the federal government have been developing educational functions, usually as activities incidental to the major purposes for which the various agencies were established. Questions of relationship between these activities and those of the Office of Education have at times presented problems of great difficulty. These relationships were discussed and made the subject of significant and commendable recommendations in the reports of both of the major presidential committees on federal relations to education which have functioned in recent years.[2]

Partly because of the influence of the work of the first committee, the Federal Board for Vocational Education was consolidated in 1933 with the United States Office of Education, a major reform which had long been needed. The work of the second committee may have had some influence in bringing about the transfer of the Office of Education to the newly created Federal Security Agency, where that Office can function in association with a number of other bureaus and divisions administering related activities.

[2]Charles R. Mann, chairman, The National Advisory Committee on Education, *Federal Relations to Education, Part I, Committee Findings and Recommendations* (Washington: American Council on Education, 1931), 140 pp.; Floyd W. Reeves, chairman, The Advisory Committee on Education, *Report of the Committee* (Washington: U. S. Government Printing Office, 1938), 243 pp.

In future years, the Commission believes, the United States Office of Education must be made an establishment of major importance for the further development of education in the United States. It should become the outstanding agency in this country for the prosecution of a wide range of fundamental educational research, which should be carried on so far as possible in cooperation with educational institutions and the state departments of education. It should be equipped also to provide a high type of leadership in making the results of research and of experience available on a broad basis to the educators of the nation.

To accomplish these results, the professional staff of the Office must be expanded in size and improved in quality. The funds available to the Office for research, demonstration, and other forms of leadership, now exceedingly small in terms of the importance of these functions, should be greatly increased. In the Federal Security Agency, in which the Office is located, there should be continuous and increasing attention to the coordination of all of the youth services for which the Agency has responsibility.

### FEDERAL GRANTS TO STATES AND LOCAL SUBDIVISIONS

For the social services under state and local administration but which require financial assistance from the federal government, the general policy should be that of making annual federal appropriations to the states for broad categories of services, to be distributed within states on a basis which will lessen existing inequalities of service between areas and population groups, and otherwise administered by the state governments in accordance with plans made by them. The field of general education is an example in which this procedure is appropriate, because in that field the states have had long experience and have made much progress in developing state systems possessing varied characteristics adapted to their own needs.

Apportionment among the states should be determined in accordance with their relative financial ability and the relative proportion of the population to be served directly in each state, as determined by objective methods whenever possible. In situations where the exercise of administrative discretion in apportionment must necessarily be resorted to, this authority should be entrusted to a quasi-legislative board of apportionment set up for that purpose alone and consisting in major part of citizens not in the employ of government at any level.

It should be noted that in all cases where grants are made to the states for social services, there should be adequate provision to protect the rights of Negroes and other minority groups. In a number of states, it is unfortunately true that the needs of minorities are habitually overlooked or treated inconsiderately. In several recent cases, the federal courts have therefore been outspoken in pointing out the right of all citizens, regardless of race, to equal protection before the law. Those responsible for federal legislation and administration should be alert in providing appropriate safeguards.

The initiative of the states and of their local subdivisions in providing in whole or in part such social services as they are able to maintain out of local revenues and under local administration should be preserved and encouraged to the utmost. Federal subsidies to the states, especially when granted for broad categories of social services in which the states are already operating, should be conditioned upon the maintenance of a reasonable level of state support. The federal appropriation should be for the purpose of supplementing, and not supplanting, the state's own contribution to the social service being aided.

The granting of federal subsidies for a narrowly defined specific purpose, accompanied with a requirement that the funds so granted be matched with equal or similar sums out of state revenues to be made available for the same narrowly defined specific purpose, is undesirable as a permanent policy. It accomplishes in effect an inflexible and generally undesirable federal control of the disposition of state revenues; and, especially when it is applied to only a few specific purposes, it may produce a distortion and malformation of the state's total program of publicly supported social services.

For the same reasons, and except in matters of equalization and the maintenance of civil liberties, federal appropriations to the states for broad categories should not be accompanied by detailed control of their disposition, either through specifications in the appropriating statute or by the exercise of discretionary authority by federal administrative offices. In these relationships the federal government would function primarily as a fiscal agency for the whole nation—a role which it can and should play in appropriate areas. The field of state and local initiative would have more scope than ever before, because it would be less circumscribed by local financial limitations.

Although some services must necessarily be fully supported and also directly administered by the federal government, even in these cases there is a large place for local initiative. In fact, the success of the federal administration of such services will depend in large part upon the ability and willingness of the people of every state and every locality to cooperate in a sponsoring capacity, and to contribute the knowledge of local conditions, local peculiarities, and local needs necessary to the best functioning of the services.

# CHAPTER
# XVII

## RESPONSIBILITY FOR PLANNING
## IN RELATION TO ACTION

---

THE care and education of youth, or any other important social responsibility, should be made a constant subject of long-range planning. The best-laid plans may not always succeed, but nevertheless assiduous fact-finding, careful interpretation, and consultation between those responsible for action can do much to lessen the harassment of one unexpected emergency after another.

### PLANNING BY PUBLIC AND PRIVATE AGENCIES

Planning for the welfare of youth should go on in orderly fashion concurrently at the local, state, regional, and national levels. At the local level the general community councils or community youth councils, embracing representatives of varied ages and interests, including officers of governmental and nongovernmental agencies, can participate in the function of local planning.

In the realm of local government, city and village councils, boards of education, and county boards of commissioners should endeavor to devote their efforts more largely to long-range policy-making and less to details of immediate administration than is now usually the case. Administration should be entrusted to competent executives, leaving

241

the local council or board free to give most of its energies to its proper function of policy determination.

The constant stream of information requisite to intelligent long-range planning can come partly from the executives, but must also come in part from some detached agency existing solely for fact-finding and advisory purposes on a broad scale. To perform this function there are already in existence hundreds of city and county planning boards. These boards in the past have mainly been concerned with physical aspects of planning. Increasingly they can and should concern themselves with the broader problems of their local areas.

The same principles apply at the state level. The American Youth Commission recommends that governors and legislatures give attention to the organization and fiscal support of properly constituted state planning boards, in order that the independent and comprehensive research and advisory service which can be thus supplied shall not be lacking. It will always be found that in a broad view of the total resources of the state, human and material, the care and education of young people will loom as a large element.

To bring increasing unity into the combined efforts of a great variety of nongovernmental youth-serving organizations existing at the state level, and to implement more effectively the large reserves of good will toward young people, the Commission recommends also that the governors of the states inaugurate annual conferences of representatives of such organizations, together with representatives of the appropriate state and federal departments and institutions in related fields.

These state-wide conferences should create standing committees to work during the interim periods on different portions of the general problem of the care and education of youth. Records of the proceedings of the conferences and of the committees should be distributed among the conferees, and to the press and public, for the purpose of stimulating public interest and increasing public knowledge of ways and means of facilitating the contribution of the state's young people to the strength and culture of the state and the nation.

Since unemployment is obviously a nation-wide problem which must be coped with by national agencies, since equality of educational opportunity is a national responsibility, since the necessity of a national health program is apparent, the need for a national planning agency for youth is bound to be greatly accentuated.

The National Resources Planning Board and its predecessors have already had eight years of experience in furnishing research and consultative service to the federal government and in stimulating and coordinating the work of planning agencies at the regional, state, and local levels. Recently it has set up a small research staff for a study of youth problems in prospect in the post-war period.

The Commission commends this activity and recommends that it be continued and expanded with the cooperation and participation of the major public and private national agencies concerned with youth. Moreover, in order that the results of planning may be made widely known and may be considered by agencies close to the scene of action, the Commission recommends the formation at an early date of a federal-state youth policy conference. The conference might well be called together by the President of the United States, it should be organized jointly by the officials of the National Resources Planning Board and of the Federal Security Agency, and the membership should consist mainly of the state and federal officials in charge of general and vocational education, public employment service, and youth work programs. Federal agencies concerned with health, recreation, child labor, juvenile delinquency, and civilian defense should also be represented, as well as the national private organizations and services for youth. The conference should meet periodically and should have a budget for carrying on its activities and planning its work. It might also have advisory committees of representatives from the fields of business, labor, agriculture, and the social sciences.

No single institution, new or old, will be able in itself to provide a complete program for youth in the coming years. An adequate program will require from all a continuous willingness to pioneer new services and to experiment with new cooperative relationships. Broadly representative conferences and other planning activities which cut across professional and agency lines will therefore continue to be of major importance at local, state, and national levels.

### PLANNING AND ACTION BY YOUTH

Many older persons are constantly tempted to feel that youth themselves are mainly to blame for any problems or difficulties which they encounter. Young people know instinctively that this is not the case in connection with major problems. Certainly it is obvious that they did not create the social, economic, and political situations out of which many problems arise.

Problems cannot be solved, however, merely by attempts to assess the blame or responsibility for original sources of difficulty. In particular, intelligent young people are well aware that to solve the problems of any individual young person, he must at the very least be an active partner and in many cases he must be the moving spirit. Much should be done to provide opportunities for youth, but personal success and security will inevitably depend to no small degree on individual qualities of integrity, courage, skill, energy, and continued ability and desire to learn.

The first duty of every young person when confronted with personal problems, therefore, is to make a self-survey of his own situation and of the available resources. The results may seem unpromising, but very few young persons are in a situation so completely desperate that it is beyond hope. Even under the adverse conditions of the last decade, a considerable number of young people were able to find ways by which to come up from situations of the most complete despair to positions of recognition and honor. The Commission salutes these young people and urges other youth to emulate their courage, persistence, and energy.

For many youth, the major resources revealed by a self-survey will be time for planning and energy for action. This should not be a cause for discouragement; nothing else is so essential.

In many instances these resources can be utilized most effectively by young people who combine their efforts to plan and carry out a course of action. During the depression years, some of the most inspiring examples of constructive activity on the part of youth were provided by the self-help job councils. These were made up of unemployed young people who joined together to train each other in methods of job-seeking and to carry on community campaigns to enlarge the number of job opportunities.

The whole field of recreation and use of leisure time is one in which mutual self-help has always been practiced by young people on a considerable scale and in which self-help methods are especially appropriate and beneficial. Young people who create and maintain their own youth centers not only provide themselves with facilities they need and want but also learn for themselves the true worth of such virtues as persistence, reliability, loyalty, and devotion to mutual service. The facilities which young people can sometimes create and manage for themselves may have greater appeal than more elaborate structures and organizations in which they have less of a feeling of participation.

Whatever their immediate prospects as individuals, all young people have a special duty to give thought to the problems of other young people and to be helpful in all possible ways. This is a duty which rests with special weight upon those who have had advantages and who find themselves in a fortunate position.

There is always a problem of mediation and interpretation between the generations. Young people who have found opportunity in a suitable occupation, demonstrated their capacity for actual service, and attained a position of personal security can sometimes be especially effective as representatives of those less privileged. Service for youth is preeminently a form of community activity which such young people should seek in discharging their obligations of voluntary service as citizens.

## PLANNING AND ACTION BY ADULTS

In the comments of the last section, the Commission has been addressing itself frankly to those young people who are thoughtfully concerned about the problems of their own generation, who have some appreciation of the character of the more important problems, and who would like to do something about them. There are many such young people, and there is much that they can do by way of planning and action for themselves and for others of their age group, although all persons of good will should lend their assistance.

To adults, however, the Commission wishes to emphasize the fact that the more difficult aspects of the problems considered in this report are concentrated among youth who are quite unlikely to solve their own problems without extensive guidance, training, and assistance in obtaining opportunity. This is especially the case when millions of young people are suspended between childhood and adulthood during long periods of general social and economic maladjustment.

In a broad view, the oncoming youth of recent years and of the present may be divided into three groups. There is, first, the group, probably much in the majority of all youth in this country, which has benefited from parental attention, available educational opportunities, and a fair balance of opportunity for self-reliant development. Second, there is the group with which this report has mainly been concerned, the group which has been left without adequate care or opportunity to the point of gross neglect on the part of society. This is undoubtedly a group of substantial size. Finally, there is a group the size of which cannot possibly be estimated but which undoubtedly exists. This group consists of the young people who have been consistently overprotected and overserved, in some instances by social agencies, but mainly by parents.

Adults are frequently dismayed at the lack of appreciation on the part of youth even when an abundance of helpful care has been provided. Yet it is one of the oldest facts of human nature that no amount of protective care or attention in which the recipient has only a passive part is likely to inspire much gratitude. In its field studies of youth, the Commission found a general absence of appreciation for the service rendered youth through the usual types of classroom instruction in the schools. Conversely, the greatest amount of appreciation came from youth who had spent a summer of hard labor in voluntary work camps, camps in which the young people were given real opportunities to be of service to others.

At all times it is essential to remember that young people develop maturity only when they have opportunities for constructive activity. When the point is reached in adolescent development where the authority of the older generation begins to be questioned, this should be regarded as the signal for emphasis upon self-help. Moreover, from this point on, advice should be given when requested on how best to plan and develop activities, but more and more responsibility should constantly be placed upon the young people themselves. It is only when young people have vital opportunities along with a full measure of responsibility for using them that adolescent immaturity can develop into adult maturity.

In recent years of peace, before youth attitudes had been caught up in the maturing pressures of the war, the current generation of young people included many who had a demanding attitude toward life unaccompanied by any willingness to put an all-out effort into life. Yet that was merely the result that might have been expected.

The peacetime provision for youth has consisted mainly of multiplying opportunities for participation in passive processes of education, while constantly postponing opportunities for productive activity to higher and higher ages. The depression years of the last decade intensified both trends. High school enrollments were expanded by 2,000,000 or more, public work programs were provided most of the time for 300,000 to 500,000 out-of-school youth under 21, but the shrinkage of opportunity for regular employment was so great that during most of the decade two or three million out-of-school youth under 21 were unemployed, as well as one or two million between the ages of 21 and 25.

A few of the unemployed youth were able to occupy their time constructively, but for most of them the period was an arid waste. Personal development was not only retarded; frequently it was so perverted that for years to come millions of young Americans will carry the psychological scars of the depression years in their personal attitudes and social reactions.

The true importance of youth unemployment is still far from fully appreciated in this country. Because we have had no political youth movement of any consequence, the effect of unemployment on young people has not been widely recognized. Adult unemployment has seemed far more serious, both from the point of view of family dependency and the consequent need for relief and from the point of view of the greater economic loss involved in a failure to use mature skill and productivity. It has been difficult to develop any general concern for young people who were provided for by their parents and who were merely waiting impatiently for the economic system to expand enough to take them in.

For a true appraisal, however, the experience of other countries must always be kept in mind. The Commission has been reluctant to load this report with references to the situation abroad; but the fact is that chronic youth unemployment in many countries has been one of the most explosive elements in the world situation of the last two decades.

Superficially, a résumé of foreign experience may seem to indicate that youth are moved by a spirit of narrow materialism and will follow any government that gives them bread. Nothing could be farther from the truth. Youth unemployment is so devastating, not because of physical suffering and material loss, even though these may be considerable, but exactly because it attacks the basis of youthful loyalty and idealism. An older unemployed person may have learned to adjust to fluctuations in employment opportunity with some measure of philosophic acceptance. To a young person, a long siege of unemployment which is shared by millions of others is an obvious demonstration of the incapacity of the present social order. In the face of such a demonstration, it is difficult to develop loyalty for the existing social institutions. Youth will turn instead to measures, however desperate, which offer promise for the future.

At the moment, youth unemployment has been greatly reduced and young people find themselves much in demand, but only because we are asking them to assume great responsibilities in industry and in the military services for the prosecution of the war. For the future, we have not yet adopted policies that give any assurance that as soon as youth are no longer needed for the war effort they will be incorporated in some other way into the effective life of the nation.

When the present war does finally come to a conclusion, many persons who have occupied positions of leadership will be emotionally worn out. Economically, the stage may be set for a period of deflation and distress. Politically, the tendency may be to let things drift, to attempt again "to return to normalcy."

The young men who have been demobilized from the armed forces, however, will not be exhausted or quiescent. Neither will be the other millions of individuals who have been moved from peacetime industries or unemployment into the war industries and out again. The number of footloose, bitter, and dispossessed individuals may be at a maximum. Such groups are much more likely than in 1921 to find political expression, and the times will be surcharged with great social tension.

In the future we shall not be allowed to say that young people are to achieve life and liberty only by struggling successfully as individuals from a morass for which we are all economically, politically, and morally responsible. Our responsibility for action is clear. In some field of labor, private or public, at all times opportunity must be provided for young people to work in a manner commensurate with their powers, with a return sufficient to sustain life and the institutions of marriage and the home, and to secure advancement in responsibility and in the esteem of their fellow citizens. Nothing less will suffice.

This Commission has great hope that the adults who control affairs will do the necessary planning to see to it that opportunities are continuously available, and it has confidence that youth will use those opportunities effectively. American youth are not of such stuff as is easily conquered by fear or defeated by seeming obstacles. They will respond to a clear call for service—sacrificial service if need be—to strengthen and defend the nation. They richly merit a prompt and supreme effort to restore and sustain their confidence in the future, to justify their faith, and to draw upon and utilize for the common good their innate self-reliance and resourcefulness.

*Part IV*

IN CONCLUSION

# CHAPTER
# XVIII

## MEANING FOR LIFE

---

Public attention is now almost wholly centered upon the war. It goes without saying that this is inevitable, sane and right. So terrible a crisis as the one into which we are plunged makes it imperative to turn our energies from the slow, long-time constructive efforts of normal life and, racing at top speed, to brace ourselves for deadly danger. Judging by appearances, the declaration of war has utterly transformed the situation and attitudes of American young people, almost from one day to the next. The question might be asked: Why think, speculate, plan for things as they were, and are no longer?

The answer is because that situation of yesterday, so altered today, will almost certainly be again one day, in essence, the same as it was yesterday. And because humanity, so poorly gifted in many respects, has a great safeguard against disaster in its capacity for forethought. That men are able to plan for the future, even in the midst of shattering catastrophe, is one of the reasons for our survival on the globe. We see this natural endowment resourcefully active now in many of the best minds of the nation. Passionately concerned with the peril in which we stand today, they are still capable of vigorously reasonable efforts to understand the deep-lying causes which have brought about the tragic situation of mankind, and of trying with an active effort of

253

the reason to plan for the future so well that the tragedy may not be interminably recurrent. Moreover, to the credit of our race be it said, the ability for long-time forethought is widespread among all men and women with experience of life. Such creative reason sees with lucid clarity that the "solution" of the youth problem offered by the necessity for war is no solution at all of vital and real difficulties which are dangerously likely to recur.

If human reason can continue to take thought for a better future in the midst of disaster, human imagination is positively aroused by the emotional upheaval of a crisis. Never was there a better time to consider what the real situation of American youth is, was, and creatively might be than when we see them snatched out of that situation of yesterday with its wonderful but neglected and unexplored new possibilities for richer life and thrust into the ancient practices of war. We now gladly vote vast sums to feed, clothe, train, teach, discipline, and occupy youth that they may protect our nation from danger. But our nation was in danger before the present emergency because we listlessly failed to make sure that youth were adequately fed, clothed, trained, occupied, and all the rest. If only we could have the chance to do it over and do it better.

It is with the courage and conviction to declare that we Americans shall have the chance to do it over, and with the firm determination that we will resolutely do it better, that this report, founded on so much research and study, is issued with this final chapter of reflections upon the actual and potential inner meaning of life in modern industrial society as it affects the younger generation.

We may as well begin with the statement that the prosecution of the war, life-and-death center of our days as it is now, is no such permanent element in American life as nation-wide employment. This is sober, factual reality, however odd a plain statement of a permanent truth may sound in a time when the trumpets of war are so thrillingly calling out our every resource and all our devotion.

But even employment, vital as it is, is not so important in modern times as it has been in other periods, when—not fancifully, but as a plain matter of fact—it was the life-and-death element in most individual lives. In the society of our days, welfare and health are dependent on having a job; but for any single individual or group literal physical survival does not depend on paid employment as survival formerly depended on success in hunting and fishing.

Instead, in times of peace and normal living there is a new problem. Then, the really searching, intimate problem for each one of us is that of how to develop, out of the new and tremendously changed conditions of modern times, a way of life which makes life worth living, a way of life satisfying and rewarding to the best and finest qualities we have—those qualities which deserve to be called creative. For, if the long-recorded experience of our race proves anything, it proves that living may become intolerable to complex human beings if it is wholly centered on material security, even when comfort is added to safety.

The raw materials which life offers to the creative instinct are infinitely various. Time itself is one—the hours in every day which recurringly offer themselves to us, empty vessels for us to fill. Another, one of the simplest, is clay, the mud from under our feet. Out of this, human beings have made uncountable objects of use, and some of supreme beauty. Another, very different, is the presence on the globe with us, of other men and women. We can conceive no finer use of the divine instinct to shape into comely form what it finds in human existence than to make of the relationship between human beings something enduring, stable, and beneficent.

To speak of God, men use the noblest words in human speech, none more noble than the phrase in the beginning of the Creed, familiar for centuries to so many million worshippers, which calls Him "maker of heaven and earth" or God the Creator. When we claim, proudly and humbly, that our human nature in which there is so much weakness and evil partakes of the Divine, we are giving the highest honor in our power to the creative instinct in us, the instinct to lay hold creatively on the raw materials of life—physical, intellectual, social, spiritual—and to shape them into usefulness and beauty.

To protect this finest of our innate qualities from atrophy caused by disuse, or from warping caused by misuse, is a first duty. To use it ardently and wisely—that is the goal of human existence. Failure to see that goal clearly, failure to advance toward it, at least to struggle toward it and to help others advance—such failure is certainly one of the greatest causes of the feelings of fear, frustration, hatred, and aggression which so often beset us all.

We cannot use the older, familiar outlets for our creative instincts, those outlets dear to us from habit. Modern society is organized in ways very different from those time-honored folkways to which our very reflexes have been automatically adjusted. This change makes it imperative for us to find new channels for the free, unhampered outpouring of the finest and most living of our human qualities. We can have no inner peace until we do.

### THE NATURE OF WORK IN OUR TIMES

The relation between work and leisure is one of the folkways that has been most completely transformed. The character, uses, and possibilities of work and leisure in modern industrial society, and their effect upon the quality of our living, have all been modified. Let us consider, therefore, what work is, in our times. Or rather, what a job is, meaning by a "job" work done for a cash payment. For a new distinction between work and a job—a concept that deeply affects our understanding of life—is beginning to emerge in our minds.

There are two new factors in earning-a-living work, brought to us by modern methods of manufacturing and distributing goods: On the one hand, the hours spent in earning-a-living employment have been shortening to a degree that would have astounded our grandparents. On the other hand, what is done in those hours, in the majority of cases, is less and less interesting to the person who does it and because of its never-varying monotony provides less and less stimulus to and exercise of the instinct for creative, self-directed activity, on which in the long run zest in life depends.

As gradually and on as huge a scale as the advance of a glacier, and hence almost as imperceptibly to ordinary men and women, the time taken from their lives by earning-a-living jobs has been shrinking. Far more vital for personality, the work itself, the small, subdivided job which falls to most people to do, is in less and less obvious relation to the whole of what society needs to have done.

This plain, material, and vital fact about modern jobs seems so distressing and alarming to human beings, who have until now found their basic, enduring satisfactions in the work they did to earn their living, that there is a natural tendency to wince at the thought of it, hastily to deny that it is true, or at least to ignore it as much as possible. But an honestly attentive look at the nature of modern work shows that, in spite of many ingenious efforts on the part of employers and educators, most jobs, being concerned with single minute processes in a complicated and subdivided system of production and distribution, do not make obvious sense to the people who do them. Their meaning as useful, indispensable parts of a necessary whole can be grasped only by a consciously intellectual effort. And what can be grasped only by human brains does not color individual human lives as do older conceptions that come to us through our emotions and our five senses and that are constantly presented to us in the frame of an old, long-accepted association of ideas.

A century and a half ago, the big boy who helped take care of the family sheep also learned from his elders how to shear the sheep, to wash and prepare the wool. He saw his mother spin thread from this same wool, weave cloth from the thread, and make garments from the cloth. It was not only through his brain but also through innumerable mental and sensory associations, through his connection with the whole structure of society, that the inescapably necessary character of his work was constantly impressed upon him. It was at the moment of performing each of his tasks, not in taking conscious thought about it, that he felt as well as knew that his work was an integral part of the process of getting clothes to wear. How very different is the reaction of the young worker of today whose job consists of pressing on a buffing wheel in a factory all day, every day, eight or ten thousand small objects, made of plastic and all exactly alike! For this modern youth the connection between his immediate task and the larger process of which it is a part is remote, shadowy, and abstract, hence incalculably harder for him to hold in mind.

Work on a family-size farm is still more of a "way of life" than almost any other modern way of earning a living, requiring, as it always has, ability to meet new situations and to devise new ways to conquer unexpected obstacles, whereas in most factory work any personal deviation from the pattern set is fatal to efficiency of production. One other exception to the quality of most modern jobs is the repair work done in smaller garages, where the "trouble-shooter" is called upon constantly to show resourcefulness, mental flexibility, ingenuity, and intuition based on experience, together with constantly more varied manual dexterity. And we have all observed what fascination a modern repair garage can have for the boys who live near it.

*Why* did the old-time preindustrial work give basic enduring satisfactions? First, because it was obviously, visibly useful and necessary and, second, because it was so little subdivided and specialized that its performance was accompanied by a steady increase in a great variety of skills. This matter of skill and its narrowing in modern work conditions will recur later in this discussion. The point to be noted here is that the life of the modern young worker in a factory is different from that of his great-grandfather not in only one but in two ways, each of which by its very nature has a prodigious influence on human personality. First, the work of the modern youth is infinitely less various, less interesting to an ordinary human mind, less stimulating to the creative instinct in him. Second, as if to compensate for this loss, it takes out of his waking time only approximately half the number of hours which his great-grandfather was forced to spend on his earning-a-living work. The inescapable conclusion, arrived at by an arithmetical process which can be grasped by any second-grade child, a conclusion which nevertheless is heatedly denied or willfully ignored by a dangerously large number of modern people, is that the young worker today has about twice the amount of free time his ancestors had.

To face and recognize this plain fact and to assume the responsibility for its consequences on human life are among the most pressing things modern young people need to be able to learn for their own good. But the change, although it has been coming gradually, has seemed to appear so suddenly that we elders are still gaping blankly at it or pretending that it is not there or refusing to admit its importance because we don't know what to do with it. And what we do not know we can hardly teach to others. Here is a new lesson that all of us, young and old, must study together on the same learners' bench.

## THE NEW PROBLEM OF LEISURE TIME

All those who have had even a short experience of living and of observing others live know that the quality of life for each one of us depends about as much on the use we make of what we have, as on what we have. What we have in modern conditions is not what our forefathers had; the quality of our present lives depends upon our learning how to use what we *now* have. The old ways of making good use of what people had in earlier days will not serve us.

We have learned that political privileges without reasonable economic security and opportunity cannot assure health, satisfaction, and enjoyment of life to mankind. We have further learned that in a complex, industrialized society, economic security and opportunity will not, just by the nature of things, be distributed widely and equitably enough to ensure that general stability which is possible only in a society where there are not large numbers of gravely underprivileged.

The realization that political liberties must be supplemented by economic ones marks a long step forward in the American effort to make opportunities for satisfactory living as widespread as is humanly possible. But quite as essential, and vastly less talked about, is the realization that it does a human being little good to be provided with the raw materials of a satisfactory and enjoyable life if he is inexpert and uncreative in his handling of those raw materials.

To the eye of wisdom, the really significant, fundamental way in which industrial efficiency has changed our daily life from that of our forefathers is not by providing the dazzling array of useful and agreeable gadgets-for-sale such as bathtubs, automobiles, steam heating, beauty parlors, which make our days physically more comfortable, cleaner, with a higher surface finish, faster, and more complicated. That new element in daily life brought to us by modern conditions which is unprecedented, momentous, and fundamental is freedom from the necessity to labor hard for very long hours every day in order to survive. In other words, much as we fear the sound of the phrase, much as we shrink from the grave and unescapable personal responsibility it lays upon each one of us, desperately as we try to camouflage the reality behind the phrase, the new life element is leisure time.

The art of creatively and resourcefully making the best of what we have is thus concentrated in our times on using for the best—in every sense of the word "best"—the new free time in our daily lives. It is seldom in our power as individuals to change the hours spent on the job. All those other hours in each day when we are not on the job are, however, in our hands. But the art of creating the best possible way of life out of what we have, absolutely essential though this art is to our happiness and satisfaction, receives comparatively little attention from those of our contemporaries who are intellectually responsible and able.

### WHY HAS THIS PROBLEM BEEN IGNORED?

There are several reasons for the persistent ignoring by most intelligent thinkers of the need to learn how we may turn our modern situation to good advantage in creating livable lives, in so far as a satisfactory use of the new free hours is concerned.

One reason is the fear—unfortunately justified—that, if we were to admit that resourcefulness and ingenuity determine the quality of a human life almost as much as do the raw materials which they shape, this admission would immediately be seized on by ungenerous and reactionary people and used as an argument to oppose efforts to distribute those raw materials more equitably.

For example, in the section of this report on nutrition, it is made clear that undernourishment is often the result of bad cooking and bad management rather than of poverty. Such a statement is made reluctantly by conscientious people because, through experience, they have come to know that it is often snatched up by the illiberal as proof either that poverty does not exist or that it needs no alleviation.

The same sort of specious reasoning has been seen in the course of the long attempt to secure better housing for the poor. Those working for better homes for wage earners hesitate to give publicity to the fact that many home backgrounds could be (in spite of the manifold disheartenments brought by poverty—bad health, poor equipment, overcrowding) greatly improved, if homemakers alertly and ingeniously used all the resources that they already have. It would be very helpful to those homemakers to receive stimulating suggestions about creative use of the raw materials available to them. But too much said about this publicly might be used—indeed has been used in the past—as an excuse for opposing the most necessary improvements in low-income housing.

As everyone knows, there are two ways to manage life. One is to make the best possible use of any situation in which we find ourselves. The other is to fight hard to make the situation itself better for us and for others less fortunate than we. Of course, the best attitude, wisely complex, is to do both at the same time. But such are the limitations of our human minds that by showing how to get more satisfactions out of a situation as it stands, we imperil our chances of getting help to improve it. Undoubtedly, the people working for human betterment are affected, more or less, by this well-grounded fear, and this is one reason for their silence about the fact that in general the right utilization of what we have is as important for our happiness as our having a great deal.

Another reason for the failure of many intellectuals to recognize that we have to learn how to use the greatest asset in most modern lives—hours free from the immediate compulsion to work for pay— is an actual ignorance of the tremendous effect upon each individual existence of the sweeping changes of industrial production and distribution. This ignorance is due partly to the fact that the transformation, although rapid from a historian's point of view, has been gradual enough to spread out over several generations. Naturally, it is always hard for people to visualize conditions which existed before they were born.

Another contributing cause is a familiar linguistic confusion arising out of the use of old words in new meanings, thus setting up a cloudy mental confusion every time they are pronounced. The "home" formerly meant the place where most of the articles used in daily life by ordinary people were manufactured and distributed. The "family" was a sizable group of actively producing workers, cooperating under one roof to take care of their own material needs. It is a far cry from that earlier "home" (which was factory, vocational school, home for the aged, hospital, and home economics laboratory) to the present one —a small shelter from which in many instances all members of the family save the very youngest go out every day, each one far from the others, to work for the money with which to buy the things that once upon a time families manufactured together. Yet, because we still use the old word "home," we hardly realize how completely new as an institution the modern home is, and hence how imperative is the need for the people in it to manage their lives in new ways, if they are to retain their mental and moral equilibrium. We know, with our purely intellectual brain centers, that a great, a decisive, a radical change has taken place, but our habits and reflexes and emotions have hardly begun, as yet, to be aware of a transformation in human life as swift and improbable-seeming as anything in a fairy story.

One more reason may be briefly cited for the more or less conscious turning away by responsible leaders of humanity from the problem of how to find in the new, modern, strange-to-us rearrangement of time in each human day the nourishing satisfaction of creative activity which gave our ancestors their vitality. The problem is one that cannot be treated in the exact terms of laboratory research. The scientist, considered today the model of intellectual dignity, indeed of intellectual respectability, sheers off from phenomena which can be neither weighed nor accurately measured, nor so simplified and divided by analysis into parts that from isolated fragments, worked upon by research specialists, verifiable data may be secured.

Human problems can seldom be studied by these methods. All human problems are complex. In each one, decisions must be made and actions taken long before data can be scientifically verified. Perhaps the very character of the problem of leisure time explains the reluctance of intellectuals to give to it anything like the respectful attention and earnest thought which they focus on the economics involved in the production and distribution of material income. The use of leisure time seems to them, probably, a vague subject that should be left to the uplifters and the emotionalists.

Yet a prophetic eye would perceive that the solution of the problem of leisure time is, in sober literal fact, one of the two or three keys without which we cannot unlock the doors to a decent human future. A seer would be appalled by the mistake we elders make in continuing to plan for the lives of the younger generation. And it does not need a prophet or a seer to see our mistake. It needs only an ordinarily intelligent person of experience willing really to look at the situation, to be staggered by the unwisdom of the preparation for life we give our young people, ignoring in it, as we do, the paramount importance to them of how they spend their free hours. Our educators struggle conscientiously to prepare our youth for what probably cannot be accurately foreseen in their future lives—the kinds of jobs in which they are going to have to earn their living. But they do not prepare them for what can with certainty be foreseen—that each one of them will have free time in his life, the use of which will largely determine the quality of the future man or woman.

We do worse than omit any attempt seriously and intelligently to prepare them to make a creative use of this new priceless treasure. By the shallow, inept mental attitude we assume, we tacitly acquiesce in the prospect that they will, like so many of us, make the wrong choice when confronted by the solemn searching responsibility for a free-will decision between materialistic, passive triviality and the opportunity to acquire that rich, expanding, deepening personality which grows up from the strong root of creative effort.

And finally, to these various natural reasons for the odd conspiracy of silence on the part of seriously thinking people about the great subject of preparing youth to do what they might in creating a satisfying way of life out of the free-time aspect of modern conditions, there certainly must be added another, natural enough, but not so respectable: the rushing pounce of the modern profit-making instinct to exploit commercially the transforming changes in modern lives. The changes that have taken place have put a larger number of the human race than ever before into a situation analogous to the traditional situation of the newly rich; they have less work to do than formerly (and that work less exhausting) and more cash to spend.

Newly rich people are by no means a new phenomenon in human history. There are well-known patterns and traditions connected with them. One is that they are gold mines for those who have objects or services for sale. Such salesmen have quickly expanded the old pattern to fit the immensely larger gold field opened up by a much wider distribution of cash and free time. What our salesmen have to offer are the same things used in all periods by the newly rich to fill up the gap created in their lives by the disappearance of long hours of enforced labor—material possessions, personal services, and amusement-for-sale.

These pleasures are new and fresh to many people, for whom they are made possible by that same efficiency of the modern industrial system which has sucked out from their lives the substantial character-food of varied, obviously useful, self-directed, stimulating work. That is, just at the time when the active pleasures of genuinely creative activity are lessened in the daily lives of ordinary people, they are offered a far greater range of passive, purchased pleasures, the sale of which provides a cash profit for an especially energetic class in society.

### FUTILITY IN THE USE OF LEISURE

It is not surprising that, without even knowing what they are doing, the people of the present day have slid helplessly into innumerable noncreative, inactive, futile ways of spending their new free time. To themselves they seem to be continuing only what humanity has always found wholesome and necessary—harmless recreation as a change from "work." They do not realize that the word "work" now means something very different from the modern job.

For one thing, in the preindustrial period of long hours spent in heavy, exacting labor, the worker was very tired at the end of the day. In the brief period of each day or each week or each month during which he was free from the necessity to work at his job, he needed not more effort but pure relaxation and pleasure. Just random fun was delicious because it was a rest from the enforced purposefulness of all his other activity. Such recreation was the icing to his cake, the butter on his bread. The cake, the bread, was his work. Now in the majority of cases when the worker, even the wage earner, ends the relatively few hours spent in earning-a-living work, only some of his muscles are tired. Moreover, although he may, with the upper layer of his consciousness, intellectually grasp the rather abstract conception that he has been doing work necessary to himself as a member of society, he has not had the satisfaction of *feeling* his work to be useful as he performed it. In other words, the worker's job no longer gives him the character-calories and personality-vitamins that build up his individuality, as the food which he eats builds up his body. The person who has done eight hours of muscularly easy work that did not call out his ingenuity or resourcefulness does not need the butter or the icing which "recreation in free hours" used to be for the old-time worker. The modern worker still needs bread—that is, serious, continued, really creative effort with its rich flowering into variegated skill that will feed his personality as the variegated responsible work of the past fed the personality of his great-grandparents. It is foolish and wrong to attempt to fill the many free hours presented him by the machine with purposeless fun, excellent as such fun is in its place, or with the static and unfruitful acquisition of possessions, or with the passive, sensory pleasures of being served by others, when what he most needs is some valid substitute for the self-directed, creative, purposeful activity and skill taken away from him by the machine and the division of labor. It is as though we were to urge a person who hadn't bread enough to keep him in health to try to make up for it by eating more butter!

One picturesque instance of giving butter in place of bread is to be found in the growth of the business called "cosmetology." In this new modern industry, the personal services formerly given only by skilled ladies' maids to rich women can be purchased in any amounts for which the buyer can find money, from the simple cutting of finger-nails up to extravagant toilet luxuries such as have not been known since the late Roman Empire. This new business, from literally nothing at all, has become in forty years one of the great industries of the nation, ranking with those whose yearly receipts represent substantial fractions of the total income spent by Americans of all classes. It is not realistic to say that in itself this extreme care for the surfaces of the body is harmful as the use of morphine is harmful. It is, rather, like the occasional purchase of silk shirts by workingmen suddenly paid boom-time wages. There is no harm in silk shirts. But to buy and wear them when what those wage earners really needed to buy with their first extra cash was dental care for their long-neglected teeth—

that, like the extravagant sums spent in our nation on the beauty parlors, indicates a lack of proportion which lowers the quality of life almost as much as does wrongdoing.

No one today escapes the importunity of those who manufacture consumer goods, the urgent insistence that people should constantly spend more and more time and money on purchasing more and more material objects, hiring expensive expert help to take care of these objects, and discarding them, not when their usefulness is lessened by the passage of time, but when they are artificially made undesirable by speeded-up changes in fashion. No more evidence of this insistence is needed than the reams of advertising in our newspapers and magazines and the prodigious growth of retail stores of all kinds. And no one need do more than open his eyes to perceive in the size and financial importance of the motion-picture industry the almost frightening eagerness for passive, ready-made amusement, bought at a price. The cinema itself is harmless enough; indeed when of decent quality, it is a delightful addition to the pleasures of life. Yet, the rocket-like growth of the industry in recent years is alarming, just as the first symptoms of pellagra are alarming, not because they are visibly serious, but as an indication of a serious malady caused by the lack in everyday life of an element vital to human health.

The effort to solve by unnecessary buying of possessions and services and induced synthetic interests and excitements the problem of the emptiness formerly occupied by varied, creative, purposeful work under the compulsion of necessity has a disquieting and dangerous result in that it obscures as by a smoke screen the fact that free time really is available for practically anyone who will put out his hand and take it. Superfluous buying and owning of objects, seeking amusement, and being served by people paid to do it occupy so much of the newly freed time in modern lives that people are fooled into believing, against demonstrable evidence, that they have no leisure. So much icing and butter is available to those with even a little cash that, except for vague persistent uneasiness and discontent, they do not perceive that they no longer have their fair share of bread. They are like muddle-headed children who, confronted with the subtraction of two from four, doggedly insist that somehow the answer is six. They know well enough that the machine has removed from each day of their lives many hours of the drudgery forced on their grandparents. Yet, incessantly rushing there and back, as the automobile almost forces them to do, and incessantly buying more than they need as the propaganda of our times, the advertisements, bid them do, they can still sincerely and bewilderedly claim that somehow they have more to do and hence less free time than those grandparents had.

All this is of the most vital importance in the training of young people, since what we set ourselves to do is to try to assist them to learn how to make the best of life as they will find it, not as it has been. It is really extraordinary that we make so little effort to prepare young people to cope masterfully and creatively and enjoyably with their free time; that we allow it to be tacitly understood that the only alternative to the ever-shortening time spent on the job is in aimless and casual pastimes. We do not even try to clear away from their minds one factor which interferes sharply with the wise use of leisure time. This is a familiar modern confusion about the nature of money, a confusion which has grown up along with the steady increase of the use of cash in more and more of the transactions of everyday life.

### CONFUSION ABOUT MONEY AS A FACTOR

All during the nineteenth century, as the principle of the division of labor was applied in more and more complete detail, human beings were unlearning the age-old habit of working in order to make or to grow or to do what they wanted and were learning the new habit of working for money, and with the money buying what they wanted. That process has gone on so long and so intensively that we have almost forgotten that, in many cases, for many people—and very often for young people—it is still possible to move directly to the satisfaction of our needs and desires without passing our effort through the medium of money. In our confusion of mind on this point, we have almost come to the attitude of the legendary Persian potentate who exclaimed that he could not understand why Occidentals, with money to pay people to dance for them, went on dancing themselves.

Without exactly meaning to, we have—judging from our young people's reactions—created around many of them a moral atmosphere which paralyzes their natural instinct to enjoy creative activity. What looks like one of the symptoms of such a paralysis is their all-too-common, taken-for-granted feeling that what they can't get paid to do isn't worth the effort of doing, *even when the result of the work would be exactly what they would buy with money if they had it*—better food, more comfort, cleanliness, neatness, and beauty in their homes, more attractive surroundings in their towns, and more amusing and active recreation. The root of this feeling, of course, is not a new flaw in the character of youth in our times. It is found, rather, in the great development of money as the most convenient and indeed as the sole medium of that exchange of services which is the basis of human society.

In so far as this use of money is one remove from the direct factual reality of any transaction between human beings, it is an abstract idea. And it is harder for human beings to grasp and hold an abstract idea than a tangible reality. The exchange of a bushel of wheat for a pair of shoes would never in any mind blur the fact that anybody who knew how to make his own shoes could just turn to and make them. But the presence of the grocer who sells vegetables for money does tend to blur the fact that many of the people who have not money to buy his vegetables might, by direct personal effort, often no greater than— although different from—the effort needed to earn the money, grow their own vegetables.

Here is a mental confusion which is very harmful, indeed poisonous, to the quality of human life. To clear away mental confusions is the peculiar province of education. This one, unlike many, is of a kind easily reached by classroom instruction and forceful pointed exposition by teachers of history and the social sciences. Seldom does a subject suited to textbook study bear so directly on how to make the best of life as does this simple conception that the satisfaction of human desires depends less than we moderns tend to think upon the spending of money, that it is still possible in many cases to have and to do what we want by working to create what we desire or by simply going out to do what is enjoyable, without passing our efforts through the bottle-neck of earning and spending money.

## YOUTHFUL APATHY DURING THE DEPRESSION

All during the dismal years of the depression, we saw laid out before us the results in the life of American youth of our social and educational sins of omission and commission. Many thousands of young people were "unemployed"; that is, they were not able to get jobs. That they were still perfectly free to work, in ways which would enormously have increased their own comfort and have given them much pleasure, did not occur to them. How could it, when their elders were conditioned, and so had conditioned them, to the idea that the paid-in-cash job is the only work worth doing? They were almost physically paralyzed by the modern axiom "no job, no work." They were in the flower of their young years, with better physical health, by and large, than any preceding generation; they had any amount of leisure; few restrictions were placed upon their activities in their free time, either explicitly, or implicitly by public opinion; the raw materials for varied creative occupation and enjoyment lay piled all around many of them. But the spoken and unspoken example of their elders had led them to feel that free time could be used enjoyably only in buying objects, services, or amusements. They had no money. Hence, so ran the unwritten but unescapable syllogism which imprisoned them: they could make no useful or enjoyable use of their leisure time.

Now, of course, their situation, being human, was complex. It cannot truthfully be analyzed in a few simple terms. They were undoubt-edly in a situation of great emotional discomfort and anxiety; they were shut out, as far as they could see, from the earning-a-living, forty-hours-a-week activity of work on a job. Human beings always suffer keenly over inability to be part of a group. But these were young people. And there is, inherent in human nature, a powerful instinct to get relief from discomfort and anxiety by whatever pleasurable activities are still open. People condemned to death continue to play games, sing, read, to enjoy what time they have. In our American unemployed youth this instinct seemed to have been numbed as by an anesthetic.

They acted as though, if they had not money to buy, there was nothing left for them to do but to drift, helplessly passive in a vacuum of idleness, or to watch what people with money did with it. All over the country, hundreds of boys deserted the innumerable active games that cost nothing to play and idled down to the town poolrooms to watch people play a game which cost money. Girls whose grandmothers had rejoiced in needlework, in preparing food, in reading (when this was a new privilege for women), in the study of natural processes, in collective sociable enterprises, sat in sorrowful solitude watching people who had money pass by in their automobiles. Those young people who lived in cities and were capable of using books could have had the printed publications of the world in their hands; those who lived in the country had the open book of nature laid out before them as before Thoreau, Burroughs, Muir, Audubon, Fabre.

Thomas Huxley has said that "the sense of uselessness is the severest shock which the human system can sustain." We forced this shock upon our younger generation by tacitly conceding the insane limitation of the concept of usefulness to paid jobs. Because those boys and girls could not, for the time being, find paid jobs, they helplessly underwent that "severest shock" although open all around them were myriads of opportunities to be useful, to their families, to society, to themselves.

Not jobs but all kinds of worth-while work could have been done by unemployed youth, especially by those whose parents were not without resources. They could have worked, consistently and seriously, to become expert baseball players or accomplished swimmers, skillful embroiderers or gardeners. They could have enriched and beautified their own homes, their persons, or their towns, with such objects of folk art in wood or textiles as are seen in village homes and country towns in Scandinavia. They could have given their young energies to help along projects for community betterment, and where there were none, they could have undertaken simple ones of their own. They could have engaged in plans for such larger-scale pleasures for themselves as were possible without the expenditure of money, through an effort in common—such as the arrangement of playgrounds on unused land, the construction of athletic fields and, in situations where the conditions were favorable, swimming pools and skating rinks. If nothing else, they could have picked up sticks, borrowed jackknives, and become expert whittlers. It is more fun to make even the sailor's whittled ship inside a bottle than to sag on a street corner, idle hands in empty pockets. In a few instances, some of these things were done under the right kind of leadership but mostly not at all. As one astonished older person fancifully observed, not one unemployed youth whom he knew thought of making even so much use of this time as to acquire and really to master the homely, not-to-be-despised art of accurate and skillful whistling which requires no apparatus not provided by nature.

### WHAT WAS THE BARRIER TO YOUTHFUL ACTIVITY?

It can be assumed that these millions of unemployed young people were like others of their years, at the age when even if their health is not in perfect condition, their imperative biological urge is toward energetic activity as a joy in itself. We could have no more solemn warning of grave errors in the education they have received at the hands of their elders than this extraordinary paralysis of the almost irresistible impulse of youth to be up and doing.

One cause, as was intimated on a previous page, was evidently the feeling that they were outside the framework of the society around them. Human beings seem able to endure great physical hardships and pain with less suffering than they experience when they have to withstand uncertainty as to recognition and acceptance by the human group to which they feel they should belong. Here is a warning to us not to limit "the group" in which membership is desirable solely to those doing work for money.

In any case, the psychological misery of not belonging to the paid-in-cash group should not have weighed on the unemployed young as heavily as it weighed on unemployed adults with dependents. The conscientious selfless fear of not being able to take care of those economically dependent on them certainly was enough to account for the tragic inability during the depression of most of the adult unemployed to make any creative or even interesting use of the free time they had so abundantly in every day. But there was no such fear to account for the tragic lethargy of young people from 16 to 21 who had no dependents—young people biologically crammed with physical stimuli to sociability, to adventure, to ardent, spirited play, to that movement for its own sake which their elders impatiently call "restlessness," young people traditionally not given to taking life too seriously or too responsibly. It is certainly well worth our while to try to discover and break down the unseen psychological barrier which held those youth back even from getting together to play the active group games which are the traditional joy of adolescence and early maturity.

It is not enough to say that the cause of the strange, unyouthful listlessness and inaction of many young people was wholly lack of jobs and resultant lack of money. That the reason is far deeper is suggested by the portrait made of the younger generation by many competent writers in recent years in well-written fiction based upon honest observation, a portrait revealing the reckless speed, fitfulness, sexual unrestraint, and alcoholism prevalent among a great many well-to-do youth. Even making due allowance for the tendency of fiction writers to heighten the prevailing color, these conditions strongly suggest to anyone at all versed in psychology a serious dissatisfaction among these young people with what it seems possible for them to do. Yet, as far as the literal facts of their situation go, it is plainly evident that there have been, open to them in reality, all kinds of activities which have always been enjoyed by other youth in other periods. The young people in these works of fiction do not seem consciously to refuse to partake of the durable and satisfactory joys, which, for all we can see, are freely open to them; they do not turn their backs willfully on the opportunities all around them for the creative use of their leisure time; apparently they simply do not dream that such opportunities exist.

Whatever the psychological barrier which prevents their even perceiving the satisfactions which might be theirs, it is not confined to those who have too little cash. It is perhaps even more poisonous an element in the minds of many who have plenty of money. These well-to-do young people become so habituated to the process of getting possessions and amusements by paying cash for them that they try to carry this process into departments of life where it has no validity at all; they attempt to buy, with results pathetically disconcerting to them, such things as interests in life or satisfactory personal relations. The idle young person lounging in listless melancholy on the street corner when he might be throwing his heart into a baseball game on a vacant lot or hiking along a forest trail is a sad example of unused human potentialities for happiness and growth. But equally sad is the case of the well-to-do youth whose parents have money to send him on an ocean cruise (such as decided the whole course of young Darwin's life) but whose mental processes have set so rigidly in the buying-for-money reflex that he goes on trying to buy pleasure and interest in the only form in which it is for sale on the ship—in gambling and alcohol.

Future commentators on our twentieth century life will be able to analyze our situation more accurately than we can today. But even we, close to the phenomenon as we are and to a great extent blocked off from satisfactions by the same impalpable barriers that block our young people, can perhaps make a guess at the reasons for this general failure so far to create out of the golden new possibilities opened to us by the lessening of drudgery in our lives a genuinely satisfactory way of life.

One of them is certainly the general tendency already noted to carry over into phases of human activity where it need not and indeed cannot apply the habit, now become a reflex, of buying possessions and services. Like all habits this one will be hard to change but, again like all habits, it should be possible to modify it by earnest and purposeful taking of thought, in the training of the younger generation, in the ordering of our own lives.

This buying habit however, bad as it is, is a small and inconsiderable element compared to what is probably the basic cause for the profoundly unsatisfactory character of our lives, which, from the material standpoint, seem freer than ever human lives were before to advance into rich and durable satisfaction. This larger element is the removal from many more lives than ever before of the oldest motive power known to humanity, that of the continuous compulsion of material necessity. The enormous productive powers of machinery have greatly lessened in most American lives the pressure which has until now been the strongest and most prevalent force that set all of us to work—to work in the grand, general, preindustrial age meaning of activity with useful or beautiful results, directly felt or seen by the worker.

Like the visible lowering of the water in a reservoir no longer fed from one of its greatest springs, there is already one visible result in our lives of the lessening of compulsion to effort derived from material necessity. That result is an apparent weakening of the impulse to acquire individual skills. The fine flower of human work done under the pressure of material need was skill—the ability to do something well. By and large the development of this ability, in one or another of its literally infinitely varied fields, is the greatest source of pleasure, satisfaction, and growth in individual human lives, and of what is known in our collective life as civilization.

### SKILL AS A FACTOR IN HAPPINESS

Year after year throughout most of each individual life, human happiness and satisfaction in the ordinary sense are far more permanently dependent on the possession and use of those skills suited to our innate abilities than upon even such fundamental elements as bodily health, mating, and parenthood. Indeed, except by casual and unusual luck, good health cannot be permanently enjoyed except by acquiring and practicing skill in living healthfully; nor can mating and parenthood bring more than fleeting pleasures without learning how to be a good mate, and at least a decent parent. For skill which can be acquired only through effort persistent and purposeful enough to merit the name of work is the only medium which allows the operation of our creative instinct to shape and form the raw materials of life, from mud to human governments, from personal relationships to wood and steel and stone.

Many thoughtful people have seen a danger in our modern situation, which, so they feel, was dramatically proved by the paralyzed failure of many young people to use free time effectively. Most people in peacetime in civilized countries are in no actual physical risk of starving or freezing to death. If that oldest, most obvious, most dramatic compulsion to effort is gone, what urge can be counted on to give human beings the push they seem to need to make them begin and then to carry on the never-ending effort to acquire and perfect skills?

A partial answer may be found in the lives of scientists, creative workers in all the arts, fine craftsmen, scholars, and saints. They are human beings, but none of them need any compulsion, save from within, to toil and struggle forward toward perfecting his skill in his own chosen field. For it was not the spur of material necessity that drove Charles Darwin impassionedly to grapple with mighty intellectual obstacles. Beethoven neither hewed wood nor carried water, nor would he have starved if he had merely taught music and never composed a page, but nevertheless he grew in creative power with every passing day. Pascal, protected from the need for all physical effort, from any need to earn the material necessities, still put forth a gigantic effort of his higher brain centers. St. Francis had so little regard for what most men feel are the material necessities of life that he was not even aware of them, much less moved by them to his prodigious effort to realize his burning aspiration to draw near to God. Leisure time and security as created by civilization have never been anything but unmixed blessings to human beings who have walked on the higher levels of life.

On the other side of the ledger, history has grimly recorded over and over again another story, when some development in human society has freed a minority of the human race, variously known as the aristocracy, the upper class, or the leisure class, from the effort by which their forefathers justified their existence. In almost every case the leisure classes of the past have turned away from a vigorous, coherent use of their best faculties and have lapsed into intellectual stagnation or become absorbed in the tinkling, brittle trivialities that comprise what is commonly designated as fashionable life. Not they personally, but the hard-working people in their pay, have become accomplished musicians, gardeners, cooks, authors, craftsmen, artists.

In partial, easy explanation of this contrast, it has been assumed that artists, intellectuals, and spiritual leaders are an elite, somehow made of different clay from that used for other human beings. Especially has it been assumed that their willingness to work in the absence of material necessity or the lure of material reward was a quality which they alone among human beings possessed. The artist, working doggedly to perfect a painting, although his bread and butter would be assured by a much less strenuous effort, was considered a creature of a different order from the workman putting plaster on a wall. But even if it were true, as has sometimes been thought, that it is for fame and prestige rather than for money that the artist works, he could often achieve his desire without that last wringing of the heart, that last desperate effort to do his best. No, obviously there is some impulse here, some compelling urge other than the most sublimated desire for money or fame. On the whole, this truth has been generally recognized and acknowledged.

Now, so long as we consider that this urge, springing from motives unrelated to material necessity, is confined to the artist, the scientist, the scholar, the saint, our outlook on modern life must be one of despair; because the need to work constantly, as a condition of survival, is unquestionably being lessened every day for a greater and greater number of people by the wider employment of labor-saving machinery and by the new organization of society. If humanity in general really has no inner urge to do something rather than nothing and to do that something well, if human beings have no will to be active except when forced to exertion by literal need, then it is distressingly clear that the long new hours of freedom now enjoyed by many workers will be used for nothing better than random, time-killing entertainment and the low-grade pleasures of possessiveness. And there is plenty of evidence in our historical records to show that too much indulgence in these passive and unfruitful pleasures results in a dangerous degeneration of human personality.

The mass of humanity has been sustained by the pressure of literal need as sea animals are sustained by the high specific gravity of salt water. Now, except in times of war, some of this motivating compulsion has been removed from all of us, and a great deal of it from the majority of us. American children get it from universally enforced attendance at school. But since the accepted assumption in our country is that no one will be allowed literally to starve or freeze to death, many unemployed youth old enough not to be forced to go to school have been entirely separated from the old literal forms of immediate compulsion to effort. Their suffering in the resultant vacuum, while not physical, has been acute and as mysterious to them as to us.

### THERE IS HOPE FOR THE FUTURE

Yet we, the great mass of humanity, may be able to find our way forward into new and richer forms of self-chosen, self-directed creative activities, carried on, as artists and thinkers and saints have always acted, solely for the sake of their useful or beautiful results, not because physical survival in any way depends upon them. The new, thin, dangerously unsustaining element before us, in which we will be called upon in peacetime to live, is free choice, in many more lives than ever before, as to what we shall do in the several hours of each day when we are under no compulsion from urgent material necessity.

The grave and momentous responsibility of free will is laid upon the human spirit in a vast new field. The choice set before more ordinary men and women than ever before is between the flabby, passive, easy, effortless use of free time which makes of any human life a tale told by an idiot, signifying nothing, and the opposite use of time in coherent, persistent effort to handle creatively the raw materials available to us in human existence. Are there innate qualities in human nature—not only in the special personalities of creative artists, scholars, and social and spiritual seers, but widely distributed among so-called ordinary people—which if developed might become the power needed to make the right choice? Pessimists, in a panic, have been quick to deny the existence of any such saving innate quality in everyday men and women. The arrogant assumption on the part of artists and intellectuals that they are made of different stuff from other men has gone unquestioned.

But when it is questioned and put to the test by a long, attentive look at what experience and observation have taught us about human nature, we see much to give us hope that there is less difference than has been assumed between the superior elite of creative personalities and the rest of humanity. And, more important yet, what difference there is, is not of quality, of an entirely different outlook on life, as we have thought, but rather of quantity. Artists and intellectuals have it in a larger proportion than others. But there is evidence that most men and women have it—at least the seeds of it. And if the seed is there, innate and alive, what grows out of it can be increased by effort and favorable environment.

There seems to be more than evidence; there is what looks like conclusive proof in support of the hopeful view that the compelling urge which is the motive power of the creative human being—artist or intellectual—is by no means restricted to the small number of men and women who have been so completely swayed by this urge as to shape their whole lives around it. By a marvelous correspondence of function, the acquiring and the practice of a skill have been not only the condition of survival of the human race but also its most enduring, most substantial joy and pleasure.

One example of this, which can stand for the numberless others which might be cited, is the familiar instance of the potter. An immediate necessity forced our primitive ancestors to lay hold on mud and make out of it vessels to hold water and food. If a reflex response to physical needs were truly the only reaction in ordinary men moving them to effort, the potter would have stopped his work when he had produced a vessel that would merely help keep him from hunger and thirst. His "job" was done when he had made a jar in which he could carry water from the river to the camp. But, except in a very few of the least developed tribes of man, no potter ever stopped there. His "work," as distinguished from his "job," went far beyond the meeting of the material need he was coping with. He went on, of his own free will, to the practice of a finer, more exacting skill in design until he had fashioned something shapely, something that satisfied an innate longing for comeliness and beauty, which, because we see its results everywhere in human history, cannot but be universal.

Today, we see everywhere in the lives of modern men and women modern manifestations of this same instinct, this same inner compulsion to go beyond the mere earning-a-living job and to do "work" for the sheer joy of creation and accomplishment, or for the satisfaction of being of service to others, of being a useful member of one's group. Industrial workers in cities, forbidden the exercise of creative skill in their daytime occupations, where any deviation from the prescribed pattern is a defect and not a virtue, spend their evenings working busily and happily in an art workshop. Hundreds of amateur scientists in Philadelphia band together for the voluntary pursuit of research and study in their fields of interest. In Cleveland, a Committee on

Private Research is offering advice and assistance to countless numbers of amateur scholars, whose studies cover a wide range, from Egyptology to American archeology, from Chinese philosophy to the psychology of humor. In a small Vermont industrial town, which gives employment to wage earners with especially developed mechanical skills, an astronomers' club has for many years included in its membership representatives of all kinds of local workers, from the men who operate the complicated machines in the shops to the president of the company.

A promising sign of new times to come, found more widely all over the United States than any of these single examples of fine, self-directed, creative use of new free time, is the miraculously sudden and widespread appearance in our American high schools and colleges of a brand-new will to acquire musical skill and practice it for the joy of it—as, long ago, the barefooted, illiterate rural people of Mexico learned to practice it. It is true that as yet those young musicians when they leave the high schools do not often organize bands which make music for the joy of it; and the members of those fine college choruses do not, as yet, always reassemble themselves in community choral groups to continue the singing of Bach. But there has not yet been time to see what, as adults, they will do in the realm of communally made music with which their education is making them familiar.

Here and in the graphic and plastic arts are fields in which Americans with a gift for music and art, like Italians, Negroes, Germans, Indians, can be counted on to enrich our nation's life with an inherited fervor, warmer and more potent than can be found in purely Anglo-Saxon backgrounds.

But it must not be forgotten that our Republic—as history goes, our venerably old Republic—has lasted so long that it is rich in traditions of its own. We are so familiar with them that we take them too much for granted, forget to give them the honor due them, even when we try to pass on to the younger generation the best of what we have received from the past. One tradition which for Americans has colored the very fiber of life to the marrow of our bones has become more than a tradition, has become a true folkway—so intimately familiar to us all that we often joke about it. This is the American tradition of "forming a committee" when we see something which needs to be done. We so instinctively shape our desires and our efforts in this mold that we often groaningly cry out against it as a burden to daily existence. Knowing little, in intimate detail, about how other peoples manage their lives, we have no standard of comparison by which to see the value of this tradition. We do not realize that this sturdy impulse to accomplish desirable ends by voluntary, unpaid, unofficial, unprofessional, spontaneously undertaken, communal effort is vividly our very own and one of the strongest taproots of our national health. Here is the great Anglo-Saxon contribution to our mighty federation, a living trait of such vitality that it grows and thrives in our soil enriched by many other social strains even more luxuriantly than in the culturally unified background from which it sprang.

Every college, every public library, every high school in the United States should have in full view on its walls some of the inspiring passages of de Tocqueville's description of this American folkway.

The political associations which exist in the United States are only a single feature in the midst of the immense assemblage of associations in that country. Americans of all ages, all conditions, and all dispositions, constantly form associations. They have not only commercial and manufacturing companies, in which all take part, but associations of a thousand other kinds—religious, moral, serious, futile, extensive or restricted, enormous or diminutive. The Americans make associations to give entertainments, to found establishments for education, . . . to diffuse books, to send missionaries to the antipodes; and in this manner they found hospitals, prisons, and schools. If it is proposed to advance some truth, or to foster some feeling by the encouragement of a great example, they form a society. Wherever, at the head of some new undertaking, you see the government in France, or a man of rank in England, in the United States you will be sure to find an association. . . .

Thus the most democratic country on the face of the earth is that in which men have in our time carried to the highest perfection the art of pursuing in common the object of their common desires, and have applied this new science to the greatest number of purposes. Is this the result of accident? or is there in reality any necessary connection between the principle of association and that of equality? . . .

In aristocratic societies men do not need to combine in order to act, because they are strongly held together. . . . Amongst democratic nations, on the contrary, all the citizens are independent and feeble; they can do hardly anything by themselves, and none of them can oblige his fellow-men to lend him their assistance. . . .

Nothing, in my opinion, is more deserving of our attention than the intellectual and moral associations of America. . . . Amongst the laws which rule human societies there is one which seems to be more precise and clear than all others. If men are to remain civilized, or to become so, the art of associating together must grow and improve in the same ratio in which the equality of conditions is increased.[1]

It was more than a century ago that this keen-eyed observer of human society came to look at our life with that discerning detachment which only an outsider can have. If he were alive today, he would observe no weakening of, but rather abundant new growth from, this old taproot. Regardless of variegated racial shades of inherited tradition, the spontaneous, voluntary use of free time in communal efforts for the betterment of human existence is constantly more accepted by general public opinion in the United States.

To set down a bare list of such activities, such voluntary service to the common good, would take many pages of this report. In every community there are men and women who serve without salary as directors of schools, hospitals, museums, libraries, settlement houses, orphanages, churches, community clubs. The national officers of such great organizations as the YMCA, the YWCA, and their fellow associations, the General Federation of Women's Clubs, the National Congress of Parents and Teachers, the various fraternal orders, the

[1]Alexis de Tocqueville, *Democracy in America* (New York: Colonial Press, 1899), Vol. II, pp. 114ff.

American Red Cross—all freely and as a matter of course give their time, thought, and effort to public service, usually without financial reward and in innumerable cases with the certainty that their contribution will never be publicly recognized. Americans have known, from the first of our national life, how to find elsewhere than in their earning-a-living jobs the stimulus to work—serious, honest work that calls for sustained and purposeful effort. It would be easy to set down a far longer list of proofs that we are more ready than we fear to face the portentous element of a freewill choice as to occupations. But anyone who is minded to see the true significance of all this self-inspired human effort must realize that the human instinct to bring order and a meaningful, finished design out of mere raw material is one of the most spontaneous, active, and widely operative forces in our world today, just as it has always been and always will be.

## CHANGED ATTITUDES WILL BE NEEDED

Here is a great door through which we can triumphantly escape from a difficult impasse. For many of us, because of our lack of the imaginative ability to adjust ourselves readily to the new conditions of living under decreased pressure of physical necessity, the door is still shut. But it is not locked. And beyond it lies a wide, sunlit realm that offers us opportunities for more universally shared, creative pleasures than mankind has ever known before. Yet we will not enter into this realm until all of us, and particularly the young people whose lives are just beginning, come to see clearly that we must substitute and develop freely chosen, spontaneously loved skills—manual, bodily, social, artistic, spiritual, or intellectual—for the older skills enforced upon humanity by necessity. For this golden opportunity to develop higher, finer powers in a greater number of men and women than ever exercised these powers before depends, like all development in adult life, upon the sowing of seed-habits in youth which will lead to fruiting-habits in mature years. That is why the way in which free time is used by young people is so vitally important. That is why it is so tragically dangerous to have intellectuals and leaders of public thought and opinion ignore or underestimate the tremendous problem created by the existence of a large amount of free time in all our lives, and particularly in the lives of youth. Unless much of the free time of people in their youth is occupied with "work," meaning spontaneous, creative activity and the acquisition and practicing of personal skills that will bring happiness and enrichment to their lives, they will enter adult life in modern times quite unprepared for a most critical danger; and our country will be headed for disaster.

It cannot be emphasized too strongly, can hardly be repeated too often, that these saving, enriching skills are never acquired without "work," that is, long-continued, persistent effort. They can never be learned as part of mere pastimes. This principle applies equally to skill in playing the piano and skill in playing baseball, to skill in writing poetry and skill in playing card games, to skill in keeping the practices of government flexible, sane, and intelligent, and to skill in gardening—one of the finest of the arts just beginning to be widely practiced by people-in-general in their free time.

What is needed most of all is a clear perception of our modern situation on the part of oncoming youth. But youth can gain this perception only if and when it has been achieved by their elders—their guides and instructors. It is positively poisonous to young people to let them grow up under the impression that their lives must be, or safely may be, divided between the "job" and mere "recreation." The meaning that is more and more attached to the word "recreation" today, namely, that it signifies aimless and purposeless play, involving no steady, individual effort, is a deadly peril to youth. How can we achieve the transition from this false and misleading idea to one that is true and constructive?

Something to our present purpose was once said in a blunt, offhand way by an American worthy who is rather out of fashion just now— Benjamin Franklin. "Time is money," Franklin told his contemporaries. He doubtless meant that as a provocative metaphor rather than as a literal truth. But, taking it quite literally, we might do a better job of spending our time if, in that expenditure, we applied some of the techniques we learn to use in spending our money. The nineteenth and twentieth centuries have taught most of us a fair degree of realism about handling our cash. The negligent and aristocratic vagueness of the elegants of earlier centuries as to whether or not their bills were paid is displayed now only by members of those social classes comprising bums, hobos, and fashionable women. And this vagueness is no longer considered as an engaging quality but a conscienceless stupidity. Why should a feeble vagueness as to the use made of time be considered as anything more creditable? In the matter of money, most of us have learned to face facts. If we had so much money and haven't it now, we ought to have something to show for it—or we have been stupid. Why shouldn't we be equally realistic about what we do with our time? We know that when we wake up to each new day there is marked on the credit side of the ledger, "So many hours freed from manual work by labor-saving machinery." Why should we helplessly write on the opposite page of the ledger at the end of the day, "Spent it all," without being able to give any account whatever of how we spent it or what we have received in return?

In addition to a new sense of responsibility about the use of time, what we need to realize ourselves and constantly to keep before the imagination of youth is the enormous scope, range, and variety of "skills" available to those who will make the effort to acquire them. We have a laughably absurd tendency to associate the word "skill" with the attempt to go against the current of the times by trying to revive some manual work of the past, now performed by modern machinery. Skill means, of course, doing something—anything reasonably worth doing—*well*. This "something" can range from such extraordinary skill as St. Theresa of Avila showed in the reorganization of convent life in her time in Spain, to the simpler skill of an American mother who tries to animate with ardor and intelligence the activities of the small local branch of the PTA in the school attended by her children. Or it can range from such a mighty manifestation of the communal making of music as the annual presentation of Bach's *Mass in B Minor* by the steelworkers and commercial employees of the town of Bethlehem, Pennsylvania, to the faithful work with a small church choir of a conscientious organist and leader. It may be such financial ability as is shown by the trustees of a great university in balancing its budget, or it may be the effort of a few wage earners to organize a cooperative store. In bringing this matter before the attention of the younger generation we must untiringly remind them of the unending, rich diversity of the activities open to them on the sole condition that they learn, first, to protect their free time with courage and firmness from triviality and commercial exploitation, and, second, to use it wisely and rewardingly.

What we should do, what we must do, is to bring up into the field of consciousness an essential truth which is already a living part of our human experience. This truth is that the heartfelt struggle to overcome one's own limitations and to force the chaotic raw material of human life to submit to shaping and design is not only the most rewarding but also the most natural effort for human beings. It is not the rare prerogative, privilege, and reward of an elite. It is an instinct innate in all human hearts, which can, if we will wisely use the new opportunities open to mankind, grow constantly into a greater and greater element in the lives of men and women.

Such efforts used to be tied so closely to the work done under the pressure of necessity that we foolishly assumed the connection to be inevitable. But now we are beginning to see that most of the saving, satisfying skills of the past were acquired not on the "job," but through the "work" that was done beyond the immediate compulsion of material need. Labor-saving machinery has made "work," in this sense, more widely possible to human beings than it ever was in any previous period of history. And added to the wider accessibility of freely chosen work is the crowning glory that it may now be adapted closely to the tastes, interests, and abilities of the individual workers. All this, literally and realistically, is within the realm of possibilities for our American future.

### A FINAL WORD ABOUT THE SPIRITUAL

"The bond between man and his God is at the same time the fundamental bond between man and his neighbor."— Father George Johnson

Of all ages of man, youth could least be deluded for any length of time into believing that passively enjoyed material comfort can ever make life worth living. That is not their danger. The young are far more apt, as we all know, to underestimate rather than to overestimate the amount of rest, warmth, and even food their growing strength requires. They are impatient of their elders' efforts to give them material protection and security. There are countless proofs that they have an appetite for physical hardship, danger, excitement, and effort. When their ardor is drivingly aroused for some enterprise dear to their hearts, they deny themselves with fierce gladness not only comfort and safety but, for the time, recreation and reasonable relaxation. No, youth is by nature not in danger, as older people are, from materialism in the shape of ease.

But are young people safe from that pale shade of bribery called prosperity? If it were possible for the older generation so to arrange life that each youth had a congenial job, opportunities for enjoyment, a satisfactory degree of worldly success, recognition as a contributing member of the community—all the reasonable advantages with which this Commission has been so long concerning itself and of which this report has treated in such detail—would youth still be in a worse danger than in the absence of all these, the danger of thinking that such success is all there is to human life? How much are they by nature aware—if only by a dim intuition—of the life of the spirit, on which alone our full integrity as human beings must be based? And what can the faithful, loving friends and helpers of youth do to aid in the expansion of this dim native intuition of the spiritual side of their lives, to make it more of a control for their growth, to release the potential beauty and power of their natures, which lie in its keeping?

They do know, perhaps every young person living knows, something by experience of those hungers and yearnings in the human heart that can only rest in a joy, in a home, beyond this world, beyond time. This knowledge is to most of them vague and fitful, as it is with most of us also. Only at intervals does it arrest their attention. Only in exceptional natures does it hold their attention. Conscious attention, that is. For there must be some recognition of the spiritual in life in every creature, *for it is fundamental*. Was there ever anyone entirely without moments of wonder, when some degree of awareness comes over him of the life his spirit lives, of the joy of which it is capable, utterly different in quality from all other joys? Is there one of us who cannot remember that in his youth there were such moments and that they were treasured? For they were spiritual joy.

For the many young people who still turn with confidence toward the familiar teaching and inspiration of their childhood faith, the ministers of that faith, whatever it be, we may be sure, are ready and eager to help. They speak a well-known language, they unfold scriptures and symbols of proved power over the soul of man. But what about the multitude of young people who have not been brought up to revere any faith? And that number, large too, who keep up the outward observances but feel no urgent and compelling reality in their inherited forms of religion? And what of those whose backgrounds have been hostile to all churches and creeds?

How provide for a need so inward, elusive of words, so personal, intimate, varied—yet so universal, vital, so prime?

If for a moment we forget to be professional counselors, members of another generation, and, as fellow human beings, look into our hearts through the deeps of our own experience, can we not find there, after all, a quite simple, large, realistic, humanly adaptable suggestion—a suggestion enjoined upon us by what great examples and authorities these many centuries!—that we seek and serve the goodness of God by being good to one another.

If we always encourage the young, whatever their nature or circumstances, to think of others, to feel fellowship with their brothers and sisters in humanity, we shall have set them on the way to find God in the practice of that aspect of spiritual life which runs through every religion as the thread through a string of pearls. The door of escape for each one from the prison of self will have been set open.

To open the door we need an attitude which we can strive to reach and hold, a never-refusing welcome towards the holy spirit of fellow feeling which is always knocking at our inner door. We need the deeper cultivation, the widening understanding of that free, frank comradeship with others, which youth so naturally delights in. We need a yoke which on very good authority is easy and a burden which is light. We need to begin by daring,

> "To seem as free from pride and guile
> As good, as generous, as we are."

This is the creative adventure of the spirit that beckons every rising generation. The future of our land and of every land depends vitally on the supply of young men and young women who will do their best and greatest to replace our old restricted love for a few, which entails antagonism for others, by fellow feeling without stint or limit. Of all the resources of our times and our democracy, what other is like this!

The anguished peoples of the earth long for peace above every other thing. And in a short, old prayer, loved by the worshippers of more than one Communion, this practice of fellow feeling has come down the centuries under the title

> "The very bond of peace."

# INDEX

# PUBLICATIONS

## *of the*

# AMERICAN YOUTH COMMISSION

BARRIERS TO YOUTH EMPLOYMENT
By Paul T. David. Probable publication date April 1942.

YOUTH WORK PROGRAMS: *Problems and Policies*
By Lewis L. Lorwin. 1941. 195 pages. $1.75, cloth.

TIME ON THEIR HANDS: *A Report on Leisure, Recreation, and Young People*
By C. Gilbert Wrenn and D. L. Harley. 1941. 266 pages, illustrated. $2.00, cloth.

YOUTH, FAMILY, AND EDUCATION
By Joseph K. Folsom. 1941. 299 pages. $1.75, cloth.

YOUTH-SERVING ORGANIZATIONS: *National Nongovernmental Associations*
By M. M. Chambers. 1941. 237 pages. $2.50, cloth.

GUIDEPOSTS FOR RURAL YOUTH
By E. L. Kirkpatrick. 1940. 167 pages, illustrated. $1.00, paper.

MATCHING YOUTH AND JOBS: *A Study of Occupational Adjustment*
By Howard M. Bell. 1940. 277 pages, illustrated. $2.00, cloth.

WHAT THE HIGH SCHOOLS OUGHT TO TEACH
1940. 36 pages. 50 cents, board; 25 cents, paper.

EQUAL EDUCATIONAL OPPORTUNITY FOR YOUTH: *A National Responsibility*
By Newton Edwards. 1939. 189 pages. $2.00, cloth.

THE HEALTH OF COLLEGE STUDENTS
By Harold S. Diehl, M.D., and Charles E. Shepard, M.D. 1939. 169 pages. $1.50, cloth.

YOUTH TELL THEIR STORY: *A Study of the Conditions and Attitudes of Young People*
By Howard M. Bell. 1938. 273 pages. $2.00, cloth; $1.50 paper.

AMERICAN YOUTH: *An Annotated Bibliography*
By Louise A. Menefee and M. M. Chambers, 1938. 492 pages. $3.00, cloth.

SECONDARY EDUCATION FOR YOUTH IN MODERN AMERICA
By Harl R. Douglass. 1937. 137 pages. $1.00, cloth.

HOW FARE AMERICAN YOUTH?
By Homer P. Rainey and others. New York: D. Appleton-Century Co., 1937. 186 pages. $1.50, cloth.

THE COMMUNITY AND ITS YOUNG PEOPLE
By M. M. Chambers. 1940. 36 pages. 15 cents, paper.

HOW TO MAKE A COMMUNITY YOUTH SURVEY
By M. M. Chambers and Howard M. Bell. 1939. 45 pages. 25 cents, paper.

SURVEYS OF YOUTH: *Finding the Facts*
By D. L. Harley. 1937. 106 pages. (Out of print)

# STUDIES OF NEGRO YOUTH

COLOR, CLASS, AND PERSONALITY
    By Robert L. Sutherland. 1942. 135 pages, illustrated. $1.25, cloth; 75 cents, paper.

THUS BE THEIR DESTINY: *The Personality Development of Negro Youth in Three Communities*
    By J. Howell Atwood, Donald W. Wyatt, Vincent J. Davis, and Ira D. Walker. 1941. 96 pages. 75 cents, paper.

COLOR AND HUMAN NATURE: *Negro Personality Development in a Northern City*
    By W. Lloyd Warner, Buford H. Junker, and Walter A. Adams. 1941. 301 pages. $2.25, cloth.

GROWING UP IN THE BLACK BELT: *Negro Youth in the Rural South*
    By Charles S. Johnson. 1941. 360 pages. $2.25, cloth.

NEGRO YOUTH AT THE CROSSWAYS: *Their Personality Development in the Middle States*
    By E. Franklin Frazier. 1940. 301 pages. $2.25, cloth.

CHILDREN OF BONDAGE: *The Personality Development of Negro Youth in the Urban South*
    By Allison Davis and John Dollard. 1940. 299 pages. $2.25, cloth.

IN A MINOR KEY: *Negro Youth in Story and Fact*
    By Ira DeA. Reid. 1940. 134 pages. $1.25, paper.

# WORK CAMPS FOR YOUTH

YOUTH IN THE CCC (tentative title)
    By Kenneth Holland and Frank Ernest Hill. Illustrated. Ready in March 1942.

WORK CAMPS FOR COLLEGE STUDENTS
    By Kenneth Holland. 1941. 32 pages, illustrated. 25 cents, paper.

WORK CAMPS FOR HIGH SCHOOL YOUTH
    By Kenneth Holland and George L. Bickel. 1941. 27 pages, illustrated. 25 cents, paper.

YOUTH IN EUROPEAN LABOR CAMPS
    By Kenneth Holland. 1939. 303 pages, illustrated. $2.50, cloth.

# STATEMENTS OF THE COMMISSION

*(Published in pamphlet form. Now out of print but available in many libraries.)*

A PROGRAM OF ACTION FOR AMERICAN YOUTH. 1939. 20 pages.

COMMUNITY RESPONSIBILITY FOR YOUTH. 1940. 12 pages.

THE OCCUPATIONAL ADJUSTMENT OF YOUTH. 1940. 16 pages.

SHOULD YOUTH ORGANIZE? 1940. 8 pages.

YOUTH, DEFENSE, AND THE NATIONAL WELFARE. 1940. 12 pages.

THE CIVILIAN CONSERVATION CORPS. 1940. 24 pages.

NEXT STEPS IN NATIONAL POLICY FOR YOUTH. 1941. 20 pages.

# THE AMERICAN COUNCIL ON EDUCATION

GEORGE F. ZOOK, *President*

The American Council on Education is a *council* of national educational associations; organizations having related interests; approved universities and colleges, technological schools, and private secondary schools; state departments of education; and city school systems. It is a center of cooperation and coordination whose influence has been apparent in the shaping of American educational policies as well as in the formulation of American educational practices during the past twenty years. Many leaders in American education and public life serve on the commissions and committees through which the Council operates.

Established by the Council in 1935, the American Youth Commission consists of the persons whose names appear on a front page of this publication. It operates through a staff under the supervision and control of a director responsible to the Commission.